The Ancient World in Alternative History and Counterfactual Fictions

Bloomsbury Studies in Classical Reception

Bloomsbury Studies in Classical Reception presents scholarly monographs offering new and innovative research and debate to students and scholars in the reception of Classical Studies. Each volume will explore the appropriation, reconceptualization and recontextualization of various aspects of the Graeco-Roman world and its culture, looking at the impact of the ancient world on modernity. Research will also cover reception within antiquity, the theory and practice of translation, and reception theory.

Also available in the series

Alexander the Great in the Early Christian Tradition: Classical Reception and Patristic Literature, Christian Thrue Djurslev
Ancient Magic and the Supernatural in the Modern Visual and Performing Arts, edited by Filippo Carlà and Irene Berti
Ancient Greek Myth in World Fiction since 1989, edited by Justine McConnell and Edith Hall
Anne Carson/Antiquity, edited by Laura Jansen
Antipodean Antiquities, edited by Marguerite Johnson
Classical Antiquity and Medieval Ireland: An Anthology of Medieval Irish Texts and Interpretations, edited by Michael James Clark, Erich Poppe and Isabelle Torrance
Classics in Extremis, edited by Edmund Richardson
Faulkner's Reception of Apuleius' The Golden Ass in The Reivers, by Vernon L. Provencal
Frankenstein and Its Classics, edited by Jesse Weiner, Benjamin Eldon Stevens and Brett M. Rogers
Gender, Creation Myths and their Reception in Western Civilization: Prometheus, Pandora, Adam and Eve edited by Lisa Maurice and Tovi Bibring
Greek and Roman Classics in the British Struggle for Social Reform, edited by Henry Stead and Edith Hall
Greeks and Romans on the Latin American Stage, edited by Rosa Andújar and Konstantinos P. Nikoloutsos
Greek Tragedy in 20th-Century Italian Literature: Translations by Camillo Sbarbaro and Giovanna Bemporad, Caterina Paoli

Homer's Iliad and the Trojan War: Dialogues on Tradition,
Jan Haywood and Naoíse Mac Sweeney
Imagining Xerxes, Emma Bridges
Julius Caesar's Self-Created Image and Its Dramatic Afterlife,
Miryana Dimitrova
Kinaesthesia and Classical Antiquity 1750–1820: Moved by Stone,
Helen Slaney
Once and Future Antiquities in Science Fiction and Fantasy,
edited by Brett M. Rogers and Benjamin Eldon Stevens
Ovid's Myth of Pygmalion on Screen, Paula James
Performing Gods in Classical Antiquity and the Age of Shakespeare,
Dustin W. Dixon and John S. Garrison
Reading Poetry, Writing Genre, edited by Silvio Bär and Emily Hauser
Sex, Symbolists and the Greek Body, Richard Warren
The Classics in Modernist Translation,
edited by Miranda Hickman and Lynn Kozak
The Classics in South America: Five Case Studies,
Germán Campos Muñoz
The Codex Fori Mussolini, Han Lamers and Bettina Reitz-Joosse
The Gentle, Jealous God, Simon Perris
The Thucydidean Turn: (Re)Interpreting Thucydides' Political Thought Before, During and After the Great War, Benjamin Earley
Translations of Greek Tragedy in the Work of Ezra Pound,
Peter Liebregts
Truth in the Late Foucault: Antiquity, Sexuality and Psychoanalysis,
edited by Paul Allen Miller
Victorian Classical Burlesques, Laura Monrós-Gaspar
Victorian Epic Burlesques, Rachel Bryant Davies
Virgil's Map: Geography, Empire, and the Georgics, Charlie Kerrigan

The Ancient World in Alternative History and Counterfactual Fictions

Edited by Alberto J. Quiroga Puertas and
Leire Olabarria

BLOOMSBURY ACADEMIC
LONDON • NEW YORK • OXFORD • NEW DELHI • SYDNEY

BLOOMSBURY ACADEMIC
Bloomsbury Publishing Plc
50 Bedford Square, London, WC1B 3DP, UK
1385 Broadway, New York, NY 10018, USA
29 Earlsfort Terrace, Dublin 2, Ireland

BLOOMSBURY, BLOOMSBURY ACADEMIC and the Diana logo are trademarks of Bloomsbury Publishing Plc

First published in Great Britain 2024

Cover image: akinbostanci/Getty

A catalogue record for this book is available from the British Library.

Library of Congress Cataloging-in-Publication Data
Names: Quiroga Puertas, Alberto J., 1978– editor. | Olabarria, Leire, 1984– editor.
Title: The ancient world in alternative history and counterfactual fictions / edited by Alberto J. Quiroga Puertas and Leire Olabarria.
Description: London ; New York : Bloomsbury Academic, 2024. | Series: Bloomsbury studies in classical reception; vol 35 | Includes bibliographical references and index.
Identifiers: LCCN 2024007263 (print) | LCCN 2024007264 (ebook) | ISBN 9781350281622 (hardback) | ISBN 9781350289666 (paperback) | ISBN 9781350281639 (pdf) | ISBN 9781350281646 (ebook)
Subjects: LCSH: Alternative histories (Fiction)–History and criticism. | Civilization, Ancient, in literature. | History, Ancient, in literature. | LCGFT: Literary criticism. | Essays.
Classification: LCC PN3448.A47 A53 2024 (print) | LCC PN3448.A47 (ebook) | DDC 809.3/8768—dc23/eng/20240314
LC record available at https://lccn.loc.gov/2024007263
LC ebook record available at https://lccn.loc.gov/2024007264

ISBN: HB: 978-1-3502-8162-2
ePDF: 978-1-3502-8163-9
eBook: 978-1-3502-8164-6

Series: Bloomsbury Studies in Classical Reception

Typeset by RefineCatch Limited, Bungay, Suffolk

To find out more about our authors and books visit www.bloomsbury.com and sign up for our newsletters.

Ταῦτα δὲ ἐγένετο μὲν οὐδέποτε, ἔστι δὲ ἀεί
These things never happened, but they occur all the time.
Salustius, On the Gods and the Universe *4.9*

Contents

Figures

Contributors

Anastasia Bakogianni is Lecturer in Classical Studies at Massey University, New Zealand. Her research and publications focus on the reception of Greek tragedy on stage and screen. She is author of *Electra Ancient & Modern: Aspects of the Tragic Heroine's Reception* (2011), editor of *Dialogues with the Past: Classical Reception Theory and Practice* (2013) and co-editor of *War as Spectacle: Ancient and Modern Perspectives on the Display of Armed Conflict* (2015) and *Locating Classical Receptions on Screen: Masks, Echoes, Shadows* (2018).

Sarah Annes Brown is Professor of English Literature at Anglia Ruskin University, UK, and has published widely on both science fiction and classical reception. She has a particular interest in the intersection between science fiction and 'canonical' literature and is currently completing a monograph on Shakespeare's relationship with science fiction. She has served as a judge of the Arthur C. Clarke Award (2014–15) and is currently the Secretary of the Science Fiction Foundation.

F. Javier Campos-Daroca is Senior Lecturer in Classical Tradition and Reception Studies at the University of Almería, Spain, as well as Senior Fellow at the Institute of Communication and Society from the same university. He has a wide range of publications on Herodotus, ancient tragedy and its reception, Utopian literature, and philosophy in the Hellenistic and Roman periods. He also has translated the works of Diodorus Siculus, Maximus of Tyre, Alcidamas of Elea, Chrysippus (collected fragments) and Marcus Aurelius into Spanish. He is currently working on the reception of Socrates during the Imperial period and modern times.

Lynn S. Fotheringham is Lecturer in Classics at the University of Nottingham, UK. Thanks to the university's Centre for Spartan and Peloponnesian Studies, most of her work on historical novels (including graphic novels) has focused on representations of Sparta: Steven Pressfield's *Gates of Fire*, Frank Miller and Lynn Varley's *300*, Kieron Gillen and Ryan Kelly's *Three*. She is working on a monograph on ideas of authenticity in popular culture representations of the ancient world, which will include material on other ancient topics, including novels about Cicero.

Ryan C. Fowler is a Research Associate in the Department of Classics at Franklin & Marshall College in Lancaster, PA, USA. His research currently focuses on ancient Greek medicine and Imperial era rhetoric. Forthcoming publications include a volume contribution on diatribe in Methodius of Olympus, a commentary in *Medical History* on the Hippocratic text *On the Heart* and an article in *Social History of Medicine* on the Alexandrian physicians Herophilus and Erasistratus.

Genevieve Liveley is a Turing Fellow, RISCS Fellow, and Reader in Classics at the University of Bristol, UK. Her particular research interests lie in narratives and narrative theories (both ancient and modern). She has published widely in books, articles, and essays on narratology, on chaos theory, cyborgs, AI, and how the ancient world and its stories might help us to better anticipate the future of our own.

Leire Olabarria is Lecturer in Egyptology at the University of Birmingham, UK. Her research interests include kinship and marriage, social memory, and the construction of ritual landscapes. She also works on the reception of ancient Egypt in popular culture and has published on the use of ancient Egyptian imagery in heavy metal music.

Elia Otranto obtained his BA degree in Classics at the University of Granada, Spain. For his BA dissertation he explored the rhetorical structure and literary devices used by the emperor Julian in his *Misopogon*. He has participated in several workshops and seminars in which he has presented papers on how the figure of Julian has been approached from the perspective of reception studies. Currently he is working on his PhD dissertation, which deals with the use of invective in the emperor Julian's works.

Alberto J. Quiroga Puertas is Senior Lecturer in Ancient Greek at the University of Granada, Spain. His research interests lie primarily in late antique literature and rhetoric, topics about which he has published several papers and books. He also has an interest in reception studies in contemporary literature and cinema.

Benjamin E. Stevens works on underworlds and afterlives, the history of the senses, classical receptions and film. He has published four co-edited volumes on receptions in science fiction and fantasy and a monograph on silence in Catullus. Since 2022 he is Lecturer in English at Howard University, USA.

Will Tattersdill is Senior Lecturer in Literature and Contemporary Fantasy Cultures at the University of Glasgow, UK. He is a literary critic who teaches and publishes on the cultural interaction between literature and science. He has written about late-Victorian magazine culture, *Star Trek*, and museum history, and his current work is on the relationships between people and dinosaurs. From 2018 to 2022 he taught an undergraduate class dedicated exclusively to alternative history.

Jesse Weiner is Assistant Professor of Classics at Hamilton College, USA. He has published numerous articles on Greek and Latin literature, drama, and classical reception studies with strong interests in monumentality, memory, aesthetics and gender studies. He is co-editor of *Frankenstein and Its Classics: The Modern Prometheus from Antiquity to Science Fiction* (2018). In public humanities, he has worked with Ancient Greeks/Modern Lives and his work has appeared in *History Today* and *The Atlantic*.

Foreword: On the Usefulness of What Didn't Happen

Will Tattersdill
University of Glasgow

'We cannot change what has happened', muses eleven-year-old Simmea, captured by slavers and sold to a group of idealists who are planning to build Plato's Republic (Walton 2015: 20). Her fatalism is interesting in the circumstances: she has been brought to Atlantis, where Pallas Athene has gathered all the people who have ever earnestly prayed to be part of the great project. There are masters from the Roman Empire, from Renaissance Italy, from nineteenth-century England, and even robot workers from the far future to help with the practical side. Time-travel, in this story – *The Just City*, by Jo Walton (2015) – is very much on the agenda. Yet as young Simmea suggests, the linearity of her own journey is unalterable. Despite the efforts of the masters to give her a new name and identity, despite their insistence that 'I should not talk about my earlier life', she remains, at least in part, a product of her circumstances (Walton 2015: 59). The results for the Just City will not be harmonious.

One of the early hints we get at this comes immediately before the line I began with, which is on the very first page of Simmea's part of the narrative. In this passage, Simmea ruminates about what her life *might have been* had it not been for the slavers, the masters and Athene. Without them, she speculates:

> . . . I might have grown up in the Delta and lived the life the gods had laid out before me. True, I would never have learned philosophy, and perhaps I would have died bearing children to some peasant farmer. But who can say that might not have been the path to happiness?
>
> Walton 2015: 20

Here, Simmea writes in what Andrew H. Miller (2012), following Stuart Hampshire, calls the 'optative mood' – she takes a moment to think about how things *might have gone*, if something had been different. The optative mood is an appropriate one with which to open this volume, since the phrase derives from the Hellenistic Greek term for a verb whose prominent function is the expression of a desire (εὐκτικὴ ἔγκλισις). Alternate history's characters, as much as its writers, are caught up in the expression of desire – if not the desire to live in a different history, then at least to know what that history would or could have looked like. In *The Just City*, the desire to live in Plato's Republic forms the basis of an experiment conducted by Walton as much as by Athene, and *with* history as much as *outside* it. But as well as being the grammar of the extravagantly weird counterfactual scenario, the optative mood is something most of us slip into every day: if I'd turned left instead of right, if I'd cycled instead of walking, if I hadn't knocked that glass, lost those keys, said those things . . .

Considered as a genre, alternate history fiction often feels perhaps overly-focused on large-scale considerations. Its books, we assume, are 'about' big armies clashing (or failing to clash), big social changes (or stasis), or important leaders, usually men, dying before (or after) their time. None of these assumptions are particularly unfair; all of them, in nascent form, can be found in Louis Geoffroy's *Napoléon et la Conquête du Monde, 1812–1832* (*Napoleon and the Conquest of the World*; 1836), the ur-text of the modern genre for many scholars. But at its best, alternate history is also interested in the personal, in moments where an individual shaped in a world different from ours is confronted by a reflection or decision in which *contingency* is key. Nothing is inevitable from the start in alternate history: even events left unaltered from actual history can be surprises, historically-informed readers can still be confounded, and choices therefore once again have meaning. There is a parallel, and not a useless one, with recent moves in (post-) classical scholarship, expressed perhaps best in Tim Whitmarsh's (2013: 6) injunction that we recall 'that when each of these poets [Vergil, Philo, Theodotus] wrote, the future was entirely up for grabs'. In short, the road not taken provides an interesting view of our 'real' history. There is no better background than this sense of reopened possibility for the exploration of Walton's true subject in *The Just City* – human volition.

Alternate history is often thought of as a working-through, in its most clichéd form less a narrative than a hypothesis. But what is being 'worked through' can go beyond differences in acknowledged events – it can be perceptions, feelings, modes, forms. This is perhaps even truer when alternate history refers to classical civilizations, our daily knowledge of which (as Walton understands perfectly) is inevitably coloured by a palimpsest of receptions stretching back hundreds or thousands of years. '[T]here is a dynamic relationship', Kathleen Singles (2013: 8) has written, 'between the point of divergence and the function of the reader in alternate history. It seems that, the less explicit the point of divergence [. . .], the more active the recipient'. Taking into account decades of historiographical insights into the reliability of any supposed objective view of the real past, how carefully can we really map our hypotheses of classical difference? Or, to put it differently, what does it mean consciously to alternate something of which so many alternates already exist? Among all the Athenes offered by today's scholarship and popular culture – and yesterday's – what does it mean to make a change?

Of course, there are some events from the classical past which we understand extremely well, and divergences from them create the subject matter for many of the essays collected in this book. Even these examples, however, may reasonably be argued to have contemporary reception near their hearts. Alternate histories of antiquity are, of course, receptions – but they are also 'about' reception, every bit as much as they are 'about' armies or great men. Indeed, reading the contents of this volume, it has increasingly dawned on me that the term 'reception' as used by classicists may well be a powerful tool for understanding alternate history more broadly. It is chiefly for this reason that I hope this book will be useful not just to its immediate audience, but to literary critics, historians and cultural theorists.

*

In all of the above, I've written about alternate history as if it is a cohesive set of texts, easy to identify, with an agreed-upon definition. Such is not, of course, the case. My opening with *The Just City*, for example, would probably make Singles unhappy, and the novel fits uneasily into the possible-world typology proposed by Marie-Laure Ryan (1991b) and recently refined by Riyukta Raghunath (2022). In part, this is because Walton doesn't propose a surgical alteration, with history running down a different track from a single point of divergence (sometimes called a nexus or Jonbar point). Rather, her historical interventions are scattershot, with periods operating more like places than times for many of the characters; though Walton is playing with time, the novel is clear that a specific future (proceeding even beyond the author's present) is inevitable, has for all practical purposes already happened. Taking place in the lacunae of this inevitability, *The Just City* might better be described as a 'secret' history (like Stevenson's *Kidnapped!* (1886), say) than an 'alternate' one: 'The gods are bound by Fate and Necessity', Athene says, 'and Necessity only allows the kind of changes in time that nobody notices' (Walton 2015: 157).[1] Moreover, the presence of Athene herself, to say nothing of the science fictional affordances like the robots, removes the veneer of plausibility from this text. 'What if Athene established Plato's Republic?' is a different category of question from 'What if the Persians lost at Thermopylae?', and we instinctively understand that the latter can be answered with more credibility.

It's because I am not convinced that this instinct is correct that I have persisted in opening with *The Just City*. Part of the beauty of alternate history comes from the fact that even the most unambitious propositions ('If Rashford had scored that penalty, England would have won') are ultimately unknowable, unfalsifiable in the Popperian sense, the property not of science but of fantasy (after all, Rashford could have scored but the opposing side could then have equalized; Rashford could have scored but a riot or natural disaster could then have stopped the match; Rashford could have scored but England could then have been disqualified later due to mismanagement or cheating). It's for this reason that 'counterfactuals' remain frowned upon by academic historians, Ferguson (ed.) (1997) notwithstanding. But it is also this quality which makes them compelling, including, if you catch them off duty, to many historians.[2] 'Fantasy', as anyone who has immersed themselves in Robin Hobb or Brandon Sanderson knows, doesn't have to mean 'unrigorous'. For me, the idea of sharply dividing the fantastic from the plausible allows 'mainstream' alternate history to get away with too much, allows us to keep thinking of it as in some way realistic despite the pointedly metafictional interventions of its most famous single text, Philip K. Dick's *The Man in the High Castle* (1962).

Alternate history, then, is difficult to define – both a highly specialized niche of military science fiction *and* a general human impulse traceable to antiquity, depending on how one slices it. Your own priorities will dictate whether it is most useful to you as a subset of historical fiction, fantasy or the optative mood. Following John Frow's (2005) understanding of genre as a quality of a text rather than a category of texts, though, I try to be less interested in 'where something fits' than I am in 'what something does'. *The Just City*, I think, *does* something very comparable (though not identical) to Walton's earlier novel *Farthing* (2006), a book with a much more traditional claim to the mantle of alternate history. *Farthing* contains a point of divergence (Rudolf Hess' 1941 mission to broker peace with the UK was a success), a manifestly counterfactual outcome (Britain is a lone independent power in a Nazi-controlled Europe), and no supernatural affordances. In both books, however, Walton is deeply interested in the ways history is shaped by individual choice, in the limits of freedom in a fair society, and in the agency of women in particular in the cognitively estranged worlds created by her deviations from history. The two novels, different though they are in certain respects, are united precisely by the way in which they use the gap between a fictitious world and the one we know to advance their thinking. For me, that's enough to make *The Just City*, and any other works dealing more loosely with the 'alternate history' label, worthy of consideration under it. 'I thought at first that it was a ridiculous dream', Walton's Sokrates says of the attempted Republic, 'but as it keeps going on and becoming more and more detailed I have decided to treat it as reality and go along with it on that basis' (Walton 2015: 115).

Even if you disagree, I hope I've begun to convince you that that value of alternate history – however defined – does not lie solely in the plausibility of specific theses about how history 'would have gone'. It is not for its realism that *The Man in the High Castle* (in which the Nazis drain the Mediterranean, for example, with 1950s technology, after the resource expenditure involved in winning a European land war) has become the genre's standard-bearer. It is not for the surety of their (re)projections that we value the acknowledged genre classics like Murray Leinster's 'Sidewise in Time' (1934), Ward Moore's *Bring the Jubilee* (1953), or Robert Harris' *Fatherland* (1992). So for me, including the literal magic of Susanna Clarke's *Jonathan Strange and Mr Norrell* (2004), the retro-futuristic artwork of Simon Stålenhag's *Tales from the Loop* (2014), or the mermaid-like wajinru of Rivers Solomon's *The Deep* (2019), is only logical. These are all texts interested in the work which can be done by removing our assumptions from history. It makes sense to think of them together.

*

For all my talk of definitions and mainstreams in the above, it remains the case that alternate history is a niche, both within popular fiction and literary criticism. Readers – even readers of science fiction (sf) – can easily pass the genre by, perhaps encountering it only when written by an author they are already reading (Dick, say, or Stephen King). For literary critics, too, alternate history has been easy to miss – the number of books and articles dedicated to it remains tiny when compared to the attention accorded to historical fiction, say, or fantasy. My sense is that this is beginning to change: readers are encountering historical contingency far outside the traditional boundaries of military sf, for example in Kate Atkinson's acclaimed *Life After Life* (2013), whilst the critical potential of the genre is reflected by, for example, the recent collection of pathfinding essays edited by Glyn Morgan and Charul Palmer-Patel (2019a). Even that essential volume, though, makes very little space for alternate history with a focus on antiquity; if alternate history is an underexplored corner of popular fiction, then alternate *classical* history is even more overlooked.

At the time of writing, the online bibliography uchronia.com lists 240 alternate histories with a divergence point between 4000 BCE and 500 CE, compared with 406 for the period 1800–1900 CE.[3] This is an incredibly crude measure,[4] but does confirm a general sense that the genre's key primary and secondary works remain focused on more recent historical contingencies – if Napoleon had won at Waterloo, if the Confederacy had won the civil war, if Hitler had triumphed over the Allies. Despite Imperial Rome's memorable presence in 'Sidewise in Time' (1934), the Leinster story for which the genre's annual awards are named, ancient history has preoccupied relatively few of alternate history's writers – and almost none of its critics. With this volume, that changes.

I have already begun to suggest, from my own position of ignorance as regards ancient world studies, why this is such a welcome move. It's true that any neglected text or subject deserves attention, but alternate history's real potential lies not just in the extra primary fodder it can grant English literature but in its connective power for multidisciplinary work. The bread-and-butter questions asked by this genre potentially involve experts from all kinds of subjects: when I wrote an alternate history module for final-year literature undergraduates, it seemed natural to invite in 'special guests' from history, philosophy, physics, creative writing and palaeontology to help students think things through. Each of these disciplines has a particular perspective on the questions of determinism and contingency upon which alternate history inevitably dwells – and there were many others I could or would have sought, had resources permitted. I also asked Leire Olabarria, one of the editors of the present volume, to talk to the students – not because we were reading anything set in the ancient past (I confess, in this respect, to having reproduced the biases of the wider genre), but because a classicist's experience and perspective seemed crucial in helping students to process the idea of historical periods as imaginative spaces. Leire's particular emphasis on architecture, reflected in her essay in this volume, gave my students a whole new set of provocations as they worked towards creating alternate scenarios of their own. Alternate history writers must synthesize social, scientific, military and personal changes and their consequences, often through philosophical lenses; it behoves its critics, therefore, to think in an interdisciplinary way. And if interdisciplinarity is useful, then Classics, the original interdiscipline, is an excellent vantage point for the overall genre.

The overall genre is also an interesting place from which to regard Classics – or ancient world studies, or ancient history. As a naïve outsider to the field, I have allowed myself a degree of slippage between these terms so far, but the contestation implied by them alone suggests a distinct value in studying the ancient world through the lens provided by alternateness. Mathura Umachandran's (2019) call to 'stop producing the idea of white antiquity', insisting on broader ways of understanding an ethnically and textually diverse past, requires not only careful and diligent scholarship, but also *imagination* – the vision to reconstruct not only a different classical world than the one we have inherited from the Victorian era, but a different Classics with which to understand it. The move is connected, in my estimation, to Ariella Aïsha Azoulay's (2019) notion of 'potential history', which asks us to deliberately unlearn our settled impressions of the colonial past. As a response to this enormously important project, my proposed study of the niche genre which builds itself around blatant contradiction of the historical record perhaps seems overly literal; it is questionable, too, on the grounds that many authors of alternate history (although certainly not all) have a *re*-connection with imperialism, not its destruction, close to the centre of their vision (see Quiroga Puertas and Otranto's chapter in this volume for a thoroughly worked-through example). Despite this, studying English literature has convinced me that alternate history *could* play a role in the decolonial endeavour, not so much because of the work done by the stories themselves as because of the challenges to the status quo implied by the questions they necessarily raise. It's for this reason that I hope classicists (using the term as inclusively as it can be imagined) will take this volume as an opportunity to think of alternate history as a source not just of material but of methodology.

*

The preceding sections of this foreword all perorate around the idea that precisely because of its inevitable engagements with questions which span genres and disciplines, alternate history has more to offer the academy than merely a new corpus of which to ask our questions; the questions themselves can be changed.

As a legacy of the generations-long process of getting popular fiction onto university syllabuses, academics who study such material still frequently practise the necessarily defensive postures of their forebears. Is sf worthy of being studied alongside the realist novel? Of course! And to make this point, we continue to ask sf the same kinds of questions that we ask the realist novel. Only very seldom do we start reading realist novels through the (famously) new questions offered to us by sf.

When I began teaching alternate history, I quickly noticed that a very fast way of getting classroom discussion moving was to ask students to practise counterfactual thinking themselves – not just by making up their own points of divergence (although I do recommend this as a classroom activity!), but with regard to the particular texts or passages we were reading at the time. Instead of saying 'why does the author use the word "violet" here?', I started asking 'how would this passage be different if the author had chosen "purple" instead?' The latter kind of question is often better for generating the kinds of insights we normally expect from the former, perhaps because it seems more concrete, perhaps because it operates in a provisional space which requires students to perform less prior knowledge. The technique scales, of course. 'Imagine a *Bleak House* where Lady Dedlock lives – how is that novel different from the one we have?' 'Imagine the exact story of Becky Chambers' *A Prayer for the Crown-Shy*, but set in poetry instead of prose. What has changed?'

I came to call this way of reading 'counterfactual criticism', and as these last two questions suggest, I was soon using it in classes which had nothing to do with alternate history per se.[5] Paying critical attention to this strange niche genre, I realized, had taught me new ways of thinking about the works my own discipline calls 'classics' – Dickens, Gaskell, Eliot. After reading the present volume, and especially the end of Anastasia Bakogianni's chapter, I am convinced that these sorts of tools can transfer into the study of *actual* classics too. In an era of widely-available misinformation about ancient cultures, such a suggestion perhaps sounds heretical: surely we should focus on the real detail of what we know rather than encouraging our students to invent? The question is an entirely justifiable one. One thing that my own teaching experience has taught me, though, is that alternate history writers generally have to be *more* engaged with the verifiable elements of actual history, if only to make their divergences from it as effective as possible. The image of a whimsical free-for-all replacing the rigour of historical study doesn't quite work – even in wildly, beautifully inventive, physically preposterous texts like Catherynne M. Valente's *Radiance* (2015), as we see in Benjamin E. Stevens' essay, a learned engagement with the source material is everywhere evident. Asked to improvise with history, most students – at least, most I have met – proceed with an instinctive caution. It is a caution I recognize from the archive, but it's also the caution I find in Tolkien, making Middle Earth brick by brick, and in the gadfly precision of Walton's Sokrates as he squares up to Athene for the final dialogue.

If none of the above has convinced you, I would ask: what if it had? What if I'd written this more persuasively, structured it better, showed a better understanding of ancient history? What if my new puppy or the ongoing industrial dispute in the UK university sector had calmed down long enough to allow me to do a better job? Could I have managed to get you to try a new way of teaching, if only for a few minutes? Could I have persuaded you that the value of the alternate lies not just in its potential to reapprehend the past but its potential to reapprehend our disciplines, and the relationships between them? Could you have found, if I'd made you want to, other still more compelling reasons to treat of alternate history on a methodological level, things that could never occur to me?

If only as an experiment, try living, for a few days, in that uncannily similar world. Is there anything from it, I wonder, that you would keep?

Glasgow University
May 2023

Notes

1 For a comparison of academic and popular understandings of 'alternate', 'alternative' and 'secret histories', see Fotheringham in this volume.

2 Just as this book goes to print, a national newspaper article calls for counterfactual history to be taken more seriously (Kettle 2023).

3 http://uchronia.com/bib.cgi/diverge.html (accessed 30 May 2023). I chose very round numbers for my date ranges for the purposes of broad illustration and am not seriously attempting to define the classical period (or, indeed, the nineteenth century).

4 Crude not only because of the site's necessarily limiting selection criteria (described fully at http://uchronia.net/intro.html accessed 30 May 2023) and my own thoughtless periodization, but because the date of a text's divergence point does not necessarily suggest the date of its setting – a text may have a classical divergence point but not be set in the classical period (although such a text, as we see in Fowler's chapter of the present volume, would still interest a scholar of classical reception).

5 For a fuller explanation, see Tattersdill (2023).

Acknowledgements

The editors would like to express their gratitude to the Bloomsbury staff for their patience and their guidance in the process of editing this volume: Lily Mac Mahon, Zoe Osman and Alice Wright. The editors also want to thank the contributors to this volume for their commitment and their confidence in the project.

When Alberto first contacted me to collaborate with him on this project, the possibility of a global pandemic would have been interpreted as a classic counterfactual. Little did we know that our explorations of what the ancient past could have been would be paralleled by discussions on the media about how Covid-19 could have been avoided or how it could have been dealt with more efficiently. With the benefit of hindsight, I know there are many things I would have done differently during the months of recurrent lockdowns – it took me too long to finally buy a piano! – but working with Alberto is something that I would not change at all. This project, with its ups and downs (granted, more downs than ups), has been an exercise in alternate history itself, but, as any good counterfactual, it is grounded on a fact: an unwavering friendship that feeds on pseudo-intellectual novels, pepperoni pizza and bad jokes. I do not know what my life without Alberto would be like, but I can guarantee that it would be more boring than in this timeline. If this book has materialized, it is all thanks to his dedication and commitment to what could have been.

(Enters Alberto). Unlike Leire, I cannot play the piano nor I have the wide set of skills she has. Having said that, I admit that I am an extremely lucky person, though I am aware that being lucky is not a virtue or a merit one works hard to achieve. Be that as it may, it has been thanks to my lucky stars that Leire accepted my offer to co-edit this volume. Her scholarly ethics, only equal to Ted Hastings' moral standards, have prevented me from making errors and taking wrong decisions on many, many occassions. In spite of her chronic injury in the left scaphoid, her efforts and extreme generosity have been decisive for the completion of this volume, for which I owe her a great debt of gratitude.

Oxford and Birmingham
August 2023 (year 14 *ab Izarra condita*; year catorse in Ohkua! calendar)

Note on Text/Translation

For the translation of ancient sources, please see editions listed in the bibliographic references at the end of the volume.

Introduction

Alberto J. Quiroga Puertas
University of Granada
Leire Olabarria
University of Birmingham

Lives of the Future Past

It is a typical English summer morning. Among the thick grey clouds, one can have a peek of a blue sky, and a single, timid ray of sun shines brightly at periodic intervals. I look through my window, and I see my neighbour Gordon enjoying a nice mug of hot chocolate and some *papadzules*. He spots me from his wrought iron garden chair and waves, ostensibly gesturing for me to open the window. He is always ready for a chat, and today is no exception. 'Good morning!', he says, 'I didn't see you at the *cantina* yesterday! Is everything ok?' 'Yes, no worries!', I reply, 'I wasn't feeling very well, that's all'. 'That is a shame', he answers, 'Maureen was serving her bean *tamales*, and the county *mariachi* provided superb entertainment'. I start sensing where this conversation is going, so I add, 'It seems I really missed out! I will be there next week!' Gordon gives me a sly smile, 'Of course you will be there next week. I know you wouldn't miss the bicentenary of Conquista Day. It is very important that we all come together as a community to celebrate our *emperador*. *Viva* Agustín VI! *Viva* the Mexican Empire!' He is obviously testing me at this point, and I don't want to get into trouble, so I unenthusiastically reply, '*Viva*! Have a nice day, Gordon. Enjoy your breakfast!'

What if Agustín I had remained in power as emperor of Mexico in 1823? What if he, inspired by an overwhelming victory against Spain, had embarked on a military conquest of the globe? What if Mexico had become the most powerful empire of the nineteenth century CE? This story, which may seem not only fanciful but even preposterous, is an example of counterfactual fiction.

On the one hand, there is a historical point of divergence that is briefly alluded to in this fragment, namely that Britain was conquered by the Mexican empire two hundred years prior to the narration. On the other, we have an allusion to a 'big man', the current emperor of Mexico, with the implication that his predecessor catalysed the aforementioned turning point in history. None of these aspects are elaborated upon in detail in this short fragment, but they provide a brief contextual setting to let the reader's imagination run wild. Why would Britain become a target of the expansion of this Mexican empire? Where would the main battles have happened? What kind of political structure would be in place in this alternate twenty-first century?

In this story, the timeline is altered by a historical divergence that occurred in the nineteenth century CE. In counterfactual fiction, divergence points tend to be placed in the not-so-distant past, perhaps because the reader's familiarity with conventional historical interpretations is required for counterfactual narratives to work effectively. For example, counterfactual reimaginings of the period of the Second World War are particularly widespread, as exemplified by *The Man in the High Castle* (1962) by Philip K. Dick, which is arguably one of the better-known alternate fictions. But what if our attention were to be turned further back in time? What possibilities would a focus on the ancient past afford in this reimagination of alternate presents?

These questions, among others, are addressed in this book, which aims to explore the use of antiquity in counterfactuals and other forms of speculative narratives in different literary genres such as historical novels, fantasy and science fiction literature. Historical novels based on counterfactuals usually make use of the variety of formal manifestations and the imaginative possibilities offered by what-if approaches. Their interpretation does not attempt to rewrite the past so much as merging two cultural codes – the one that belongs to the period of the author and the historical event around which the plot unfolds. As Evans (2014: 176–7) stated, 'counterfactuals are ironical because, ultimately, they always cast more light on the present than on the past'. The intention of the contributions of this book is, hence, to offer a new insight into how cultures of the ancient world are perceived and what these exercises in critical speculation may tell us about ourselves. Approaching the antique world through the lens of 'what-if' plots and alternate scenarios contributes to negotiating our bonds with the past in a time when long-established cultural patterns are being challenged and contested.

Categorizing Counterfactual Thinking: What if it couldn't be done?

Counterfactuals are unrestrained by the limits and notions of reality and, as such, they are notoriously difficult to define. They could be understood, as Christopher Prendergast (2019: 2) puts it, as 'a category of thought and language' activated by an in-built mechanism that allows us to think about alternative courses of events, to reconsider our past decisions, or – as in the opening story – to carefully speculate about divergences in the outcome of historical episodes.

Being perceived as a mode of thought and an argumentative method, the heuristic value of the 'what-if' is appreciated in a number of different disciplines, from medicine to economics, which make use of the counterfactual as a tool to explore alternative scenarios and propose solutions to incumbent problems. For example, counterfactual analysis, also known as 'potential outcome model', is the methodological basis for some approaches to areas in the biomedical sciences, such as epidemiology (e.g. Höfler 2005), although the limitations of this type of inference model are also noted (e.g. VanderWeele 2020), or physics, a field in which debates over its use have led to disagreements (e.g. Elitzur and Cohen 2020; Vaidman 1999). Counterfactual reasoning is regarded as a potentially productive heuristic model in philosophy, playing a key role in discussions about agency, free will and rationality (Starr 2022). In politics, counterfactual impact evaluation is used to assess the effects of new policies implemented by means of a variety of methods, for instance, a curated comparison between one social group that has been exposed to the policy and one who has not (Gertler, Martínez, Premand, Rawlings and Vermeersch 2016: 47–62). Counterfactual thinking has also been a popular area of psychological research since the 1980s, with a recognition of the overall beneficial effects of what-if speculation on individuals (e.g. Mandel, Hilton and Castellani 2005). As proven by the contributions of Tattersdill, Fowler, and Bakogianni in this volume, counterfactuals also have a pedagogical potential to be exploited in the classroom. Their speculative nature encourages students to question the factors behind a historical episode and to reflect on how that episode would have changed should those factors have been different. While some dismiss historical counterfactuals as an intellectual trifle (e.g. Carr 2001), others argue that counterfactual speculation should be seen as a method for historical analysis in its own right (e.g. Bunzl 2004, Gallagher 2018) that allows to explore the limits of what is possible and/or inevitable. For example, Tetlock, Lebow, and Parker

(2006) bring our attention to the way in which counterfactual argumentation can be used to question and challenge the reasons for the 'rise of the West'. In a similar way, Evans (2014: 38) has stated that the influence of econometric history or military history has played a major role in the admission of counterfactuals in historiography as they serve to deploy 'an element of what did not happen in order better to explain the consequences of what did'. In addition to its heuristic role in different scientific disciplines, counterfactual modes of thinking can also be used in the arts to recreate alternative worlds and play with the limits of imagination. In this context, as noted by Will Tattersdill in his Foreword to this volume, analysis of counterfactual science fiction has traditionally been the domain of literary critics. As a result, the potential of an interdisciplinary approach to the analysis of counterfactuals has been largely overlooked. For all of these reasons, counterfactual thinking should be understood as an umbrella term that covers different and overlapping forms of reimagining the past.

This flexibility of counterfactual approaches results in a polymorphism of manifestations that cannot be contained within the boundaries of rigid taxonomies or applied to restricted contexts. Delineating analytical categories for imaginations of what did not happen is an elusive task; yet, the richness of the counterfactual field has led authors to propose potential ways of classifying this phenomenon. One option would be to focus on whether a counterfactual is expressly outlined or not. In these cases, it is possible to talk about 'explicit counterfactuals' when the premises of the what-if scenario are fully elaborated and explicitly stated, like the short story that opens this introduction. But there are also 'implicit counterfactuals', that is, scenes and contexts that invite to develop an alternative story by inference. Thus, stating that vaccines have saved millions of lives implicitly intimates that millions of people would have died if vaccines had not been discovered.

Other possible criteria to try to classify counterfactuals are based on the traits of the new alternative reality that is being constructed. Among these forms, uchronia stands out given its ample presence in literary fiction. The French author Emmanuel Carrère, in his novel *Le Détroit de Behring* (1986: 9), defined uchronias as any text whose purpose is to modify what already happened. Thus, uchronias require the full development of an alternate reality that encompasses the narration of the events prior and posterior to the nexus point, that is, the point of divergence in which the outcome of an actual historical episode is sustituted by an imagined one. In turn, the degree of the difference between the reimagined past – and its resulting alternate world – and the actual world will depend on to what extent the principle of minimal departure is activated in the narrative. The principle of minimal departure advises to (re)construct the new reality as close as possible to the real world. For example, in the imagined story at the beginnig of this Introduction, the new reality would involve Britain being conquered by Mexico, one of the most powerful political and military stakeholders in a reimagined nineteenth century CE, but the principle of minimal departure dictates that readers would imagine that Britain remains otherwise as close as possible to the reality that is known to them. Uchronias are sometimes catalysed by time-travel, which is both a sf subgenre and a literary ploy at the heart of counterfactual narratives.

Another form of counterfactual thinking is alternate history (also known as 'parahistory' or 'allohistory'), a term that refers to hypothetical scenarios created by historians as part of their attempts to contextualize the causes leading to a particular historical event. Often considered intriguing and fascinating by the general public, the interest in counterfactual history has resulted in a growing number of publications that gauge the impact of what-if narratives (e.g. the recent volume edited by Morgan and Palmer-Patel 2019a). However, there is no scholarly consensus about their usefulness in historiographical studies. Richard Evans has assesed this debate in a monograph (2014) that puts a strong emphasis on the downsides of applying counterfactuals in historiographical analysis. Evans is partly refuted in Catherine Gallagher's study, as she understands that counterfactuals are not only a methodological approach, but also (2018: 9) 'a historical object, whose long term development and motivations might give us some significant insight into our ways of making history meaningful'.

What all these forms have in common is the invention of scenarios that do not correspond with reality as we know it, yet they differ in their extension, scope and purpose. In some instances, they overlap and interact; for example, the plot of some uchronias can revolve around time-travels and share literary devices with science fiction. Sometimes they may also be used interchangeably, highlighting the difficulty of establishing clearcut boundaries between them.

Whatever term or classification one opts for, counterfactuals grant us the ability to think beyond the margins of reality. Indeed, what may draw our attention to counterfactuals is not what they are, but rather what they allow us to do. In the opening story about Agustín I of Mexico, for example, we encourage readers to identify and separate aspects of the story that are 'authentic' – the British summer weather, the typical garden furniture – from those that point towards an alternative reality – the food, the entertainment venue. In this sense, these types of speculative narratives are, by definition, unfinished pieces that are shaped by means of a process of critical reflection undertaken by the reader.

Counterfactuals rely on the shared recognition of a past that allows for creative engagements with the present, something that Singles (2013: 7) characterizes as a latent tension between artificiality and authenticity. In this framework, counterfactuals introduce a creative dialogue with the past that allows us to reflect on our present and future.

Time, What Is Time?

In our volume we are interested in exploring precisely how ancient historians and classicists approach alternative narratives, and what role they feel these play in the reimaginations of the ancient past as conceptualized by both ancient and modern authors.

Not only modern authors have concerned themselves with the possibilities of altered times as a narrative device. Indeed, we can explore how intellectuals throughout antiquity engaged in discussions about the nature of time as well as the narratological and philosophical possibilities offered by breaking the linearity of time. One of the main reasons that has encouraged us to explore the potential offered by modern reimaginations of the past is that Graeco-Roman literature exhibits a comparable tendency to break the linearity of time. Philosophers, rhetoricians and even bishops pondered on the nature of time and how it can be manipulated for literary and rhetorical purposes. For example, in the fourth century BCE Aristotle considered that time could be defined as 'the dimension of movement in its before-and-afterness, and is continuous (because movement is so)' (Aristotle, *Physics* 4.11), even though the philosopher also had to acknowledge that time was such a complex and slippery notion that made one 'suspect either that there is really no such thing as time, or at least that it has only an equivocal and obscure existence' (Aristotle, *Physics* 4.10). In the fourth/fifth centuries CE, the bishop Augustine of Hippo, on his part, linked time with the concepts of memory and God, although the bishop only managed to give a humorously aporetic definition of it: 'So what is time? If no one is asking me a question about it, I know what it is; but if I want to explain it to the questioner, I do not know how to' (Augustine, *Confessions* 11.14).

However, the difficulties to pinpoint a precise definition of time did not stop ancient authors from experimenting with it in their writings and, especially, via counterfactual thinking and the composition of hypotheticals. The possibility of imagining what could have happened outside of time and outside of reality was dealt with by Aristotle in his *Poetics*. In a passage in which the philosopher digressed on the different tasks of poets and historians, he claimed that

> it is not the poet's function to relate actual events, but the kinds of things that might occur and are possible in terms of probability or necessity. The difference between the historian and the poet is not that between using verse or prose (...) No, the difference is this: that the one relates actual events, the other the kinds of things that might occur.
>
> Aristotle, *Poetics* 1451a–b

Along the same lines of Aristotle's reflection is Cicero's understanding of the differences between *historia* and *argumentum* (Cicero, *On Invention*, 1.19.27): '*Historia* is an account of actual occurrences remote from the recollection of our own age (...) *Argumentum* is a fictitious narrative which nevertheless could have occurred'. In addition to these considerations, it should be mentioned that hypotheticals and counterfactual periods were composed thanks to the articulation of *eikos* ('probable, likely'), a philosophical and rhetorical notion that helped in the creation of what-if scenarios.[1]

The presence of instructions on how to produce a counterfactual passage in the *progymnasmata* bears witness to the relevance of this mode of thinking in Graeco-Roman literature. *Progymnasmata* were rhetorical exercises of increasing difficulty that were designed to help students improve their skills in the composition of encomia, comparisons, invectives and other literary operations. An example of the presence of counterfactuals in these educational materials can be found in the collection of *progymnasmata* attributed to the rhetor Theon (first century CE), in which he recommended students to speculate about historical facts as a way to find materials to praise someone (*Progymnasmata* 110): 'It is useful also to conjecture about the future on the basis of past events, as if one were to say about Alexander of Macedon, "What would he, who overthrew many great peoples, have done if he had lived a little longer?"'. A similar purpose is detected in another treatise from Imperial times, Menander the Rhetor's *On Epideictic Speeches*. In the section devoted to the composition of a monody, Menander (434.10–437.4) strongly relied on the use of counterfactual thinking. After giving instructions on dividing the facts narrated in the monody into three different times (past, present and future), Menander advised to elaborate on what the addressee would have accomplished if they had not died: 'Share the grief of the father and mother, and amplify the pathos by showing what hopes they have been robbed of. You should also argue from the point of view of the city, saying what kind of man he would have been to it, how he would have shown himself as a benefactor, how indeed he did' (Menander Rhetor, 436).

The intellectual toolkit developed since Aristotle until Menander found its most notable expression in the *History of Rome* by Livy. The historian conjectured what would have happened if Alexander the Great had decided to march against Rome (9.17–19). Livy punctuated his historiographical digression with counterfactual clauses that helped him show that Alexander could have reached Rome, but that he would have been finally defeated by the Roman army given its superiority. Given the level of detail and the thoroughness of the historian's conjectures, Livy's text is one of the few examples in Graeco-Roman literature that can be considered as an uchronia.

Therefore, we think that the study of counterfactuals and their different manifestations offers new research avenues for the study of the relationship between antiquity and modernity. In this sense, the Postclassicisms Collective (2020: 24) has posed this question: 'If the conceptualization of historical time changes – "the times they are a-changing" is the anthem of modernity – how, then, does the study of antiquity change with it?' Some of these changes are actually addressed in the contributions to this volume, as the authors of the novels that have been analysed have toyed with time following cultural and political agendas.

Disrupting Time

The reworkings and reinterpretations of the ancient past present in these novels are dealt with from the perspective of reception studies, a field that has gained momentum as an academic discipline within the last two decades, particularly instigated by the publication of two handbooks (Martindale and Thomas 2006; Hardwick and Stray 2008), followed by the creation of a dedicated journal (*Classical Receptions Journal*) by Oxford University Press in 2009. These publications helped delineate the discipline and establish reception firmly within the study of Classics. While at its inception reception may have been more focused on what was traditionally regarded as 'high culture', the remit of reception has expanded over the last few years to cover many areas of popular culture as well, as demonstrated by recent studies of the impact of classical culture on comic books (Kovacs and Marshall 2011), heavy metal music (Fletcher and Umurhan 2019), videogames (Rollinger 2020), and science fiction and fantasy media (Rogers and Stevens 2019).

In this volume, we propose to highlight this intersection of Classics and popular culture by exploring the role that counterfactual narratives and uchronic scenarios play in the perception and reception of ancient cultures. Our interest in novels and short stories is motivated primarily by methodological reasons. As stated above, the manifestations of counterfactuals are numerous, so we consider that focusing on their presence in a particular form (namely, literary fiction and historical novels) will avoid ambiguities and overlappings. These novels and short stories allow us to approach counterfactuals from the perspective of literary practice, with an emphasis on the narrative devices – from metalepsis to ekphrasis – that different authors use to create a timeline that never was. A focus on popular literature – rather than works perceived as 'literary classics' – is not the only way in which the present volume disrupts conventional understandings of classical reception. We advocate for a reconceptualization of what Classics means by embracing a broader definition of classical tradition that looks beyond 'Classical Greece and Rome' to encompass other places – such as Egypt – and times – such as Late Antiquity. This decision is prompted by the current intellectual questioning of disciplinary boundaries in the study of the ancient world, a matter to which Will Tattersdill also alludes in the Foreword.

In line with the heuristic approach advocated above, our understanding of counterfactuals and uchronias will be broad and inclusive, being mediated by playful reinterpretations of time. In some cases, the works surveyed in this volume are set in alternate pasts resulting from a different outcome of a major historical event in antiquity (e.g. *Roma Eterna*, by Robert Silverberg). This point of divergence serves authors as a template to explore chance and contingency in human affairs, or to inquire into issues that have a special relevance in our society, such as certain political ideologies. In other instances, the chosen novels are set in a present that is portrayed as an alternate timeline to our own. In these imagined new worlds, some of the usual counterfactual tropes operate by articulating strong subtexts and intertextual references to the ancient world (e.g. *Fireball*, by John Christopher). Either in the shape of uchronias, alternate histories, science fiction tales or time-travel stories, the novels analysed in this volume can be considered as an exercise in ideological ventriloquism that modern authors have practised to voice their opinions, concern and fears on contemporary issues.

As it is shown in the ten chapters of this volume, reimagining the past through counterfactuals has more to do with our attempts to redefine what the ancient world means to us than with efforts to try to rewrite history. For example, a story in which Alexander the Great survives long enough as to expand his conquests even further (*A Choice of Destinies*, by Melissa Scott) or a novel based on the supremacy of Egypt in modern times (*Three Princes*, by Ramona Wheeler) encourage us to think of the geopolitical implications that these alternate scenarios would have had today. Similarly, time-travelling in order to instruct Aristotle on the use of modern technology ('Aristotle and the Gun', by L. Sprague de Camp), or to witness the triumph of Celtic peoples over the Roman Empire ('Delenda Est', by Poul Anderson) not only reveals our necessity to establish a dialogue with the past, but also evidences that concepts like 'progress', 'civilization', 'culture' or 'history' – as well as the very concept of Classics – are being reconsidered thanks to the pedagogical and cognitive toolkits afforded by counterfactual narratives. What-if narratives and speculative scenarios, then, are understood in this volume as cultural mechanisms through which the authors explore how our relationship with the ancient world is continuously reshaped.

Overview of the Book

This volume is organized in three thematic sections, which showcase some of the opportunities provided to us by the use of counterfactuals. These sections delve into, respectively, the limits and potential of counterfactual history as a literary genre, the capacity of counterfactuals to provide commentary on past and present political and cultural circumstances, and the impact of both fictional and historical artworks on the creation of counterfactual narratives. The contents of these sections necessarily overlap, but the organization into separate parts allows us to keep a focused and bounded approach.

Section 1 is entitled '*Fortuna Imperatrix Mundi*: History between Chance and Determinism'. This section explores to what extent ideas of chance, contingency and determinism play a role in the construction of counterfactual scenarios in narrative. Would Rome have become an empire, had Julius Caesar not been murdered by Brutus in 44 BCE? Was the so-called Amarna revolution inevitable after the reforms introduced by Amenhotep III in the fourteenth century BCE? Historiography, theology and philosophy, among other disciplines, have long debated the concept of inevitability and the role of chance in the unfolding of history. The four contributions in this section reconsider the epistemological and narratological possibilities offered by the use of counterfactuals in uchronic narratives and how these may contribute to new understandings of ancient cultures.

The first chapter, '"Delenda Est": Counterfactual and Narratological Obligations in Poul Anderson's Gerundive History' by Genevieve Liveley, uses

Poul Anderson's 1955 short story 'Delenda Est' as a case study to explore unwritten rules about creation of counterfactual dynamics. The world presented by this short story is one in which Celtic peoples took over the Roman Empire. Understanding counterfactuals as 'gerundive history', namely a history of that which must have happened, Liveley questions whether there are any limits to our counterfactual imagination and interrogates to what extent those limits may be based on perceived laws within which history (and counterfactuals) operate. In the second article, 'Counter-Apostate, Counter-Christianity in John Christopher's *Fireball*', Ryan C. Fowler explores historical determinism through a timeline journey to an alternate 1981 pagan England where a Christian uprising is allegedly about to change the course of history. The survival of Julian the Apostate in his Persian campaigns of 363 CE is presented as the point of divergence that allowed for paganism to thrive and Christianism to be thwarted, but the 1981 uprising gives Christopher – and Fowler – the chance to pose questions about inevitability and the very concept of history in the context of the classroom and beyond. In '"All That Is Solid Melts into Air": Destabilizing History in Robert Silverberg's *Roma Eterna*', Sarah Annes Brown delves into the use of counterfactual explorations for social commentary. In his novel, Silverberg plays with multiple points of divergence: we witness a timeline where Rome remains the dominant political stakeholder, the Exodus did not occur, and Muhammad is murdered before he could unite Roman citizens under a single god. Thus, this 2003 novel exploits and subverts reader recognition of key moments and characters in history in order to raise subtle questions about determinism. Finally, Javier Campos-Daroca in 'What if Aristotle Had Known (Better)? Technological Counterfactuals in L. Sprague de Camp's Short Fiction "Aristotle and the Gun"' makes the short story 'Aristotle and the Gun' ([1958a] 2002) the centre of an exploration of the value of science and technology in counterfactual argumentation. In his efforts to accelerate 'progress', an engineer travels in time in order to introduce Aristotle to scientific advancements, with disastrous results. This contribution constitutes a fascinating take on determinism and inevitability that goes beyond event- and character-centred perspectives. Overall, the chapters in this section provide a useful and necessary starting point to issues of historical determinism and contingency.

From the narratological mechanisms used to create counterfactual narratives, Section 2 moves towards the role that individuals played in these alternate accounts. This section, entitled 'Narratives of Power in Uchronias: between "Big Men" and Underrepresented Voices', investigates how the nature and reach of personal power is represented in uchronic narratives. As also seen in the previous section, counterfactual works may sometimes focus on the weight of an individual's charismatic personality in the unfolding of historical events, while determinism may question their pivotal role, and this section explores that latent tension. In addition, it was our intention to transcend the usual focus on 'big men' by giving voice to underrepresented groups whose role as key historical stakeholders is often dismissed. Through their stories, the reader has the chance to reimagine the world and seek social justice by means of reflective engagement with the ancient past.

In 'The Triumph of Greek Civilization? Projecting Ancient Greece into an Alternate Future', Anastasia Bakogianni raises questions about the alleged responsibility of 'big men' in political developments, taking the opportunity to reflect on the embedded misogyny of these overly masculine counterfactual works. Through the analysis of a novel (Melissa Scott's *A Choice of Destinies*, 1986) and a short story (Lois Tilton's 'Pericles the Tyrant', 2005), Bakogianni investigates how the lives of Alexander and Pericles respectively have been used as a lever to craft an alternate world in which Greece is one of the main political superpowers, highlighting how contemporary political anxieties are subtly interwoven with the characterization of power in counterfactual narratives. The second article in this section, 'Emperor Julian's American Dream', by Alberto J. Quiroga Puertas and Elia Otranto, centres on the complex reception(s) of Julian the Apostate, taking Mario Farneti's *Imperium Solis* (2009) and *Gladius Imperii* (2012) as their case study. In these novels, Julian is presented as not only escaping his tragic death, but also managing to arrive in the American continent, where he brings progress and development to an allegedly primitive land. The authors explore Farneti's political agenda and its impact on the presentation of Julian as a modern Prometheus of sorts. This contribution reminds us of how counterfactuals are not only meant to destabilize the socio-political *status quo*, but they can also be used to perpetuate bigotry – in this case, in the form of a racist paradigm of Western superiority. The final contribution to this section is 'Alternat(iv)e Fiction in T. S. Chaudhry's *The Queen of Sparta*: Unrepresented Voices and Counterfactuality', by Lynn S. Fotheringham. This 2014 novel is used to explore the boundaries between literary genres in the characterization of counterfactual narratives, paying particular attention to the gaps between academic and popular understandings of uchronias. In addition to this interrogation of traditional definitions of genre, Fotheringham sees Chaudry's work as a unique opportunity to raise questions about the way Greece is traditionally represented. Indeed, the novel places the focus on historically unrepresented groups, namely female (the Spartan queen Gorgo) and non-white characters (a fictional Indo-Scythian prince called Sherzada), who are said to have founded a settlement in the Indus valley that would eventually be destroyed by Alexander the Great, quenching any potential subversions to the course of history as we know it. Section 2, in sum, explores the implications of alternative political systems and ideologies through counterfactual reimaginings of the past. The chapters highlight the relevance of counterfactual explorations, which can creatively contribute to achieving a deeper and more reflective understanding of contemporary events.

The three contributions in the final section, 'Art, Culture and the Poetics of Counterfactuals', explore the impact of works of art in the crafting of alternate times and places. Artistic expressions – from literary works to architectural environments – play a key part in counterfactual worldbuilding, either by familiarizing or de-familiarizing a given setting. On the one hand, some of them may be directly taken from or inspired by historical pieces, providing a concrete anchoring point to alternate reimaginations. On the other, authors may concoct original works of art to populate these worlds creatively and help them develop new symbolic messages through metatextual means.

The first chapter in this section is '"A Picture That Can Only Ever Come in Parts": Alternate Histories of Film in Catherynne M. Valente's *Radiance*', where Benjamin E. Stevens proposes that art raises insightful questions about how historical knowledge is constructed. In Valente's 2015 novel, a fictional film from an alternate Hollywood's Golden Era is inspired by a well-known but fragmentary poem by the seventh/sixth-century BCE female poet Sappho. In this complex and metaleptic novel, classical reception is brought to the forefront in the interpretation of a counterfactual work of art that highlights the poetics of historiography, which is also made up of fragments and ekphrastic recreations. In 'How Place Creates Time: Imagined Architecture as an Expression of Identity in Ramona Wheeler's *Three Princes*', Leire Olabarria explores how worldbuilding – rather than the detailed description of a historical divergence point – may be the key to the creation of an alternate time. *Three Princes*, by Ramona Wheeler (2014), presents us with an alternate nineteenth century CE in which an immense Egyptian empire is one of the most influential stakeholders in international politics, together with Tawantinsuyu, which encompasses South and Central America. Wheeler's narrative focuses on descriptions of surrounding natural and built environments, creating a sense of familiarity as well as displacement. A reimagined Egypt is still populated by colossal buildings that reinforce the widespread view of Egypt as a 'culture of monumentality' and as a never-changing, static society. Architecture contributes to the construction of the identity of the protagonists, something that in this paper is addressed from the theoretical perspective of cultural hybridity. Finally, in 'Antiquity Interrupted: Partial Receptions as Counterfactuals', Jesse Weiner relies on a poetics of counterfactuals that allows him to propose that translations and adaptations can effectively produce counterfactual reimaginings of literary works. He uses three case studies to characterize these receptions as 'partial' – because they only engage with sections of the source texts – and 'terminal' – because they truncate ancient narratives, providing alternative endings that can radically transform the message and purpose of the work. Overall, the third and final section of the volume plays with works of art – ancient and modern, real and fictional – and explores the creative impact they can have on counterfactual narratives and their receptions.

It is our belief that counterfactual narratives allow us to establish a dialogue with the past that facilitates critical reflection about the present. By pondering over what may have been and playing around with alternative outcomes, academics, students and the general public can explore issues of agency, contingency and chance as well as the impact they have on history-made-present. What if the study of the ancient world were relevant after all?

Note

1 As noted by Wohl (2014: 2), '*Eikos* arguments thus draw on – and provide an invaluable window onto – the Greek's shared assumptions about human psychology, social norms, and narrative verisimilitude'. See also Gagarin (2014: 15–29).

Section 1

Fortuna Imperatrix Mundi: History between Chance and Determinism

1.1

'Delenda Est': Counterfactual and Narratological Obligations in Poul Anderson's Gerundive History

Genevieve Liveley
University of Bristol

Introduction

In *History Boys*, Alan Bennett (2004) famously characterized counterfactual history as 'subjunctive history', the imagination of that which *could* or *might* have happened in the past.[1] This chapter considers instead whether counterfactual history might rather (or as well) be described as 'gerundive history' – the imagination of that which *must* have happened – and explores some of the rules and laws under which this form of historiography typically operates. It investigates the obligations limiting the scope of that which should or ought to happen in such speculation about the past – including the deontic dominance of the actual historical timeline. In particular, it reassesses the six criteria of good counterfactuals proposed by Philip Tetlock and Aaron Belkin (1996: 16–31): clarity, cotenability, historical consistency (the 'minimal rewrite rule'), theoretical and statistical consistency, and projectability. The chapter takes Poul Anderson's 1955 short story 'Delenda Est' as its case study – a time travel counterfactual in which Anderson's Time Patrol discovers a world in which 'it looks as if something upset the Roman empire and the Celts took over' (Anderson 1955: 11) – and it re-evaluates both the counterfactual dynamics of this narrative and the criteria that Tetlock and Belkin suggest help to make it a good example of the form.[2] Blending close reading of Anderson's original 1955 text and its 1960 'alternate' revisioning with detailed consideration of the wider theoretical issues that the narrative(s) stage(s), it demonstrates that 'Delenda Est' exhibits an aptly anticipatory recognition of both the limitations and obligations of counterfactual 'laws'.

Gerundive History

In Anderson's short story or 'novelet', first published in the December 1955 edition of *The Magazine of Fantasy and Science Fiction*, Time Patrol agent Manse Everard, 'American, mid-Twentieth A.D' (Anderson 1955: 3), bored by a hunting trip back in time to the Pleistocene era, attempts to take a vacation in his own milieu – 1950s New York.[3] His time 'machine' – something like a motorcycle or scooter without wheels (Anderson 1955: 5) – takes him to 'lower Manhattan, 23 October 1955, at 11.30 A.M' (Anderson 1955: 6). But when he materializes in this time and place, Everard fails to recognize the world around him. The people are fair, 'with a great deal of red hair', they speak 'in some babble' Everard cannot understand, and they wear a strange costume:

> The men wore loose colorful blouses, tartan kilts, a sort of Scotch bonnet, shoes and knee-length stockings. Their hair was long and many favored drooping mustaches. The women had full skirts reaching to the ankles and tresses coiled under hooded cloaks. Both sexes went in for massive bracelets and necklaces.
>
> Anderson 1955: 6

Everard and his companion have indeed travelled to New York, 1955 but have somehow arrived on 'Another time line. Somebody has managed to change history' (Anderson 1955: 8). Crucially, within the logic of Anderson's storyworld, this is not presented as an 'alternate history' – a parallel possible world to that with which we and Everard are familiar. This changed alternate timeline has replaced the original. The world that Everard knows has been destroyed, over-written by this new history. His uncomfortable duty is, therefore, to discover what caused this change and to undo it. The hybrid plot that ensues is part counterfactual history, part 'whodunnit', and part 'whendunnit' as Everard hunts for the rogue time travellers who have disturbed the time continuum by interfering with some crucial 'nexus' event.

Everard sees it as his 'plain duty to restore the original time track' (Anderson 1955: 31). Since the new timeline has effectively written the Time Patrol and its founders out of history, its deletion is presented as imperative: 'One perquisite of an agent's office was the longevity treatment of the Danellians, . . . the supermen who were the shadowy chiefs of the Patrol' (Anderson 1955: 4–5).[4]

> To protect themselves, the Danellians had recruited the Patrol from all ages, a giant secret organization to police the time lanes. It gave assistance to legitimate traders, scientists, and tourists – that was its main function in practice; but

> always there was the watching for signs which meant that some mad or ambitious or careless traveler was tampering with a key event in space-time.

However, keeping history on track is more than Everard's narrative function in this story. Time Patrol agent Manse Everard embodies the rules and obligations of Anderson's alternate history. Everard metapoetically polices the laws of both time travel and counterfactualism in the storyworld of 'Delenda Est'. And it seems wholly appropriate that the very title of this story expresses his future-inflected responsibility. As a helpful footnote to the original short story confirms (Anderson 1955: 35), Anderson's choice of 'Delenda Est' as the Latin title for this counterfactual appeals to the political motto famously attributed to Cato the Elder: *Carthago delenda est* – literally, 'Carthage must be destroyed'.[5] And, following the Roman annihilation of Carthage in 146 BCE in the aftermath of the Third Punic War, the phrase came to denote an uncompromising appetite for 'total war' (on this trend in the 1930s and 1940s see Little 1934 and Adcock 1946). By using only a fragment of this familiar phrase as the title for his counterfactual and thereby supressing the name of the city, Anderson himself linguistically (and metapoetically) places 'Carthage' under erasure – at once a reflection of Rome's historic razing of the city and an anticipation of the eradication of the alternate world that his story will (re)present. Once Everard locates the 'switchpoint' (Anderson 1955: 11) at which the course of history was disrupted and his own timeline erased, he must go back and undo it, thereby eradicating the new timeline and the entire alternate world it has produced.

The force of this obligation weighs heavily upon Anderson's character: interviewing one of the inhabitants of the alternate timeline, trying to figure out when their histories separated, he reflects silently that 'my job is to condemn you and your entire world to death' (Anderson 1955: 18); 'tell me what I must do to destroy you' (Anderson 1955: 19). Interrogating this sense of obligation, Anderson has Everard justify his responsibility to history (to remember 'his purpose' – Anderson 1955: 19) by appealing to 'the little things and the little folk' (Anderson 1955: 21) he knew and loved in the original timeline – all of which have been destroyed by this new history. It is, therefore, 'no abstract sense of duty which compel[s] him' (Anderson 1955: 21) but the memory of his parents, a college girlfriend, old friends, a pet dog, Shakespeare, the Golden Gate Bridge, the 'billions of human creatures' who 'had never been' (Anderson 1955: 10). Other characters test and explore the nature of duty too. One of Everard's quasi-Russian captors, who plans to use the agent's time machine 'to soar above enemy cities and pelt them with fire' (Anderson 1955: 27), confesses that he would rather not go to war but that he and his people 'have our obligations ... it is necessary' (Anderson 1955: 25). When another Time Patrol agent offers to go into battle to fix the temporal anomaly that has disturbed the timeline, Everard insists: 'I've got to go ... I don't know why, but I've got to' (Anderson 1955: 32). The narrative thus unfolds within a strict deontic frame – a teleological matrix in which rules, duties and obligations of various kinds are repeatedly foregrounded.[6] In this respect, Anderson's narrative sets the stage for the laws and rules that would come to govern the 'genre' of counterfactual history in the late twentieth century – among them the six criteria for judging good counterfactuals proposed by Philip Tetlock and Aaron Belkin (1996: 16–31; see also Levy 2015 and Morley 2019).[7]

Clarity

Tetlock and Belkin (1996: 18) recommend that a 'good' counterfactual should always 'specify and circumscribe the independent and dependent variables (the hypothesized antecedent and consequent)'. That is, the counterfactual should clearly identify the nodal point or nexus connecting the counterfactual antecedent to its consequences and stipulate the temporal-causal connections between them.[8] In 'Delenda Est', the point of divergence (and its second-order consequences) is not immediately revealed, but only gradually comes into focus. Just as the strange new world into which the Time Patrol jump is initially 'registered in bits and pieces' (Anderson 1955: 6), Everard slowly puts together various clues in order to clarify what has happened to cause this alternate history: or rather, 'what had *not* happened' (Anderson 1955: 20). Everard has 'studied history ... with a thoroughness that should have earned him several PhDs' and is also able to consult a 'Classical Scholar' (Anderson 1955: 7, 12), so is able to determine that 'The Second Punic War, or rather some key incident thereof, was the turning point' (Anderson 1955: 20) – namely, the untimely death of the Scipios at the battle of Ticinus in 218 BCE.

Under their rubric of 'clarity', Tetlock and Belkin highlight the popularity of such 'assassination' tropes in counterfactual histories: in such cases 'it is so easy to imagine "getting away with" changing only a few causal antecedents and producing a consequential result ... These possible worlds are only a muscle twitch or nightmare removed from the actual world' (Tetlock and Belkin 1996: 20). Indeed, illustrating the value of this trope as the nodal point for a counterfactual, Anderson himself uses assassination as an example to explain the rules of time travel and history modification (Anderson 1955: 11; on the 'political reversal' story as a standard of the genre see also Raghunath 2020: 7–8). What is more, the Time Patrol in which Everard serves has its own technical terminology to refer to such a tipping point or pivotal node: the 'nexus' – defined by Anderson (1955: 11) as 'Some one happening [at] a nexus of so many world lines that its outcome [is] decisive for the whole future'.[9]

The Minimal Rewrite Rule

By pinpointing the death of the Scipios at Ticinus as the nexus or tipping point for his counterfactual, Anderson also neatly observes the 'minimal rewrite rule' or rule of historical consistency (Tetlock and Belkin 1996: 23–5): the rule that recommends 'altering as few "well-established" historical facts as possible'. Everard's powers of 'total recall' tell him that in his own history 'both the Scipios were at Ticinus, and very nearly killed; the son saved his father's life during the retreat' (Anderson 1955: 30). Anticipating the 'minimal rewrite rule', Anderson (or rather, his rogue time traveller) needs to alter this single 'turning point' or 'key event' (Anderson 1955: 29) – positing something that might plausibly have happened in actuality – and then to imagine the trophic cascade of consequences that might ensue from this alternative antecedent. In fact, Anderson extends the 'minimal rewrite' rule to other pivotal events within this cascade, including in the 1960 reworking of 'Delenda Est' one further hypothetical consequence of his original hypothesis: the idea that Judaism was destroyed along with the Romans, for 'without the balance-of-power effect of Rome, the Syrians did suppress the Maccabees; it was a near thing even in our history' (Anderson 1960: 152).

Cotenability

Indeed, an additional rule proposed by Tetlock and Belkin (1996: 21–3) is that of 'logical consistency or cotenability'. That is, a good counterfactual will need to think beyond a single tipping point and consider its imbrication within a wider historical milieu, imagining what other inter-connecting historical factors might also change, what compounding and complicating principles might also be brought into (or taken out of) play. It is important that such connecting factors be both logically and internally consistent if the counterfactual is to maintain plausibility and, in 'Delenda Est', Anderson's anticipatory observation of such a rule is relatively robust – and self-consciously performed. For example, Everard is able to make sense of a strange map illustrating the alternate geopolitical configuration of Anderson's counterfactual world by 'filling in the gaps of his knowledge with what sounded logical' (Anderson 1955: 10 – this line is missing from the 1960 revision). Such logical reasoning also allows Everard to reconstruct the chain of interconnected events (and non-events) that have cumulatively resulted in the emergence of this alternate world: the Scipios – both father and son – are killed at Ticinus during the Second Punic War between Rome and Carthage; thus, there is no Publius Cornelius Scipio to undermine the Carthaginian base in Spain, no cutting off of their Iberian life-lines, no stranding of Hannibal in Italy, no Third Punic War, and no Roman defeat of the Carthaginians when they face Scipio Africanus at Zama. Instead, in this alternate history, Hasdrubal Barca moves into Spain unchallenged and reinforces the Carthaginian troops, allowing Hannibal to destroy Rome in 210 BCE.[10] With Rome and its institutions lost, the 'Gauls and Cimbri and Parthians [go] ramping through the shattered Classical world' (1955: 30). A short-lived Carthaginian Empire ('the Carthaginian government was too venal to endure' – 1955: 20) sees the Parthians, Gauls, Celts and Germanic tribes carving up Europe and North Africa between them. Then:

> As ships improved, there was trade around Africa with India and China. The Celtanians discovered Afallon [North America] ... but were thrown out by the Mayans. The Brittic [British] colonies further north had better luck, and eventually won their independence. Meanwhile Littorn [Lithuania/Russia] was growing vastly. It swallowed up central Europe and Hyperborea for a while ... [Now] The Asian countries have shaken off their exhausted European masters and modernized themselves, while the Western nations have declined in their turn.
>
> Anderson 1955: 20

Significantly, this long causal change effectively results in an alternate history that is not radically dissimilar to that of actual history and the real geopolitical landscape of 1955 (or 1960). In Anderson's counterfactual, global politics and economics appear to follow a path that initially deviates from their actual historical course, but over time (broadly, 2000 years) they come to run along closely parallel if not intersectional lines. In fact, several constants appear in the alternate timeline. War is 'always the same' (Anderson 1955: 32) and the rule of law is also presented as largely unchanged in the shifts attending Anderson's alternate world: Everard is arrested by agents clearly recognizable as 'police' (Anderson 1955: 8), albeit wearing 'coppery breast-plates and helmets', who use handcuffs, carry guns, hustle Everard and his companion into their vehicle ('A black Maria is much the same in all times'), and lock them in a 'cell with an iron-barred door' (Anderson 1955: 7); the 'police chief' who later interviews them has both office and desk (Anderson 1955: 8). In fact, both 'Government and traffic' look strangely familiar to Everard, who recognizes some distinctive Gallic 'French' character in both (Anderson 1955: 15).

Similarly, although social, cultural and technological principles are ostensibly subject to major changes in the counterfactual world of 'Delenda Est', the differences between counterfactual and actual history turn out to be relatively minor. Everard's impression of 'a technology roughly equivalent to the 19th Century' (Anderson 1955: 8) suggests a world in which science and technology may have developed at a different pace but which nonetheless follow a familiar historical trajectory to that of the industrial and scientific revolutions and discoveries experienced in the actual world. Thus, Everard learns that 'In the eleventh century, the Celts began tinkering with steam engines. They seem to have gotten gunpowder too, maybe from China, and to have made several other inventions. But it's all been cut-and-try, with no basis of real science' (Anderson 1955: 18).

The steampunk aesthetic of the new order is revealed by the presence of 'steam cars' oddly styled like Viking boats with 'sharp prows and figureheads' (Anderson 1955: 6) and with 'oil-lamp headlights' (Anderson 1955: 15). Everard subsequently discovers that this culture has slavery 'though not on racial lines' (Anderson 1955: 14); that 'they had approximately the same time units [t]here as in his world, both descended from the Babylonian' (Anderson 1955: 27); they enjoy wine, books and cigars (Anderson 1955: 16–17); the women wear cosmetics (Anderson 1955: 12); they have gas light and matches (Anderson 1955: 8, 17), navigational compasses (Anderson 1955: 25), 'clumsy iron bridge[s]' (Anderson 1955: 15), steam boats, hot air balloons and glider planes (Anderson 1955: 22). The world 'had gradually developed a rule-of-thumb mechanics', Everard reasons, 'but no systematic science' – thus, 'They don't have atomic bombs, . . . neither do they have penicillin' (Anderson 1955: 14).

The robust efforts that Anderson makes to ensure that this kind of logical consistency and 'cotenability' informs his counterfactual seem to limit the alterity of his consequent world. And this limitation extends beyond the typical conventions attending the narratological 'principle of minimal departure' in such counterfactual storyworld design. According to Marie-Laure Ryan (1980: 407; 1991a: 58), the principle 'applies to all statements concerning alternate possible words' and entails that 'whenever we interpret a message concerning an alternate world, we reconstrue this world as being the closest possible to the reality we know' (Ryan 1980: 403; 1991a: 51).[11] In the case of 'Delenda Est', the 'principle of minimal departure' primarily concerns the real timeline and course of history that we know. For, as we have seen, the corollary to contenability appears to be a fixed, deterministic model of history. The alternate timeline that emerges as a consequence of the Scipios dying at Ticinus seems only to delay rather than to radically disrupt the teleological progress of history. The tacit footnote to Everard's observations on the new world's lack of systematic science is that they don't have atomic bombs . . . yet.

Projectability

Further expanding the rule of cotenability is that of 'projectability' which mandates that the counterfactual should 'tease out testable implications of the connecting principles and determine whether those hypotheses are consistent with additional real-world observations' (Tetlock and Belkin 1996: 18; 30–1). While the notion of 'testability' in any counterfactual situated in the ancient world is necessarily problematic, 'Delenda Est' offers a rare opportunity to observe an author revisiting and teasing out some of the principles and hypotheses of his original model in the light of additional (including 'real-world') observations.

Five years after its first publication, Anderson included 'Delenda Est' in his 1960 collection of Time Patrol stories, the *Guardians of Time* – a paratext to which acknowledges that an earlier version appeared 'in slightly different form' in the 1955 *Magazine of Fantasy and Science Fiction.* Some differences between the original and the alternate version are indeed slight: a handful of dates are refreshed so that instead of travelling to 1955, Everard and his companion arrive 'in lower Manhattan, 23 October 1960, at 11:30 a.m.' (Anderson 1960: 136). Other changes seem designed to add greater historical accuracy and verisimilitude to the original: the historians in the new 1960 timeline more plausibly refer to the 'Punic Wars' as the 'Roman Wars' and to 'Spain' as 'Hispania' (Anderson 1960: 155). When Everard joins a Roman battle-scene in the 1960 version, Anderson's narrator acknowledges that 'Only a few captains and scouts were still mounted; as often before stirrups were invented, what started to be a cavalry battle had become entirely a fight on foot after the lancers fell off their mounts' (Anderson 1960: 172). There is no reference to stirrups or the lack thereof in antiquity in the 1955 version of the battle. Similarly, new historical knowledge on the part of both author and character seem to inform Everard's observation in the 1960 text, that 'In Everard's history, Julius Caesar had been astonished to find the Veneti building better vessels than any in the Mediterranean' (Anderson 1960: 156). This new detail also helps to bolster the logic of Anderson's counterfactual in terms of the plausibility of its premise concerning the Celtic world's early colonization of North America as well as its historic sea-trade with the Far East.

Indeed, Anderson takes other opportunities to strengthen the plausibility of his counterfactual in this 1960 reworking. In both stories he extends the multi-order consequences of a world and a history in which 'the Romans vanished early' (Anderson 1955: 18), but in the 1960 story he adds a further logical consequence and an explanation that is absent from the original (Anderson 1960: 152): 'So, I'm pretty sure, did the Jews. My guess is, . . . Judaism disappeared and therefore Christianity never came into existence. But anyhow, with Rome removed, the Gauls got the supremacy'. The absence of Christianity, its institutions and technologies, is no less critical to Anderson's counterfactual than the absence of the Roman Empire. However, in order to explain the non-existence of Christianity as a world-faith, the 1960 reworking acknowledges that Anderson (also) has to account for the non-existence of Judaism. In a seeming throw-away addition to the 1960 text, Anderson notes that 'Judaism seems to have disappeared, and Buddhism hasn't been very influential' (Anderson 1960: 151). Yet, the omission of other world religions, especially Islam, from his counterfactual vision – and the failure to factor in their likely expansion in these conditions – stands out as a glaring oversight in Anderson's logic. And moves to patch-up this logic in the 1960s version of 'Delenda Est' only serve to draw our attention to some of the flaws of the foundational premise. For example, in the 1955 original, Everard attempts a 'minimal rewrite' to explain the conditions of the new timeline, positing that: 'it looks as if something upset the Roman empire and the Celts took over' (Anderson 1955: 11). Yet, in the 1960s revision, Anderson has Everard address a potential weakness in this theory. He maintains the original premise that (Anderson 1955: 15) 'If his own Western civilization had developed out of the decaying Roman Empire about, say, 600 AD', then the absence of Rome as a world power would have had radical implications for the shape of that civilization. However, his 1960 revision acknowledges that if the Roman Empire really were to have been upset, this would still leave the culture, science and technology of the ancient Greeks to shape the development of Western history. Everard's addition in the 1960 version hypothesizes that 'it looks as if something upset the *Graeco*-Romans and the Celts took over' (1960: 143) – but quite how the legacy of classical Greece is also erased in this new history is never directly addressed.

Omissions and modifications such as these may seem of only superficial significance, but they complicate the 'basic theory' of time and temporality that Anderson posits for his storyworld. For, as Everard explains

> Events are the result of a complex. *There are no single causes.* That's why it's so hard to change history. If I went back to, say, the Middle Ages, and shot one of F.D.R.'s Dutch forebears, he'd still be born in the late nineteenth century – because he and his genes resulted from the entire world of his ancestors, and there'd have been compensation. [. . .] But every so often, there must be a really key event/ *a really key event does occur*. Only with hindsight can we tell what it was, but some one happening was/*is* a nexus of so many world lines that its outcome was/*is* decisive for the whole future.
>
> Anderson 1955: 11; additions in 1960: 143, text in italics

Quite why no equivalent 'compensation' emerges for the assassination of the Scipios in the counterfactual, it is not clear. Nor is it self-evident why, if 'there are no single causes', a single event can serve as a nexus that radically changes the whole course of history. Similarly, Anderson's attempt (in a rhetorical prolepsis focalized and vocalized via Everard) to explain in the 1960 version why this new timeline has only 'now' appeared seems defensive rather than persuasive: 'Don't ask me why they weren't 'always' wiped out; why this is the first time we came back from the far past to find a changed future. I don't understand the mutable-time paradoxes. We just did, that's all' (Anderson 1960: 144).

Theoretical and Statistical Consistency

Mutable-time paradoxes aside, Anderson takes care in both versions of his narrative to justify his counterfactual consequents and to authorize their plausibility by appeal to wider theoretical principles. Tetlock and Belkin (1996: 18; 25–30) maintain that the counterfactual must 'articulate connecting principles that are consistent with "well-established" theoretical [and statistical or probabilistic] generalizations relevant to the hypothesized antecedent-consequent link'. This is important if the counterfactual is to avoid developing fanciful or 'far-fetched consequences' that are implausible or improbable and so strain the counterfactual's credibility (Tetlock and Belkin 1996: 25). In cases of counterfactuals involving ancient history and long temporal-causal chains, such as we encounter in 'Delenda Est', multiple theories and a plurality of internally consistent 'well-established' generalizations are necessary (if not sufficient) to satisfy this condition (on the virtues of such plurality see Levy 2015: 395).[12]

Anderson (1955: 17) draws upon two popular theories concerning the history of science in order to justify why the people of this counterfactual world 'should be so backward intellectually, and still have combustion engines'. Explicitly citing the ideas of Lewis Mumford and Alfred North Whitehead, Anderson hypothesizes that a relative lack of scientific sophistication is concomitant with a corresponding lack of organized religion:

> As Whitehead pointed out, the medieval idea of one almighty God was important to science, by inculcating the notion of lawfulness in nature. And Mumford added that the early monasteries were probably responsible for the mechanical clock – a very basic invention – because of having regular hours for prayer. Clocks seem to have come late in this world.
>
> Anderson 1955: 17

In the absence of the Roman Empire and the Holy Roman Empire, there would be no Christian tradition to foster scientific innovation. The superstitious pagans of the alternate timeline still believe in witchcraft, their nearest equivalents to engineers, scientists, and doctors are 'artisans', 'wizards' and 'Druids' (Anderson 1955: 16, 29). Anderson's 'generalization' here owes much to Mumford's 1934 study of *Technics and Civilization*, especially his influential theory that 'The clock, not the steam-engine, is the key machine of the modern industrial age' (Mumford 1934: 14–15). No less important is Whitehead's 1925 thesis (as set out in *Science and the Modern World*) that 'the development of modern scientific theory ... is an unconscious derivative from medieval theology' and that modern science and technology originates in 'the medieval insistence on the rationality of God' (Whitehead 1925: 18). In the context of these theoretical generalizations, the steampunk aesthetic of Anderson's alternate world is the logical and necessary consequence of a superstitious rather than religious worldview.

Indeed, Anderson's appeal to Whitehead's history of science carries wider significance for our understanding of his own theory of the rules of historical counterfactualism as staged in 'Delenda Est'. For Whitehead (1925: 18), 'the greatest contribution of medievalism to the formation of the scientific movement ... [is] the inexpugnable belief that every detailed occurrence can be correlated with its antecedents in a perfectly definite manner'. This proposition not only aligns neatly with the counterfactual rules of clarity and contenability proposed by Tetlock and Belkin, but – as we have seen – also provides the foundation of Anderson's own 'scientific' approach to alternate history. That is, the obligation that every detail in his counterfactual timeline must be traceable back to clear correlating antecedents and (indeed, *because*) there exists a kind of rational 'lawfulness in nature'.

Yet this lawfulness imposes certain limits upon the direction of history as upon time itself. For example, in a passage of brief exposition that is cut from the 1960 reworking of 'Delenda Est', Anderson attempts to explain the natural laws that make time travel and the mutability of history possible:

> Travel into the past involves an infinite discontinuity; it was the discovery of such a principle which made the travel possible in 19352 A.D. But that same discontinuity in the conservation-of-energy law permitted altering history. Not very easily; there were too many factors, the plenum tended to 'return' to its 'original' shape. But it could be done.
>
> Anderson 1955: 5

Anderson appeals here to classical physics and to both the first and second laws of thermodynamics – or what Menke (1998: 969) describes as 'the thermodynamic nature of history'. That is, the laws of physics which say energy can be neither created nor destroyed and that time's arrow flies forward in one irreversible direction. The standard demonstration of these laws is the cup of hot tea which grows cool over time as its heat energy is transferred into the space of the room in which it sits: over time the tea will always grow colder and never become hotter again – as heat will aways flow to cold and never in the opposite direction. The energy once used to heat the water for the tea is not destroyed but it is lost; it is transformed into unusable energy or *entropy*.[13] There is, then, a strongly deterministic (even teleological) property to the conservation of energy law and its correlate law on the irreversibility of natural processes, since together these laws demand the future destruction of life, the universe and everything – 'the tragedy of the inevitable "heat-death" of the universe, a time when all energy [will] be dissipated into entropy and all order into anarchy' (Menke 1998: 970). Arthur Eddington, whose popular works on these laws Anderson does not directly cite but with which he is certainly familiar, describes this as 'the running-down of the universe', likening the workings of the universe to that of a clock (Eddington 1929: 84). Indeed, Anderson's (1955: 5) explanation that it is a 'discontinuity' in the first law of thermodynamics that permits time travel seems explicitly to evoke Eddington's (1929: 85) own disinclination to accept any such 'discontinuity' in the divine regulation of the clockwork-like physics of the universe. These 'well-established' theoretical historical and scientific generalizations offer important insights into the dynamics of Anderson's counterfactual history and help to explain his apparent reluctance to accept the co-existence of multiple timelines and universes in 'Delenda Est' – as well as his determination that the counterfactual world 'must be destroyed'.

Conclusion: Historical Necessity

The Magazine of Fantasy and Science Fiction in which 'Delenda Est' first appears introduces the story with a brief editorial preface which asks the magazine's readers: 'can you deduce the historical turning point which created this World of If?' (Anderson 1955: 3). Within the narrative's storyworld the key turning point turns out to be the Battle of Ticinus in late November 218 BCE, but Anderson's 'World of If' is also created by another, external, historical nexus: the testing of the first atomic bomb in New Mexico in mid-July 1945 CE and the subsequent bombing of Hiroshima and Nagasaki in August that year. The magazine cover depicting a 'sun becoming a nova' – an exploding sun, and a mushroom cloud arising from a desert planet – serves to reinforce this atomic connection. And although Oppenheimer would not characterize himself as 'destroyer of worlds' until his infamous television interview in 1965, he had described himself in an interview for *Time* magazine in 1948 as 'shatterer of worlds' – an echo of which may be heard in Anderson's description of his counterfactual in 'Delenda Est' as 'the shattered Classical world' (Anderson 1955: 30; on Oppenheimer, see Thorpe 2006).

Seed has suggested that Anderson's counterfactuals respond directly to the fears of nuclear apocalypse and the perceived inevitability of a Third World War that dominated global politics (and literary responses thereto) in the 1950s and 1960s. Indeed, we might regard this as another facet of the 'principle of minimal departure' that colours Anderson's narrative. Yet, as 'History . . . is scrutinized for the scripts whose replay might shed light on the "plot" of the present . . . [friction] emerges in Anderson's fiction between nuclear apocalypse and historical continuity' (Seed 1999: 41; on the eschatological plotting of Anderson's narratives see also Hellekson 2001). Such friction can certainly be seen in 'Delenda Est' in Anderson's struggle to reconcile the competing dynamics of historical determinism and contingency – nicely characterized in another of his short stories, 'Cold Victory' (first published in 1957) as a conflict between the aleatory 'dice of future history' and the teleology of 'Historical Necessity'. In 'Delenda Est' Anderson sets out to explore the effects of a small yet key causal event (the virtual throw of the dice that decided whether the Scipios should live or die in 218 BCE) turning out differently. But his counterfactual thought experiment is circumscribed on every front by 'historical necessity'. The alternate history reverts (more or less) to the actual course of history. Thus, in the counterfactual 1955 (or 1960) of 'Delenda Est', Afallon (North America) is on the brink of another war with Littorn (Lithuania/Russia) – just as the USA and USSR were imagined to be in the actual 1950s and 1960s while both global super-powers fought to win the nuclear arms race (see Roland 2010). In fact, such a grim prospect is one of the factors that helps mitigate Everard's guilt that he must destroy the new world:

> This culture might not have the ruthless will and sophisticated cruelty of Western civilization; in fact, in some ways it looked strangely innocent. Still, that wasn't for lack of trying; and in this world, a genuine science might never emerge, man might endlessly repeat the cycle of war, empire, collapse, and war. In Everard's future, the race had finally broken out of it.
>
> Anderson 1955: 21

Here we see an optimistic glimpse of future continuity and progress, but this positivity is tempered – even contradicted – by a scepticism born of Everard's own experience of history (Anderson 1955: 6, ellipsis in original): whenever 'a city went up in radioactive flame, something wept. He could understand the fanatics who had tried to change events. It was only that their work was so unlikely to make anything better . . .'.

For Anderson, then, counterfactual history is fundamentally concerned not with what *might* but what *must* happen. His attention to the rules and obligations of counterfactualism – clarity, cotenability, projectability, historical, theoretical and statistical consistency – focuses upon micro-scale details, upon the small things, the minor characters, the lesser battles, the insignificant events (the 'little things and the little folk', Anderson 1955: 21) which nevertheless have the potential to cause critical disruptions with major consequences. Yet, at the macro-scale, the historical plenum must always '"return" to its "original" shape' (Anderson 1955: 5). As Hellekson (2001: 98) points out: 'Anderson always squashes the alternate timeline and returns time to its "normal" path'. This, after all, is precisely what the Time Patrol is deployed to do. For Anderson, then, counterfactual history is less concerned with aleatory possibility than with historical necessity: it is history in the gerundive.

Notes

1 See also Tetlock and Belkin (1996: 4), for whom counterfactuals are 'subjunctive conditionals'.

2 Contrary to Hellekson (2001) who reads Anderson's fictions as a kind of 'anti-alternate history'. She does concede that: 'In one sense, Anderson works as a

meta-alternate historian: his works prefer to deal with the structure and nature of history and history making' (2001: 98).

3 The magazine also includes stories by Isaac Asimov, P. G. Wodehouse, Edgar Allan Poe, and Saki.

4 This section of text is subject to major revision in the alternate 1960 edition of 'Delenda Est': 'he had seen that history rewritten in minor things – not by God, which would have been endurable, but by mortal and fallible men – for even the Danellians were somewhat less than God; . . . he was forever haunted by the possibility of a major change, such that he and his entire world would never have existed at all' (Anderson 1960: 135).

5 Recorded in Plutarch, *Cato* 27; Pliny, *Naturalis Historia* 15.74; Aurelius, *De Viribus Illustribus* 47.8; Florus 1.31. Anthony Boucher, editor of the 1955 magazine in which 'Delenda Est' originally appears, adds this gloss to the story (Anderson 1955: 35 – omitted from all subsequent reprintings): 'For any readers victimized by a modern anti-classical education, I might insert this footnote: that Mr Anderson's title stems, of course, from the political war-cry uttered by Marcus Porcius Cato ('Cato the Elder') in 157 BC and incessantly for a decade thereafter: *Delenda est Carthago* (Carthage must be destroyed), resulting in as insensate an act of barbarism (what we today would call genocide) as any military victor has ever perpetuated – and yet an act which laid the foundations for the world in which we exist'.

6 As Hellekson (2001: 102–3) suggests, 'Anderson prefers to play by rigid rules: the past is hard to change in all his texts'.

7 Given Anderson's interest in rules (and this chapter's focus on the same), Tetlock and Belkin's 'rules' for evaluating counterfactual thought experiments seem both relevant and appropriate here. See also Evans (2014: 81–7) for similar criteria against which to assess a 'good' counterfactual.

8 Levy (2015: 388) further suggests that this clarity should also extend to the representation of 'the nature of the relationship' between the two timelines, and a clear sense of whether the relation is deterministic or probabilistic.

9 Anderson's stories provide the origin of the term 'nexus event' in Hellekson's (2001) taxonomy of counterfactuals. On the importance of such nodes in counterfactuals see also Dannenberg (2008); Ryan (2006: 657, emphases added), for whom: 'Alternate . . . history fiction creates a world whose evolution, *following a certain event*, diverges from what we regard as actual history'; and Singles (2013: 7), who defines the 'point of divergence' as 'the moment in the narrative of the real past from which alternative narrative of history runs a different course'.

10 Despite its eventual demise as a political force in this timeline, the legacy of Carthage and its leaders is retained in the names of some of the characters in Anderson's (1955: 19) story world: Cadwallader Mac Barca, Hamilcar ap Angus, Finn O'Carthia.

11 On the 'principle of minimal departure' in counterfactuals see especially Raghunath (2020).

12 Significantly, Anderson (1955: 26) disavows some of the problematic 'generalizations' and discriminatory theories that *could* have informed his counterfactual: for example, he has Everard affirm that 'He was no respecter of windy theories about inborn racial traits'.

13 For an accessible explanation of these laws see especially Menke (1998).

1.2

Counter-Apostate, Counter-Christianity in John Christopher's *Fireball*

Ryan C. Fowler
Franklin & Marshall College

Introduction

Though scholars have argued for some time whether it is appropriate in the twentieth and twenty-first centuries to apply the term 'post-Christianity' to some parts of the world (e.g. McDonagh 2001), we may have cause to wonder whether the world impact of the religion – starting as a Second Temple Judaic sect in the first century CE in the Roman province of Judea – *necessarily* had to have taken the historical path it did. This line of thinking has given rise to several questions. What would a non-Christian 1981 Britain have looked like? What if there had been no Holy Roman Empire governing Central Europe for a thousand years? How would the world be different if Christianity had not taken hold within the Roman Empire in the fourth century CE? These are precisely the types of questions at the heart of John Christopher's young adult novel *Fireball* (1981), in which the story's contrafactual pivot point is the early death of the anti-Christian Roman Emperor Julian 'the Apostate' at thirty-two years old.[1]

In what follows, I will discuss the challenges John Christopher (one of several pen names used by Christopher Samuel Youd) faces in his *Fireball*: that is, to make accessible to a young audience an incredibly complicated historical development – the move away from an effectively Christian Roman Empire by the last 'pagan' Roman emperor, who himself was a complicated thinker and author – as an invitation to ask larger questions about the nature and development of history and religion. To this end, Christopher must work along two axes: he must be attentive to historical accuracy to ensure his audience recognizes the characters involved, while preventing the novel from devolving into a tedious scholastic historical–study; he must also develop his alternative historical timeline in a way that is plausible enough within the limits of the genre to convince his readers to continue reading.

I will first provide a summary of the novel, then, for context, discuss our timeline's Julian, Christopher's Julian, and the uses of religion and technology within the novel. I will then turn to some of the literary techniques Christopher employs in *Fireball* that relate to the genre of contrafactual history, including issues of personal identity and the friction between determined and contingent events, ending with some of the questions I suggest Christopher wants to raise for his readers, perhaps in the classroom. My argument is that Christopher's *Fireball* is an important example of one of the ways counterfactual narrative can be used to explore historical causation and the deterministic paths of religious movements with a young adult audience in mind. I end by briefly discussing the possible use of this novel as a pedagogical tool to encourage critical thinking within the classroom.

Fireball, a Summary

The general plot of *Fireball* is as follows. A British teenager and his visiting American cousin are drawn through a ball of lightning into what at first seems to be another world. In fact, the two find themselves in Roman Britain, but in an *alternative* 1981 CE, one in which the Emperor Julian had actually survived the Parthenian battle in which, in our own historical timeline, he was killed in 363 CE. As a result of his survival in this new alternate timeline, however, this counter-Julian was able to successfully direct the Roman Empire away from the path it had taken after the Emperor Constantine's Edict of Milan in 313 CE, in effect restoring a general Hellenistic polytheism as the state religion, and thereby relegating Christianity to the status of an underground cult.

After over a millennium and a half of this second-class status, Christopher's character 'Bishop', a powerful figure within the church, interprets the appearance of the British teen and his cousin as a sign from God to begin his long-planned revolt aimed at overthrowing the Roman army, the emperor, and pagan Rome itself – his goal was to establish what he envisions as Christianity's rightful place within the empire. In the final part of the novel, readers follow the tactics used in the various battles that make up the revolt, all of which proved to be successful, primarily because of the introduction of two as yet unheard-of military advancements helpfully furnished by the teens: the stirrup (not invented until the eighth century for the Frankish cavalry), and the longbow (invented by

Edward the First in the thirteenth). Near the end of the novel, readers confront some of the aftermath of the revolt, including the revolutionary Bishop's introduction of capital punishment against those who are unwilling to follow only Christ. In the novel's final pages, the teens escape alt-1981 Roman Britain to (slightly) less fraught shores: the New World.

Fireball is the first in a trilogy by Christopher in which this alternate timeline remains throughout: after the protagonists leave Roman Britain, in the second book in the series they travel to the New World, at first encountering the indigenous people who live there, and eventually coming in contact with an unchanged Aztec civilization. They end their journey in the third book when they are brought by slavers to the Imperial Court of China.

In what follows, I will focus on the political and religious aspects of *Fireball*, the novel's use of signs and omens, and its approach to historical determinism and contingency, especially as they may relate to the history of Christianity.

Our Julian and Religion

In any contrafactual narrative, there will always be a negotiation between a reader's knowledge of the generally accepted account of history in our timeline, and the alternative events presented by the author. There have been some interesting recent studies about how to incorporate a reader's preexisting sense of history within a reader–response theoretical framework.[2] To that end, having a sense of the usual account of Julian's rise to power and death can be helpful to many readers.

Julian's rise to power in our timeline was quick, and the covert revelation of his Hellenistic pagan revival when emerging from within a decidedly powerful Christian family was deftly handled. As a student of philosophy in 351 CE, Julian encountered so-called pagan Neoplatonists, and was initiated as a theurgist by Maximus of Ephesus; for the next ten years, however, given his family's Christian commitments, Julian's so-called pagan conversion remained a prudently kept secret. After his Christian uncle Constantius ordered the transfer of choice detachments to the east, the army mutinied, and in February 360 CE (likely with some prompting), Julian was proclaimed Augustus. It is possible that Constantius' death later that year averted civil war, but, in addition, Julian was able to publicly declare his so-called paganism. He entered Constantinople unopposed in December of that year, and a general purge of the Imperial court quickly followed, drastically reducing its officials and staff.[3]

Throughout his life, Julian was a prolific writer. He was a poet, having written two major hymns: to the mother of the gods, and to the god Helios. He wrote several panegyrics (two for Constantius and one for Eusebia) and several letters (though the authenticity of some has been questioned; see Wright 1923: xxiii; xxxvi; lxv–lxi). Yet philosophy was never very far from Julian's mind, evidence of which is found in nearly everything he wrote, but especially found within his works criticizing the Cynics (*To the Cynic Heracleios* and *To the Uneducated Cynics*) and his letter to the philosopher Themistius. One of the most important of his lost works is his anti-Christian critique, *Against the Galileans*, of which only fragments remain; but from his other writings, we can see that his own philosophic ideology was deeply rooted in Iamblichan-influenced Neoplatonism and theurgy. Questions remain as to how forcefully his own personal religious system impinged on his more general 'pagan' public religious reforms; for example, some scholars wonder whether his administrative decisions were directed more toward the founding of a Neoplatonist-infused pagan church than toward a restoration of a more traditional Graeco-Roman polytheism (see Greenwood 2021). In a different counterfactual account than *Fireball*, one that focused specifically on Julian's philosophy of religion, such details might be important. In the long run, for example, perhaps Julian's appeal to the mass of contemporary, traditionally minded Graeco-Roman pagans might have been relatively limited. But while this line of inquiry remains interesting, in Christopher's account, and given the possibly limited theosophical background of his younger audience, such details would likely be distracting.

In our timeline, though Julian targeted wealthy and educated Christians, his aim was not to destroy Christianity per se. Rather, as Peter Brown (1971: 93) writes, his goal was 'that Christianity should sink out of the governing classes of the empire – much as Buddhism was driven back into the lower classes by a revived Confucian mandarinate in thirteenth-century China'. Julian's edicts in effect do reveal a clear preference for a reinstated Hellenistic paganism.

In February 362 CE, Julian promulgated an edict to guarantee freedom of religion, which declared that all the religions were equal before the law and that the Roman Empire return to its original religious eclecticism, according to which it did not impose any religion on its provinces. Subsequently, though advertised as a general religious toleration, his actions regarding the Imperial court foreshadowed a vigorous programme of pagan activism in the interest of a general 'Hellenism': namely, that the temples and finances of the ancestral cults were to be restored. A hierarchy of provincial and civic pagan priesthoods was appointed, while the Christian churches and clergy lost the financial subsidies and privileges previously gained under Constantine.[4] Two particular results seem to emerge from Julian's edict: first, it was seen by some as an act of favour toward Jewish citizens specifically in order to upset Christians. In addition, while it might be seen as an instance of tolerance of various religious views, the return from exile of certain Christian bishops who had been censured or excommunicated by the Church may instead have been an attempt by Julian to foster schisms and divisions between Christian rivals, since disputes over what constituted orthodox Catholic teaching were often vitriolic. As the fourth-century historian (and fellow soldier of Julian) Ammianus Marcellinus (22.5.4) puts it:

> On this [Julian] took a firm stand, with the result that, since this freedom increased their dissension, he might afterwards have no fear of a united populace, knowing from experience that no wild beasts are more dangerous to human beings as are most of the Christians in their deadly hatred of one another.

A second, seemingly innocuous proclamation is Julian's *School Edict* of June of 362, in which Julian required that all public teachers be approved by the emperor – justified because the state supplemented or paid a large portion of their salaries. Ammianus (*Res Gestae* 22.10)[5] explains that the real reason for this edict (he refers to it as *inclemens*: 'inhumane' or 'harsh') was as a way to prevent Christian teachers from using pagan texts (such as the *Iliad*, which was widely regarded as divinely inspired) that formed the core of classical education. At its heart, the edict was an attempt by Julian to remove some of the influence of the Christian schools, which at that time used ancient Greek literature in their teaching in an effort to present the Christian religion as superior to paganism. There was also a likely economic purpose: by depriving them of students, the edict also dealt a severe financial blow to many Christian scholars, tutors, and teachers within the empire.

The Religious Implications of the Death of Our Julian

Ammianus (23.1–2) tells us that, after a winter in Antioch and a failed attempt to restore the temple in Jerusalem, the emperor set out against Persia in 363 CE to settle Rome's long-running war with Sapor II. Despite some early successes, the army found itself in serious difficulties, and, while withdrawing on 26 June 363, during the minor Battle of Samarra near Marangathe, Julian suffered a spear wound in the abdomen. After three days of treatments, the spear wound proved fatal. We are told by Ammianus (25.3.3) that Julian, in a rush, had happened to rejoin the battle without his protective coat of mail.[6]

As in the case of Julian's hastily forgotten protective chain mail, the idea of 'coincidence' is a natural handmaiden to the development of contrafactual narrative (see Dannenberg 2008) – in this case, we might speculate whether his gear might have stopped the type of wound he received, or at least prevented the spear or javelin strike from proving fatal. However, Christopher's novel need not go into details of Julian's survival of the battle. His point, given his younger audience – according to the publisher, the target age range is nine to thirteen years old – is to present a simplified, bifurcated alternate timeline that is generally plausible enough to raise important questions about the nature of history and the ways in which religions develop over long periods of time.

We might compare Christopher's novel with examples of *ancient* contrafactual 'what ifs'. For example, the fourth-century CE sophist Libanius (*Oration* 17.19) suggests that Julian could have accepted the Persian embassy's peace proposal, were it not for the fact that Julian considered a desire for peace tantamount to treason (προδοσία).[7] In the case of Christopher's novel, however, Julian's survival is not used to make a political point, or even a *particularly* religious one, but is used instead to develop a reasonable point of divergence that could postpone the creation of a Christian Rome as a contrafactual hypothetical possibility when compared to our own timeline.

To be sure, Julian's death in our timeline was immediately religionized; soon after Julian was killed, Libanius (*Oration* 18.274), who supported Julian, writes that the emperor was assassinated by a Christian – one of his own soldiers, no less. Less than a century later, the fifth-century Church historian Sozomenus (*Historia ecclesiastica* 6.2, written between 440 and 443) proposes that Julian was killed by the Christian Saint Mercurius.[8] Not long after Sozomenus' account, the fifth-century theologian Theodoret (*Historia ecclesiastica* 3.25, completed in 449–450 CE) reports that Julian's dying words were νενίκηκας Γαλιλαῖε ('You have won, Galilean'), suggesting that Julian had understood that with his death Christianity would again become the official religion of the Roman Empire.

Similar to the situation in *Fireball*, then, in our fourth century CE, Julian's death was understood within a religious framework from the very start. While it is generally understood that under the reigns of subsequent emperors after Julian's death there existed a policy of relative tolerance toward paganism,[9] Julian's immediate successor, the short-lived Emperor Jovian, quickly re-established Christianity's privileged position within the empire.[10] But though the divergence of *Fireball*'s historical timeline is at its core religious, in a sense

Christopher is able to raise particular points about culture, technology, and the path of history without making the Christian–pagan dichotomy the only focal element within the novel's action.

Christopher's Counter-Julian and Counter-Christianity

One of Christopher's primary assumptions in the novel is that, because the persecution of Christians by past Roman emperors had seemingly only strengthened Christianity, many of Julian's actions in our timeline were designed solely to *harass* Christians and undermine their ability to organize resistance to the re-establishment of paganism in the empire. So, though expressly opposed to violent persecution of Christians, Julian overtly discriminated in favour of pagan individuals and communities in his appointments and decisions. Measures such as his ban on the teaching of classical literature and philosophy by Christian professors and his encouragement of charitable expenditure by pagan priests signal a determination to marginalize Christianity as a social force.[11] Julian's installation of a pagan hierarchy in direct opposition to the Church's was a result of his desire to create an empire in which every aspect of the life of its citizens was connected to the emperor, who would be understood to be their ultimate provider and protector. Any parallel systems, such as the Church's hierarchical power structure or the system of Christian charity (both of which he took as models for his renewed and reorganized pagan practices), would simply distract from this primary relationship between *imperator* and *populus*. In this way, Christopher's novel follows the actions and decisions of our Julian, which in turn supports the plausibility of his alternative history for many readers.

In Christopher's novel, however, readers experience a Julian much less explicitly preferential toward his reformed paganism – in fact, his rule is presented as nearly irreligious. There is no overt reference in the novel to any of our Julian's extensive tenets about theology or theurgy, and, as a result, he is not recognizably the author of the *Hymn to King Helios* or *Hymn to The Mother of the Gods*. Instead, by removing any of the problems that emperor-deification would cause among the monotheistic Christians, Christopher keeps his focus on the consolidation of attention and patronage toward the figure of the Roman Emperor. Christopher, then, can refrain from dealing with religious nuances: it need only argue for a general polytheistic, decidedly non-Christian state religion in which emperors are not deified within their lifetimes. After the pagan Roman Empire is reinstated, however, alt-Julian could be worshipped as 'god-emperor' without repercussion, but only well after his death in his eighties (Christopher 1981: 159). As a result, Christopher can avoid any of the larger complications and controversies that may have resulted from having to delineate Julian's actual vision for religious renovation. What matters for the action of the novel is that the surviving counter-Julian avoided the outright persecution of Christians, as well as any problems that could have emerged from the forced worship of a living emperor.

For Christopher, then, few of these smaller academic details matter: his primary purpose is to invite his young readers to think generally about the nature of history, and specifically, perhaps, about Christianity itself. In what follows, I will suggest a few questions that are brought forward most prominently by Christopher's *Fireball*: in particular, the role of the interpretation of omens and signs and its connection to military technology in the novel.

Julian's Interpretation of Divine Signs and Omens

We learn in the course of Christopher's alternative history that his Julian, by not only surviving but in fact winning the battle in 363 against the Persians, 'stabiliz[ed] the world' by 'diffus[ing]' the Christian problem (Christopher 1981: 101).[12] As mentioned above, by decreeing that no living person could be deified, especially the Roman emperor, Julian ensured that Roman allegiance was to a ruler, not a god (though a false god in the eyes of fourth-century CE Roman Christians and Jews). So, Christians were able to be subdued, and in the end 'tolerated' instead of persecuted, because no conflict arose from forced worship, oath-taking, or, at least early on, even acknowledgement of another god; for this reason, the Christian 'movement ran out of steam' (Christopher 1981: 102).[13] But since the arrival of our two protagonists was interpreted by the local Bishop as a sign from God to rebel against their status as second-class citizens and take power from 'Roman pagans', the alt-1981 Christian revolution that makes up the latter part of *Fireball* gained renewed power and immediacy (Christopher 1981: 97, 170, *passim*). While their arrival was first described by the Bishop as a miracle ('God has sent a sign' [Christopher 1981: 114]), later in the novel, we read second-hand that he described their appearance as a sign from 'the Holy Ghost or a very senior angel'. Regardless, their arrival showed they were 'instruments of divine will' that enabled 'the followers of the Lord to destroy the slaves of false gods' (Christopher 1981: 129).

This divine omen that drives Christopher's narrative could remind younger readers of the reports of Constantine's so-called sign or vision before the Battle of the Milvian Bridge in 312 CE. Importantly, the reports of historians writing in the fourth century CE do not agree in detail. Lactantius, in his *On the Deaths of the Persecutors* (*De mortibus persecutorum*, written after 316 CE) (44.5), reports that Constantine was directed in a dream to mark the 'heavenly sign of God' [*caeleste signum dei*] on the shields of his soldiers before committing to battle. Having marked on their shields the letter *chi* (X) with a perpendicular line drawn through it and turned at the top, denoting Christ with the 'cross-rho'[14], his troops advanced to victory. Eusebius does not mention a sign per se in his *Ecclesiastical History* (published 326 CE), but only intimates that God helped Constantine. Stressing that he had heard the story much later from the emperor himself, in his unfinished *Life of Constantine* (28–32), Eusebius gives a detailed account of a vision. In his version, Constantine and his army were marching when he looked up to the sun and saw a cross of light above it along with the inscription ἐν τούτῳ νίκα. Typically translated into Latin as *in hoc signo vinces*, 'in this sign you will win', the literal translation of the Greek phrase is 'in this [*sc.* sign], conquer'. We are told that at first Constantine was unsure of the meaning of the vision, but the following night he had a dream in which Christ explained that he should use the sign against his enemies. In his report of the events, Eusebius then goes on to describe in detail the *labarum* (☧, made by combining the first two letters of Christ's name: chi and rho), which was also the military standard used by Constantine in his later wars against his colleague and rival, Emperor Licinius. Therefore, we have record of two slightly different signs, used for the same purpose – both interpreted as a symbol of God's assistance and a guarantee of Constantine's victory over his rival Maxentius and his forces.[15]

In readers' experiences of the novel, then, one of Constantine's signs can be connected with the appearance of the protagonists in the alt-1981 timeline as an indication that the time for battle – and victory – was at hand. In addition, this interpretation by the Bishop in the novel, in its consideration of unnatural or remarkable natural events as signs, might also point readers back to Ammianus' own Julian narrative (books 23–24).

In his historical account, the fourth-century CE historian tells us that, during the beginning of the preparations for the Parthian campaign, reports arrived that Constantinople had been struck by an earthquake, a sign that 'those skilled in such matters' insisted was not a favourable omen for a ruler planning to invade another country (23.1.7). In fact, Julian's own advisors had tried to dissuade him from the untimely enterprise, declaring that such signs ought to be disregarded only in the case of attack by an enemy (since the defence of the empire by every possible means and effort was always a priority). At nearly the same time, however, it was reported to Julian by letter that the Sibylline books had been consulted concerning this war, as he had ordered, and had given the reply that the emperor must not leave his borders that year (*imperatorem eo anno discedere a limitibus suis, aperto prohibuisse responso,* 23.1.7). Ammianus also tells us (24.5) that, while the emperor was lingering at Cercusium to allow for his army to cross the Abora on a bridge of boats, Julian received a letter in which the prefect of Gaul, Sallustius, begged that the campaign against the Parthians might be put off, arguing that Julian should not leave himself open to inevitable destruction without having yet prayed for the protection of the gods (23.5.4). Finally, Ammianus (23.5.6) adds that around this time an *additional* unfavourable omen appeared: the appearance of the outstretched corpse of an attendant who had been recently – and mistakenly – executed. Disregarding all of his cautious counsellors and these compounded negative omens (and others besides), the historian tells us that Julian in the end pushed confidently on, 'since no human power or virtue has ever been great enough to turn aside what the decrees of fate had ordained' (*quoniam nulla vis humana vel virtus meruisse umquam potuit, ut quod praescripsit fatalis ordo non fiat,* 23.5).[16] In fact, so sure was Julian about his victory that, immediately upon crossing the bridge, he ordered it to be destroyed, so that no soldier in his army might entertain hope of a return (25.5.5). Given all the reports of his seeking advice about the interpretations of various signs, signals, and natural events, then, it must be with a touch of irony that Ammianus (25.2.8) tells us that 'the emperor was opposed to the whole "science of divination" (*vaticinandi scientia*)': actually, Julian was only opposed to omens that opposed his plans.

Christopher gives his revolutionary Bishop this same sense of certainty and destiny. He shows no signs of hesitation or holding back, and systematically makes his way to Rome, winning battle after battle, absolutely confident in his mission to create a Christian Empire with the blessing of God. As the Bishop tells the two protagonists: 'A miracle brought you here, and God's wonders are not worked for nothing. Nor must they be wasted. This generation is blessed, but only if it seizes its blessing and uses it' (Christopher 1981: 114).

Signs and omens were not ignored in our own timeline's fourth-century CE Rome any more than in Christopher's alternative twentieth-century Roman Britain. As in the case of Julian's selective faith in the *scientia vaticinandi*, the deciding factor is the confidence of the individuals in power – no matter the century, or whether Christian or pagan. On one level, then, Christopher is on firm footing when he invokes omens and signs within his narrative. That said, though, plausibility – or perhaps as Lebow (2007: 156) puts it, 'reasonableness' – is determined by the reader. To my mind, Christopher is clever to straddle the extremes in contrafactual narrative between 'miracle and plausibility' (Lebow 2007: 153). Once readers make it past the 'miracle' of the fireball that places the protagonists within the alternate timeline, 'plausibility' takes over: they are asked to imagine the survival of a single individual and the possible future effects of that one event. Still, the 'miraculous' once again plays a significant narrative role in the action of the novel, in the form of the Bishop's interpretation of the divinely inspired, sudden appearance of the protagonists.

That said, regarding the idea of plausible action within *Fireball*, Christopher's novel asks readers to accept two significant effects of Julian's survival: first, that the survival of this one (admittedly quite powerful) individual could lead to a renewed pagan Roman Empire that would remain stable, able to contain a placated Christianity for the next 1,600 years. Second, readers must accept that this stability of the state would result in a nearly compete stagnation of any technological advancement, which is an important element of the action of the novel that I will briefly discuss below. In Christopher's conception of his alternative timeline, however, this reasonably imagined technological stagnation is supported in a sense by the Bishop's religious interpretation of the arrival of the cousins as a miracle from God.

Uchronic Literary Techniques: Metaphysics and Personal Identity

Throughout his *Fireball*, Christopher uses several literary strategies frequently found in science fiction and uchronias. In many contrafactual narratives, there is often some attempt to explain how the alternative history works within the 'metaphysics' of the text, at least to some extent; that is, how the alternative timeframe is understood to be connected to an original historical path (such as utopic paths, pivotal links, portals, *vel sim.*). Considering the continuity of the personal identities of the two protagonists between the two timelines in *Fireball*, we might be tempted to recall two other, rather different works of speculative science fiction. In H. G. Wells' groundbreaking 1895 *The Time Machine*, the narrator of the novel recounts the tale of the Time Traveller, who, after travelling a few hours into the future, then hundreds of thousands of years forward (i.e. 802,701 CE), finally travels millions of years into the future. Travelling back in time again, he arrives home mere hours before his original test of his time machine, his identity completely unchanged. Another similar literary example is the rather complicated use by L. Sprague de Camp in his influential 1940 short story 'The Wheels of If' of a number of *alternate histories* – called wheel-mates, or 'rooms on a wheel' – alongside *infinite worlds* (de Camp 1940: 44). In that story, the personal identity of the main protagonist is delivered unchanged into a few different alternative timelines before someone manages to force the 'wheel' to stop.

In a similar approach to these two stories, Christopher's alt-1981 Roman Britain is part of 'parallel worlds [that] exist side by side'. In the case of *Fireball*, however, the worlds 'occupy ... the same space and time, yet separate' (Christopher 1981: 103). Over the course of the novel, the young audience is offered occasional guides for how they might think about such a scenario: for example, at one point, one of the protagonists takes note of a lake that reminds him of one like it in St. James Park, and wonders to himself whether it could be the same place, and 'if at this spot in that other universe Horse Guards might right now be clopping their way to changing of the guard at Buckingham Palace' (Christopher 1981: 161).

When in chapter 6 of *Fireball* the protagonists confront the revolutionary Christian Bishop, Christopher's readers might reasonably be led to imagine that this explanation of an alternative-1981 Roman Britain (or, rather, as we are reminded in the novel: 2500 *ab urbe condita*), in which digital watches and denim jeans exist, might be met with great scepticism. However, the Bishop takes the explanation of alternative histories in relative stride because of his theological commitments: 'He who made one [world] could make two – a million if He chose' (Christopher 1981: 113). By exhorting a type of strong theological determinism, the Bishop's confusion about time-travelling teenagers is mitigated.

One of the common protocols of counterfactual historical study is the negation of a turning point. Such a process includes, as Lebow (2007: 166) puts it, assessing and defining the contingency of any given pivot event, as well as the aggregate implications of the counterfactual experiment. This requires isolating significant turning points and allowing readers the opportunity to understand the implications of the negation without worrying excessively about the intrinsic interconnectedness of events. By assuming that everything else within, around, and after the pivot point in question remains constant, readers can imagine a world in which 'everything (else) remains equal' (*ceteris paribus*) so that they may have the opportunity to think deeply about the connections between *specific* antecedents and consequents, as well as ask focused questions about historical causation and inevitability. As we have seen, in *Fireball*'s case, Julian's death is the negated, contingent pivot point between a Christian and a pagan Rome.

In the end, Christopher's novel does not – and, to my mind, need not – confront the idea that if Julian's early death had been negated and another timeline followed, our two protagonists either would not have existed, or would have been different from the individuals who show up in this alternative 1981.[17] Instead, Christopher's younger audience is asked to imagine that personal identities remain fully intact between alternate worlds, similar to the situations found in *The Time Machine* and 'The Wheel of If' mentioned above, where an individual's identity can move between worlds without any other significant changes. In all of these examples, any travel between historical paths does not create a so-called Jonbar hinge, where the smallest detail changes the entirety of the alternative timeline, so that the reader does not lose track of larger narrative designs.[18]

Determinism and Contingency

Beyond the narrative requirement of the plausibility and, ideally, the probability of a contrafactual account, any literary work of this sort likely needs to negotiate a relationship between historically contingent and historically determined events. Contingency/determinism discussions within a variety of academic disciplines are ongoing and quite outside the limits of this article.[19] For the purposes of the current discussion, we might define contingent events as occurrences that lack necessity or necessary causality, and deterministic events as occurrences that are understood as necessarily the case or a part of a necessary causal chain. A literary example of determinism that includes the 'inevitability' of certain 'fixed points in time' can be found in Effingham (2021: 1322):

> In Simon Wells' *The Time Machine* (2002), Dr. Alexander Hartdegen's fiancé is killed by a mugger. To save her, Hartdegen invents a time machine, changes the past, and saves her. However, she is then run over by a carriage. Hartdegen realises that no matter what he does, he'll be unable to stop her from being killed – every time she is saved, she'll simply die in a different manner. Her dying can be changed in certain respects (e.g. from her being killed in a mugging to being killed in an accident) but not others (e.g. she must always die at roughly that time). Her death is a 'fixed point in time'.

There is, then, in *The Time Machine*, a sense of the inevitability of the fiancé's death: in that story, it is a determined event, under any and all circumstances, no matter how those conditions might be altered. In the world of *Fireball*, Julian's death is an alterable, contingent event. A question we might ask, then, is whether Christopher wants his readers to imagine Christianity as an inevitable or deterministic event: as something (as it were) bound to happen, at some point.

Historical Cause and Effect

Counterfactuals are increasingly being recognized as essential tools in historical scholarship in order to hone the types of questions we might ask of the past; they help us reconsider ready answers by confronting biases and conceptions of inevitableness. That said, it is clear that 'what if' literature and studies also benefit classroom discussions about historical events. In other words, we might consider them to be, as Lebow (2007: 157) puts it, 'essential teaching tools and critical to establishing claims of causation'.

As mentioned above, Christopher suggests that *Fireball*'s alt-Roman Britain did not undergo dramatic technological development due to the absence of the Renaissance and Age of Enlightenment, which at least to some degree developed out of a reaction against the Church. Younger students, then, might find this explanation ironic when discussing *Fireball* since they may have learned previously that it was the look back to and desire to surpass the ideas and achievements of classical antiquity that ushered in these shifts from the sixteenth or seventeenth through the early nineteenth century. Though it is not extensively explained in the novel, Christopher's readers are invited to imagine that it was the postponement of Christianity in this alternative historical path that prevented the scientific revolution as a cultural reaction specifically geared to undermine the authority of the Catholic Church. What the novel does explain (e.g. Christopher 1981: 101), however, is that since there was no Christian Rome, there was no Muhammed – at least one who was known as a divine prophet – and that since, we are told, 'it was probably out of Islam that the ideas came that led to the Renaissance and later to science and engineering … [t]his world … scarcely changed in two thousand years' (Christopher 1981: 101). We can see, then, that Christopher plays with the idea of historical cause and effect by using an alternative pivot point that begins with a seemingly small change – the survival of Emperor Julian in 363 CE – that itself could be attributed to Julian simply donning his protective chain mail before returning to battle.

As proposed above, Christopher's novel presents a young audience with an opportunity to discuss the inevitability of Christianity in the modern era. Though in our timeline the religion was embraced by the most powerful and educated within the empire at that time – emperors, bishops, popes – Christianity also appealed to the underclasses and under-resourced throughout the empire. In his *On the Works of the Monks* (*De opere monachorum*) (22.25), for example, Augustine shows concern that too many from the lower classes might flock to monasteries to improve their social status. Thus, in Christopher's novel, as long as Christians did not hold positions of power, and were tolerated as second-class citizens, the religion could continue underground for another sixteen centuries after Julian without a re-emergence of the previous legitimizing power and authority provided by Constantine's conversion and subsequent councils and edicts. This line of argumentation might raise further questions in the classroom about whether Christopher is suggesting that Christianity – as a doctrine of the most powerful and educated, a belief system that allows those with the least status and power to find community, or both – would necessarily become the dominant religion at some point, perhaps starting in the fourth century CE, or in an alternative 1981 CE. This argument of equifinality might provide young readers an opportunity to ask themselves whether it was the prowess of various brilliant theologians – such as the fourth- and fifth-century CE bishop, Augustine of Hippo – that compelled so many people of various social statuses to be drawn toward Chistianity at the same time, and so somehow *guaranteed* its appeal and, as a result, its remarkable proliferation. A fruitful discussion in the classroom might be, then, again assuming *ceteris paribus* – no small concession, given theories of interaction and 'butterfly effects' – whether 1981 CE Britain would be, in one way or another, *necessarily* part of a Christian Roman Empire.

Conclusion

As the use of contrafactual history becomes more widespread in the study of history, as well as within the classroom, we can imagine the benefit to students and instructors alike (cf. Roberts 2011 for example). Christopher's *Fireball* invites questions that relate to the very heart of the study of history: the role of coincidence, the nature of cause and effect, and the idea of historical 'inevitability' and determinism. His novel can be seen to invite young readers to ask themselves what sorts of events or developments in the past seem to have been inevitable given various relationships between humankind and either the natural, biological, and physical world, or, alternatively, material and economic forces. Contrafactual and alternative history need not provide any certain answers to be effective: such examples of an 'If world' – as Christopher's characters describe it (Christopher

1981: 98) – can aid readers in productive ways as they think about the nature of history.

As one of the protagonists in *Fireball* puts it: 'It's not our fight. [. . .] Not our world, even' (Christopher 1981: 149). With Christopher's work, young readers have the chance to think about what they would do under the same circumstances: in this case, whether they would conform to an overwhelmingly powerful and magnetic organizational ideology, or stand up and dissent, *especially* when faced with a powerful, charismatic leader. These types of questions are at the heart of some of the many young adult titles that utilize contrafactual history, notably those that take the Third Reich as a pivot point; take, for example, Julie Mayhew's 2015 *The Big Lie* and Sarah Cohen-Scali's *Max* (published in English in 2016). This is the sort of conflict of conscience any reader can respond to, but it is particularly significant and timely for a younger audience.

Another fruitful classroom discussion that *Fireball* could lead to stems from the ways Christopher presents conflict and differences between cultures. In the novel, after passing through the fireball and becoming separated, the cousins are eventually reunited and discuss their respective experiences (Christopher 1981: 94–104). While both recognize they are in the Roman Empire, only one works out that they are in a (very different) parallel twentieth-century version, and he does so through the various cultural differences he takes note of, which he interprets through the lens of his prior education about antiquity. In fact, it is the American cousin's knowledge of Latin and ancient Rome that allows both cousins to survive at all. Yet these types of cultural differences are foreshadowed in the novel by the dissimilarities between the British protagonist and his American cousin. For example, when the two first meet at the start of the novel, they discuss American football – about which neither knows very much, for different reasons – and try hard to avoid the incongruities between baseball and rounders. Hostility between the cousins begins when the American discusses his appreciation for skiing, tennis, golf, and windsurfing, none of which the Brit has any experience with. In the end, the first punch thrown in *Fireball* is sparked by an off-colour joke made by the British cousin about the cowardice of 'the Americans' (Christopher 1981: 13). There is perhaps a deeper dramatic irony here, given that they will end up in the New World by the end of the novel.

A final, related confrontation that might strike young readers as they reach the end of the novel could include the introduction of the 'pendulum'. Built at the request of the victorious Christian Bishop, the mechanism is described as a swinging blade mounted in a way that, at the lowest point in its arc, the blade would fail to strike someone accused of heresy for choosing to kneel before a statue of Christ (many will think immediately of Poe's 1842 story, 'The Pit and the Pendulum'). This particular detail might inspire classroom discussion concerning the use and purpose of such a device, installed immediately after the overwhelming victory of the Christian revolt. In turn, this topic of conversation might lead to discussions that touch on various historical religious persecutions, crusades, and forced conversions found throughout our own historical timeline.

Notes

1 In this this article, the terms 'alternative history' and 'counterfactual' or 'contrafactual history' will be used interchangeably. The former is often associated with science fiction, and the two latter variations with historical facts that stem from a 'realistic' point of divergence (Roberts 2011: 117). Christopher's *Fireball* contains elements of both: for example, the 'fireball' of the title, described as 'roughly spherical, eight or ten feet across, blindingly white . . . float[ing] a foot or so above the ground', is a type of device found in some works of science fiction (e.g. Sprague de Camp's 'wheel' of time); Julian's survival in battle is a hypothetical historical possibility discussed even among ancient historians.

2 On this point, see, most recently, Raghunath (2020), especially chapter 3, where she addresses the idea of 'Reader Knowledge Worlds'.

3 On Julian's life and rise to power, see Bowersock (1978), and more recently, Teitler (2017). Also see Adrian Murdoch (2008), who argues, much like Christopher in *Fireball*, that, had Julian survived, Christianity would have been checked in its rise.

4 For more on the edicts of Julian, cf. Kirsch (2005: 247–8) and Kahlos (2013: 76–8).

5 Cf. Ammianus Marcellinus (1999).

6 Alternatively, the twelfth-century Byzantine historian Zonaras (13.13, B) says that Julian had taken it off because of its weight and the excessive heat.

7 Cf. other examples of ancient contrafactuals in Libanius, *Oration* 18.1, 3, 5, 26, 255.

8 According to various later medieval traditions, either this Mercurius or the Virgin Mary herself appeared to the Cappadocian Church father Basil in a vision – in some versions, Libanius himself is also involved – to communicate that 'Saint Mercurius' had killed Julian with a spear; cf. Cribiore (2013) for discussion of the various versions of this story.

9 The non-Christian writers Ammianus (30.9) and Themistius (*Oration* 12) both praised Valens and Valentinian for their religious tolerance.

10 Cf. Watts (2015) for discussion of Jovian's edict of toleration declared while he re-established the Roman Christian standard and revoked Julian's anti-Christian edicts.

11 Ammianus 20.10.7; 25.4.20; on the School Edict, cf. Hardy (1968: esp. 132) and Potter (2009: esp. 288).

12 Julian surviving the Persian campaign is a scenario imagined in the novels analysed also by Quiroga Puertas and Otranto in this volume.

13 Later in the novel, readers do find out that even though Julian was relatively successful stabilizing religious conflict by removing a religious oath of allegiance, Christian resentment nonetheless simmered for the next fifteen centuries (Christopher 1981: 132).

14 Thereby creating a 'staurogram' (⳨).

15 There are other interpretations of Constantine's sign: some scholars (e.g. Weiss 2003) have considered Constantine's vision as a solar event (including perhaps a so-called solar halo), which may have preceded the Christian beliefs later expressed by him. The solar deity *Sol Invictus* is found on a number of emperors' coinage, including those of Constantine (cf. Berrens 2004). Coins of Constantine depicting him as the companion of a solar deity were minted in 313 – a year after the Milvian Bridge; in fact, Constantine's official coinage continues to bear images of Sol until 325–326. In this context, it may be worth noting Carroll's (2002: 186) suggestion in *Constantine's Sword* that it was only after the pragmatic advantage of an alliance with Christian groups became clear, in particular after the 324 CE Battle of Chrysopolis (i.e. twelve years after Milvian) – in which Constantine defeated his last political rival, Licinius – that the identity of the emperor became finally, firmly, and publicly Christian (Carroll 2002: 193): '[i]t is at this moment [his account of the sign given to Eusebius at the Council of Nicaea in 325 CE], far more than in 312, that a unifying and universalizing symbol can serve the emperor's purpose'. Readers of *Fireball* should also note that this novel includes references to a conquering *Sol Invictus* (Christopher 1981: 176).

16 It surely did not help that the philosophers in Julian's circle, whose opinions certainly mattered to him, disagreed with all the interpretations of the soothsayers, and opposed all these types of concerns (cf. 23.5.11, 13–14, etc.).

17 Effingham (2021) discusses one way to think about alt-history in which two timelines could be (as it were) 'kept separate' through 'hypertemporal' models; for example, any time travel at all (even within the same moment) creates an alternative 'hyper-timeline' (e.g. in *Fireball*, the alt-history can be described as $t1981–T_2$), which would cause any new events to be happening in a timeline other than the 'original' one ($t1981–T_1$).

18 In some literary narratives, authors may choose to change the past with time travel; they might make it impossible to do so for literary purposes; or they might even make it possible to change some things, but not other, 'fixed points in time'; cf. Effingham (2021).

19 One high-stakes version of the contingency/determinism discussion can be found in the life sciences. On the one hand is the suggestion that determinism is required for

the very activity of scientific investigation; for example, as Morowitz (1993: 13) writes, 'we also reject the suggestions of Monod that the origin requires a series of highly improbable events and cannot be recovered from the laws of physics', because it is (Morowitz 1993: 3) 'only if we assume that life began by deterministic processes on the planet are we fully able to pursue the understanding of life's origins within the constraints of normative science'. Note this view's counterpoint is usually framed in terms of (instead of 'chance', 'randomness') the notion of *contingency* – since there are so many factors involved in – sometimes very long – causal chains, each with different statistical weights, to change one contingent condition is to make any given later event unpredictable. As Gould (1989: 1) famously puts it: 'run the tape again, and the first step from prokaryotic to eucaryotic cell might take 12 billion years instead of two . . .'; for discussion, cf. for example Luisi (2003).

1.3

'All That Is Solid Melts into Air': Destabilizing History in Robert Silverberg's *Roma Eterna*

Sarah Annes Brown
Anglia Ruskin University

Introduction

Robert Silverberg's 'fix-up' novel *Roma Eterna* (2003) charts the history of the Roman Empire in a timeline where the Exodus failed and the Jews remained in Egypt. It comprises eleven separate episodes which take us from 450 CE – or *ab urbe condita* 1203 – to 1970 CE.[1] The last story in the book was the first to be written, in 1989; the others were published at irregular intervals between then and 2003. The key significance of Silverberg's chosen divergence point appears to be the erasure of Christianity, and the impact of its absence on the Empire's success – rather than falling in the fifth century CE, Rome is still the dominant world power in the twentieth century.[2] But Silverberg never quite loses sight of the obscure Aegyptian Hebrews, and they return centre stage in the very final episode.[3]

Central to the experience of reading alternate history science fiction is an interplay between the familiar and the strange – whether one is spotting a faint uncanny shift in a fictional world otherwise identical to our own or, by contrast, suddenly recognizing an unchanged detail in a radically altered reality. Linda Hutcheon's (2013: 116) account of the distinctive pleasures provided by literary adaptations is also relevant to the experience of reading alternate histories: 'Part of this ongoing dialogue with the past, for that is what adaptation means for audiences, creates the doubled pleasure of the palimpsest: more than one text is experienced – and knowingly so'.

Alternate history also confronts us with a palimpsest, but with history, rather than a literary text, providing the hidden layer beneath the surface. Robert Silverberg's engagement with the interplay between these layers in *Roma Eterna* is particularly varied and inventive. He plays with the tropes of alternate history, complicating its familiar patterns. He manipulates the reader's knowledge of historical events, setting up expectations only to subvert them. But it is perhaps in his treatment of the forces which lie *behind* historical events – forces which are the focus of much philosophical and political debate – that Silverberg creates his most subtly destabilizing effects.

Alternate History and Determinism

The relationship between alternate history and determinism is a complex one. All alternate histories play with points of sameness and difference, and require the reader to recognize these, but the nature and significance of these patterns will vary depending on each author's attitude towards history, contingency and determinism.[4] In some texts a single change – perhaps in the life of one individual – will have a major and continuing impact on the course of history; this approach upholds the 'Great Man' theory, whereby outstanding individuals can radically reshape the world. In Kingsley Amis' *The Alteration* (1976) for example, Martin Luther's adherence to Catholicism and eventual ascent to the Papacy ensure that Roman Catholicism remains supreme in twentieth-century Western Europe. In Stephen Fry's *Making History* (1996) by contrast, the prevention of Hitler's birth by time-travellers is not enough to stop the Holocaust, for the pressure of larger historical forces ensures that another genocidal leader takes his place.[5] Silverberg's own novel offers a series of disruptive variations on these different approaches, self-consciously reflecting on the extent to which history's patterns can be thrown off course by a single adjustment, whether in relation to wars and revolutions, religious upheavals, cultural achievements or linguistic developments.

Prologue: The Failed Exodus

This process begins in the novel's brief prologue, set in 1203 AUC (450 CE). The protagonist, Lentulus Aufidius, is a historian who is writing a biography of 'the great Emperor Titus Gallius' (Silverberg 2013: 1). Although this figure is an invention, his predecessor, 'the madman Caracalla' (Silverberg 2013: 1), is not. Silverberg himself noted in *Phases of the Moon* that there is little divergence in the novel's version of history until the fall of Rome – or rather its failure to fall

(Silverberg 2004: 565). This is still a Rome troubled by 'the growing menace of the northern Barbarians' (Silverberg 2013: 1). However it is soon possible to detect some significant ripple effects stemming from this alternate history's remote divergence point in its distant past. Because the Jews never left Egypt, there is no trace of Christianity in this world, and Rome has not abandoned its pagan cults. Indeed we learn that the late Emperor, Titus Gallius, had been concerned by the popularity of various 'mystical Oriental cults', fearing they could 'weaken the fabric of the state' (Silverberg 2013: 1). Here Silverberg is clearly steering the reader to infer a decisive link between the prolonged success of Rome and the absence of Christianity, imagining how the future would have looked if the Diocletian persecution of Christians had continued and Constantine had never converted.

Aufidius' friend, Hermogenes Celer, has made a particular study of Eastern religions. He has a special interest in one obscure group – 'the Hebrews of Aegyptus' (Silverberg 2013: 2). The two men's conversation on this topic introduces a dual familiarity into this (slightly) strange version of Rome. First, Celer's musings about what might have been chime strongly with the path taken by history in our own world. He has found records of a failed Exodus from Egypt led by a chieftain named Moshe. This discovery prompts him to imagine an alternate reality in which the Jews had succeeded in settling in Palaestina, and in which a new faith had sprung up, a synthesis of Judaism and various Eastern cults. This, he imagined, might take over Rome until even its emperors became converts and weaken it from within, allowing it to be overthrown by barbarians.

The second and quite different reason why readers may find this conversation familiar relates to genre expectations. Celer has written an entire book based on his counterfactual version of history, a project which Aufidius dismisses as 'sheer fantasy': 'Perhaps, yes, perhaps no. I find speculating about such possibilities very stimulating' (Silverberg 2013: 4).[6] Thus just a few pages into the novel we are offered an example of one of alternate history's favourite tropes, the existence of an inset work of alternate history which reflects our world, or something very like it, back to the reader. If anything – and here a note of difference as well as sameness is struck – Celer's book tracks our own history with an uncharacteristic exactitude. The best known example of an alternate history within an alternate history is probably *The Grasshopper Lies Heavy*, a fictional work which plays a significant role in Philip K. Dick's *The Man in the High Castle* (1962).[7] Whereas Dick's novel famously portrays a world in which the Axis powers were victorious, Hawthorne Abendsen's inset novel tracks our own version of history closely, presenting an Allied victory and a New Deal. But later elements in the narrative, including a Cold War between the USA and United Kingdom, deviate from reality.

'The Reign of Terror'

Roma Eterna goes on to both mirror and invert our own version of history, creating a range of different effects, and constantly wrong-footing the reader's expectations. Apparent clues, based on an assumed knowledge of (our) history, point in one direction – which may turn out to be a misdirection. Parallels – like intralingual 'false friends' – can be deceptive. The eighth episode, 'The Reign of Terror' (2568 AUC, 1815 CE) is a good example of this slipperiness. The reader who enjoys working things out independently may be disappointed that Silverberg seems to lay all his cards on the table here; the story's bluntly allusive title apparently overdetermines its relationship with our own reality. However although in some ways the narrative does indeed track that of the French Revolution of 1789 – an extravagant emperor is overthrown and executed, and many of his closest companions put to death – the episode's *telos* is in fact the deliberate and successful containment of revolutionary forces by the Roman patricians.

The sybaritic excesses of Emperor Demetrius II mirror those of Louis XVI – and more particularly Queen Marie Antoinette – which so enraged the French revolutionaries. We learn of food tinted different colours each night, chariots pulled by camels and lions, and a swimming pool steeped in saffron (Silverberg 2013: 238). Demetrius' thrifty consuls, Apollinarus and Torquatus, are determined to put an end to this extravagance, but favour different approaches. Torquatus seeks to eliminate all those who most encourage the Emperor's improvidence – in a bloody purge he executes not only Demetrius' close companions, but more peripheral figures such as the craftsmen who provide his luxuries. But, even though the horrifying procession of carts to the scaffold echoes accounts of the Terror – 'the city grew more pure, and much more frightened' (Silverberg 2013: 262) – they are killed to protect the empire, not destroy it. When justifying such steps to the alarmed emperor, Torquatus unconsciously invokes the French Revolution as a terrifying counterfactual when he (misleadingly) claims his targets have revolutionary sympathies, and sketches the future horrors he has averted: 'Senators hunted down, some of them slaughtered in their beds, and, above all, the massacre of the royal family . . . The Emperor himself, Demetrius II Augustus Caesar, crucified in the Forum' (Silverberg 2013: 251).

Later in the episode the shadow of our own history peers out once again. Torquatus is reined in by his less zealous fellow consul Apollinarus in order to 'make an end to this reign of terror' (Silverberg 2013: 266). Apollinarus has Torquatus arrested, but then learns of a plot – a genuine one this time – to overthrow the empire, and restore the Roman Republic. We learn how many plebeians had hoped to see the entire ruling class destroyed, not just a few corrupt individuals, and how they had planned to 'divide their property among the common folk for the welfare of all' (Silverberg 2013: 277). Apollinarus is adamant that democracy must be avoided at all costs, fearing the effects of 'the rule of the mob' (Silverberg 2013: 271).

The phrase 'Reign of Terror' is used by a character in a later episode to describe this final purge carried out by Apollinarus (Silverberg 2013: 320), not an offshoot of revolution, like Maximilien Robespierre's, but a bold pre-emptive strike to preserve Imperial Rome. The specifically royal resonances of the word 'reign' – which may lend a muted irony to the familiar phrase – gain a revived charge when applied to the title of Silverberg's altered history. The words have stayed the same but their significance has been completely transformed. Apollinarus finally has Demetrius killed, but only in order to save the empire; he has already selected Laureolus, an honourable and worthy young man of imperial blood, to replace him. The killing of the emperor is thus not a revolutionary, but a counter-revolutionary, act. As we have seen, Silverberg strongly hints that one of the major factors behind the failure of revolution in this timeline is the non-existence of Christianity, or of a similar faith which might offer the populace 'the fantasy of a happier life in some imaginary existence beyond death' (Silverberg 2013: 280). The new Emperor Laureolus underlines this point when he declares that: 'A cult that promised salvation in the next world would inevitably weaken the common folk's loyalty to the state in this one' (Silverberg 2013: 280).

Colonialism and Race

The next chapter, 'Via Roma', is less suggestive of a specific parallel episode from real history. However, it resonates with many narratives in which colonized subjects experience complex and often painful relationships with the heartlands of empire. It is set in what in our world would be the Victorian era – 2603 AUC (1850 CE) – and the continuing survival of Rome into this more modern age of pocket-watches and picture postcards invites the reader to trace parallels with the British Empire (Silverberg 2013: 287). Its central character is a traveller from a remote outpost of the empire whose experiences mirror those of colonized peoples in our own reality. However, a piquant difference is introduced when we learn that the self-conscious young outsider, Cymbelin, is 'Britannic'. This episode persistently reflects the British Empire back at us through a defamiliarizing lens with Britain in the subaltern position.[8] We learn that some still yearn for self-rule, declaring 'Britannia for the Britons!', a slogan which echoes calls for both Irish and Indian independence *from* Great Britain (Silverberg 2013: 303). As a comment on the workings of history, its message seems to be that the broad dynamics of empire are constant, but the players may easily change.

Cymbelin is an aristocrat in his own society, but socially out of his depth in Rome, 'a brawny bumptious Celt from one of the outer edges of the civilized world' (Silverberg 2013: 290). He has been brought up to think of Rome as 'Roma Mater', a little like a Caribbean child of the Windrush generation being taught that Britain was the 'motherland'. He is othered and exoticized by the young Roman Lucilla, who quizzes him pruriently about British ways:

> 'What do you imagine we are? Savages?'
>
> 'Of course, darling! Of course! Great lovely golden-haired savages!'
>
> There is a gleam in her eyes. She is teasing, but she means what she says as well.
>
> Silverberg 2013: 306

The Romans see him as a novelty; he describes how they 'stare openly at me, the way I might stare at a giraffe or elephant parading in the streets of Londin' (Silverberg 2013: 291). By invoking animals from Africa and India, Silverberg filters Cymbelin's experiences more obtrusively through the similar objectification of foreigners by colonial Britons in our own history: 'Have they never seen a Briton before? Is yellow hair so alien to them?', he goes on to muse (Silverberg 2013: 291).

Rome's supremacy is defended by its patrician leaders in a way which further draws it together with Britain's colonial project as the supposed guarantor of stability; its 'logic, efficiency [and] superb engineering' have 'brought light where only the darkness of barbarism would have existed otherwise' (Silverberg 2013: 297). One effect of the particular type of estrangement the reader experiences in 'Via Roma' is to encourage reflection on the flimsiness and artificiality of racial taxonomies. India and China are invoked briefly as distant lands, but the only 'racial' divide which figures in the story is that between the Celts and the Romans. Silverberg's nineteenth-century Romans could have looked back to the architect and engineer Vitruvius for confirmation of their superiority over Northern

Europeans: 'southern nations, with their keen intelligence due to the heat, are very free and swift in the devising of schemes, while northern nations, being enveloped in a dense atmosphere, and chilled by moisture from the obstructing air, have but a sluggish intelligence' (Silverberg 2013: 297). Later figures from our own world would of course draw on similarly flawed reasoning to find rationales for racism which placed Northern Europeans at the summit of a racial hierarchy.

Dialect and Language

There is one element in the *Roma Eterna* future which stands out from the distorting mirror maze of alteration and reversal which confronts the reader, one aspect of European culture which remains apparently unaffected by the novel's geopolitical swerve from our own reality. This is the way in which Silverberg presents the fragmentation and mutation to which Latin is subjected over the course of fifteen centuries. In 'Waiting for the End' (1951 AUC, 1198 CE) the reader learns that both Latin and Greek have changed since the days of Sophocles and Virgil, and later chapters offer more insights into this process. It seems clear that these language changes are similar to those familiar from our own history. However, the quite different political situation means that these processes are framed in different ways. One character bemoans the loss of 'our pure and beautiful Latin' which has 'degenerated into a welter of local dialects', each with 'its own babbling lingo' (Silverberg 2013: 216). The very loaded rhetoric underlines the tension between the centripetal forces of government and the centrifugal impulse towards linguistic dispersal. Particularly interesting is the insistence on the word 'dialect' – as so often in the real world, the category boundary between 'dialect' and 'language' is shaped as much by political and social conditions as by any logical criteria. The counter-revolutionary Apollinarus is even more repelled by 'dialects' – 'coarse, vulgar versions of Latin mixed with primitive regional words' (Silverberg 2013: 258). He is particularly irked by the emergence of a 'dialect' in Roma itself – but it is not until the 'Via Roma' episode that we hear a few phrases of the new tongue: '*Venga qua, signore* … *Si, si, capisco*' … '*Allora, Andiamo*' (Silverberg 2013: 287). It is apparently identical to modern Italian.

Language and narrative inevitably mediate our access to the past. Both the third person narrator who relates some of *Roma Eterna*'s episodes and its various first person narrators experience the world refracted through a lens of Roman exceptionalism. This altered political context affects the language used to describe changes in language itself. This is yet another of the variations Silverberg plays on alternate history, and one which reflects debates over postmodern approaches to historiography, and its claims that 'History, as a literary endeavour and therefore based in language and narrative, is inherently relativistic' (Thiess 2014: 16). The transformation from Latin to Italian is apparently identical in both the real and fictional timeline; only the discursive context, the way Silverberg's characters perceive the shift – and thus the way historians tell the story of its change – has been altered.

The Great Man Theory of History

Several episodes could be said to engage with the Great Man Theory of history, as they hinge on teasing the reader with either the absence or the presence of some towering figure from our own reality. This view of history emphasizes the role played by individuals with outstanding innate abilities in shaping historical events. Thomas Carlyle articulated this theory at length in his collection of essays *On Heroes, Hero-Worship, and The Heroic in History* (1841, see Sorensen and Kinser 2013), including prophets and poets as well as kings and commanders in the category: 'They were the leaders of men, these great ones; the modellers, patterns, and in a wide sense creators, of whatsoever the general mass of men contrived to do or to attain' (Carlyle, cited in Sorensen and Kinser 2013: 21).[9]

The Great Man Theory has been countered vigorously by those who emphasize larger social and economic forces and the role of more obscure men (and women) in effecting change. The philosopher and sociologist Herbert Spencer was one of the theory's most prominent early critics, insisting that: 'Before he can remake his society his society must remake him' (Spencer 1996: 316).[10] Tolstoy, in the epilogue to *War and Peace*, is particularly emphatic in dismissing the importance of great men, such as Napoleon: 'Every act of theirs, which appears to them an act of their own will, is in an historical sense involuntary and is related to the whole course of history and predestined from eternity' (Tolstoy [1869] 2016: 650).[11]

Marxism's more deterministic view of history is also inimical to the Great Man Theory. However in Marx and Engels' *The Holy Family* ([1845] 2010: 93), there is an insistence on human agency, a rejection of fate, which contrasts with Tolstoy's ([1869] 2016: 804) assertion that 'a king is history's slave': '"history" is not, as it were, a person apart, using man as a means to achieve its own aims; history is nothing but the activity of man pursuing his aims'. Silverberg's novel offers an array of different ways of dealing with our own putative 'Great Men'.

These open up a complex and playful dialogue both with different theories of history and determinism and with the conventions of alternate history science fiction. Anna McFarlane's (2019: 97) description of Lavie Tidhar's *Osama* as 'a novel in conversation with alternate history as a discourse for understanding historiography' might also be applied to *Roma Eterna*.

Leonardo and Napoleon

Perhaps the most straightforward 'Great Man' in *Roma Eterna* is Tiberius Ulpicius Draco, the protagonist of 'Getting to Know the Dragon' (2543 AUC, 1790 CE). Yet again – as in the prologue – there is a double dynamic of recognition in play for the reader. Draco is a Hispaniard, and works in the service of the emperor's decadent, extravagant son, designing fantastical palaces for him. Draco is a polymath – an artist, historian and inventor – and Silverberg makes it difficult for the reader to miss the implied parallel with Leonardo da Vinci here:

> I have painted great paintings and fashioned splendid statues, I have written epic poems and books of history, I have even designed a flying machine that I will someday build and test successfully. And there is much more besides that I have in mind to achieve, the secrets that I write in cipher in my notebooks in a crabbed left-handed script.
>
> Silverberg 2013: 214

Draco's tragedy is to have been born out of his time: 'I like to think of myself as a man of the Renaissance, the last of my kind, born by some sad and unjust accident of fate two centuries out of his proper time and forced to live in this imbecilic decadent age' (Silverberg 2013: 215).

This is where the reader may experience a further, more subtle, moment of recognition, one based on genre expectations rather than a knowledge of history. Draco's position strongly echoes the predicament faced by the protagonist of Stephen Vincent Benét's early alternate history, 'The Curfew Tolls' (1935). The English narrator is impressed by a retired French major he meets while travelling in France in 1788. The major appears to be a brilliant strategist, yet is frustrated by his failure to fulfil his potential: 'I would be a Marshal of France; if I had been born twenty years ago, I would mold a new Europe with my fists in the next half-dozen years. Why did they put my soul in my body at this infernal time?' (Benét 1935). The punchline comes when, at the end of the story, the general learns the major has died, and writes the epitaph for his tomb:

Here lies
NAPOLEONE BUONAPARTE
Major of the Royal Artillery
of France.
Born August 15th, 1737
at Ajaccio, Corsica.
Died May 5th, 1789
at St. Philippe-des-Bains

Like Draco he was born at the wrong time – but too early rather than too late.

Christ and Muhammad

Silverberg's handling of his Leonardo *manqué* is a little heavy-handed – the reader is not so much nudged as bludgeoned into recognizing the allusion. But other great men are invoked in more inventive and unexpected ways. A notable absent presence in the novel, one of history's 'Great Men', is Christ – as we have already seen, a significant factor in Rome's survival is the erasure of Christianity. The reader who is familiar with the conventions of alternate history will be primed to spot any hints at an alternative Christ – along the lines of Silverberg's alternative Leonardo. Such a figure would have the potential to pull history back on track. As noted in my introduction, some science fiction texts are predicated on a kind of Teflon-coated history which robustly resists any attempts to change its trajectory, and swiftly compensates for any disruption in its path. History, in such texts, returns to its tramlines even after apparently significant changes. Leiber's 'Try and Change the Past' (1958) is a striking example of this approach: 'owing to the "Law of Conservation of Reality": a man laboriously saved from being shot in the head is nevertheless killed by a micrometeorite which inflicts a closely similar wound' (Edwards and Stableford 2017). The emergence of the micrometeorite suggests that mysterious forces are at work to protect the path of history. At first glance this could be seen as an example of what Stephen Baxter describes as 'the role cosmic chance plays in our existence': if the meteorite which wiped out the dinosaurs had followed a slightly different trajectory, Baxter (2019: 6) reminds us, humanity would probably never have evolved. But Leiber's fortuitous micrometeorite seems to reflect cosmic planning rather than cosmic chance. By contrast, the non-appearance of Christ in the second episode of *Roma Eterna*, 'A Hero of the Empire' (1365 AUC, 612 CE), appears to emphasize the power of contingency.

'A Hero of the Empire' might at first seem to be following the same pattern used in both Fry's *Making History* (1996) and in 'Getting to Know the Dragon'. In both those examples an entirely new, fictional character is created to fulfil a similar role to someone – Hitler and Leonardo respectively – from our own history. In 'A Hero of the Empire' we are introduced to a bearded prophet whose charisma, eloquence, hatred of cruelty and compassion for the powerless will map onto many readers' ideas about Christ, and this invitation is strengthened when the episode's Roman narrator Corbulo, who has been exiled to the Middle East, wonders if the gracious zealot with piercing eyes is a Hebrew (Silverberg 2013: 87). However this character is not an 'alternative' Christ, a science fictional creation that demonstrates that the loss of a single individual cannot hold back the tides of history. He is 'Mahmud', the Prophet Muhammad, murdered in this timeline so that his desire to sweep Rome clean and unite everyone under the One God will never be achieved. However, details which may entangle him with Christ in the reader's mind continue to accumulate. It is tempting to excavate an 'alternative' Christ from the narrator's admiring account of a prophet who preaches so passionately, and stirs up the resentment of the local Saracens, his own people, who have no wish to change their ways. His early death – a deviation from our own reality – reinforces this affinity. Like Christ, he is destroyed by Rome, betrayed by his friend Corbulo. Corbulo's admiration for Mahmud grows – but so does his fear that his teachings are so powerful they may destroy Rome.[12] In tempting the reader to misread a historical figure as a fictional, alternate character, Silverberg's story resembles Kim Stanley Robinson's *The Years of Rice and Salt* (2002), an alternate history of a world in which the Black Death wiped out the European races. This novel places episodes from history which are largely unfamiliar to Western readers at its heart, creating a potential confusion between what is truly 'alternate' in the novel, and what is merely unfamiliar. As with Silverberg's 'alternate' history of the development of Italian, the facts remain the same, only the lens is altered.[13]

In 'A Hero of the Empire' we can identify yet another of the specific mechanisms by which Silverberg plays with alterity. At several points in the novel he includes sly allusions to texts which are well known in our world but cannot possibly exist in *Roma Eterna*. One of the most familiar of these irruptions from our reality comes when Corbulo imagines the emperor exclaiming: 'Well done, thou good and faithful servant', and summoning him back to court. The fact that this is a quotation from the Parable of the Talents (Mt. 25.23) reinforces that effect of slippage between Christ and Muhammad. And on the next page, there is yet another Biblical allusion, when Corbulo complains of being 'a stranger in a strange land'. This – as well as being the title of Robert Heinlein's famous novel – is a quotation from the King James version of Exod. 2.22. It is Moses – who hovers persistently in the background of Silverberg's novel – who is so described. Although I have suggested that Muhammad and Christ are aligned in *Roma Eterna*, one further effect of these allusions might be to invoke the sometimes uneasy relationship between the three great Abrahamic faiths, given that they imply a bond between the killer of Muhammad and both Christ and Moses.

Moses and Marx

Perhaps the most audacious example of Silverberg's use of reader recognition to invoke one of history's Great Men comes in the final chapter, 'To The Promised Land' (2723 AUC, 1970 CE). The story opens in Aegypt with the kidnapping of the narrator, Nathan ben-Simeon, by two of his fellow Hebrews. Their leader Moshe – or Moses – is trying to succeed where his namesake failed; he plans to lead an Exodus of his people to a distant planet to start a new life. The prototype starship, like Noah's Ark, is thirty cubits in length. Where earlier episodes implicitly invoke debates about the nature of history, through the character of ben-Simeon, Silverberg now engages with these directly. For ben-Simeon is a theorist of history. He was sought after by Moshe's group because 'no one has a firmer grasp of the logic of history, of the inevitability of the processes that flow from the nature of human beings' (Silverberg 2013: 373). Whereas Eleazar, a zealous follower of Moshe, thinks the Hebrews would have become a world-leading power if the Exodus had succeeded, ben-Simeon hypothesizes a more modest alternative future in Palaestina, under Roman rule, which closely resembles historical reality. Before long, ben-Simeon is converted from scepticism, and filled with hope for Moshe's vision of change. He is dissatisfied with the stagnancy of Rome's rule and looks forward to a time when 'all that is solid melts into air, all that is holy is profaned, and man is at last compelled to face with sober senses his real conditions of life' (Silverberg 2013: 376). He hopes that Moshe's Exodus will bring this vision about.

The irony here is that the narrator is quoting from Marx's *Communist Manifesto* (1848), a book never written in *Roma Eterna*'s timeline. The context alters the meaning of Marx's original words – ben-Simeon is less concerned with poverty and inequality than with the way Rome has hollowed out the sacred, eroding faith through its lazy tolerance: 'a society without faith is one without a rudder: without even a course' (Silverberg 2013: 377). The test flight fails and

Moshe is killed, but ben-Simeon is persuaded to become his biographer and keep his dream alive. He is not sure if he is fitted for this task, but is eventually convinced that the group needs 'someone with a deep understanding of the long currents of history' to create a record 'that had the profundity and eternal power of Scripture' (Silverberg 2013: 380). An association between Moses and Marx offers, appropriately enough within the context of an alternate history, a blend of incongruity and familiarity. Both, in very different ways, offered the chance of an escape from bondage. The phrase, 'to the promised land' (the title of this episode), is often applied to Marx, or to socialism more generally, and more than one cartoonist has created humour by conflating the two bearded prophets.[14]

Marx was of course a thinker strongly associated with a form of historical determinism. Elana Gomel (2010: 95) suggests that he viewed history as a quasi-scientific process, and that this enabled him 'to chart the future course of history with the same assurance with which a physicist could chart the future course of a two-body system'. Silverberg's own take on Marx simultaneously reinforces and utterly subverts a deterministic view of history. The uncanny echo of Marx's exact words suggests that the forces of history are ineluctable, their emergence in a world which diverged from our own so long ago implies that Marx must be a supremely Great Man. Yet the transformation of Marx, who (though Jewish) was hostile to Judaism, and to religion in general, into the biographer of a Jewish Messiah who thinks a society without faith is rudderless, can be read as a playfully subversive reversal of both Marxism and determinism.[15] Although ben-Simeon calls for people to 'throw off the shackles of their masters', echoing Marx's claim that workers have nothing to lose but their chains, he is concerned much more with their spiritual than their material wellbeing (Silverberg 2013: 384). ben-Simeon is admired within his own timeline for his understanding of history's inevitable currents – but his ironic status as a kind of anti-Marx points to the flaws in his thinking, for there *is* no unalterable 'logic of history' after all.

Conclusion

The relationship between *Roma Eterna* and our timeline is perhaps more of a dance than a dialogue – the two histories part and come together in a series of agile, elegant and thought-provoking moves. But what of the bigger picture – what impact did Rome's endurance have on the world Silverberg creates, and what larger implications does the answer hold? In the snapshots of history we are offered, although war, violence and revolution are significant presences, it seems that Rome did at least succeed in preventing some of the most horrific episodes in twentieth-century history. 'To the Promised Land' subtly underlines this difference by making the reattempted Exodus so comparatively weakly motivated. Ben-Simeon can come up with no more damning verdict than this: 'For twenty centuries Roma has strangled mankind in its benign grip. By its shrewd acceptance and absorption of the alien gods and alien ways of the peoples it has conquered, the empire had flattened everything into shapelessness' (Silverberg 2013: 376). Ben-Simeon voices concern that Rome's sway may be coming to an end, heralding great violence. However, his final judgement, given on the novel's last page, seems more convincing: 'Perhaps I am wrong that the Republic is doomed. What is more likely true, I suspect, is that this world was meant to be Roma's; so it has been for thousands of years, and evidently it always will be, even unto eternity' (Silverberg 2013: 384).

Because it takes place in the twentieth century, we may see the Hebrews' second attempt at an Exodus as a mirror of Zionism and the founding of Israel in our timeline. This parallel highlights further the ways in which the world of *Roma Eterna* may be seen as less violent and threatening than our own. Although ben-Simeon feels the Jews have a God-given mission to strive for greatness, they are no longer victims of persecution or discrimination. Moshe's disciple Eleazar speaks with horror of the thousands killed in the original failed attempt to cross the Red Sea and escape the Pharaoh: 'half our nation, perished in a single day in horrible fear and panic' (Silverberg 2013: 368). This account of ten thousand deaths reads like a faint before-echo of the *Shoah*, and may prompt the reader to notice that no Hitler figure emerges in *Roma Eterna*. It would have been easy to depict the Hebrews of Aegypt being targeted for an alternate, Roman Holocaust, and being forced to seek refuge in space. Perhaps the cosmopolitan Roman Empire, a little like the historical Austro-Hungarian Empire, helped to keep racist or nationalist impulses in check through embracing so many different peoples in a single loose polity. Although it is far less didactic than Renouvier's emphatically secular 1876 novel, *Uchronie*, *Roma Eterna* could be said to offer a similarly positive verdict on Rome's pluralist hegemony.

Notes

1 'Ab Urbe Condita' means 'from the founding of city' and the initials were placed before dates in classical antiquity to indicate the length of time since 753 BCE, the supposed date of the founding of Rome.

2 There are some parallels between *Roma Eterna*'s focus on the marginalization of monotheisms and Charles Renouvier's *Uchronie* (1876). In this novel Christianity exists but is kept at bay by a strictly secular revived Roman Republic which ensures a peaceful and prosperous future for Europe (Gallagher 2018: 58–60).

3 In his review of the novel, Darrell Schweitzer (2010: 170) suggests that Silverberg cheats slightly in introducing 'an extraordinary series of lucky breaks', alongside the failure of the Exodus, which combine to ensure Rome's survival.

4 For a detailed discussion of the political and philosophical implications of these different emphases see Evans (2014: 47–89).

5 Kathleen Singles (2013: 57) asserts that alternate history is wedded to history's 'Great Men' as drivers of change in a reactionary way: 'Alternate histories rely on the Rankean notion that a single event can be pivotal, for example that a change in political leadership can decisively alter the following course of events, that a given battle can change the outcome of war, that a single person can change the course of history'. However, Silverberg and Fry both demonstrate that the genre's relationship with theories of history is more complex and varied than this. Singles (2013: 215–33) also offers an extended discussion of Stephen Fry's *Making History* (1996).

6 Craig A. Gibson (2004) notes that the rhetorical exercises recommended by classical writers such as Aelius Theon in the first century CE resemble alternate history in their encouragement of creative responses to hypothetical historical scenarios.

7 Alternate history is full of such ingenious self-referential effects. Another example is Lavie Tidhar's *Osama*, which Anna McFarlane (2019: 97) describes as an extended 'alternate' version, not of history, but of *The Man in the High Castle*, a 'palimpsestuous rewriting of a novel that was already a rewriting of history to begin with'. For a discussion of generic self-referentiality in alternate history see Singles (2013: 60–4).

8 A recent alternate history which creates a similar effect is Laurent Binet's *Civilisations* (2019). This satirical thought experiment depicts a world in which Europe is colonized by the Incans. Sameness intertwines with difference in a world in which Thomas More is imprisoned for refusing to recognize that Henry VIII is the son of the sun, and the Casa de la Contratación was established by the Incans, not the Castilians.

9 For other discussions of the intersection between Carlyle's writings and alternate history see Morgan and Palmer-Patel (2019b: 18–19).

10 Historian Richard Evans (2014: 28) also advises caution when evaluating the role played by 'Great Men'.

11 Adam Roberts (2019: 31–45) discusses the role played by Napoleon in both *War and Peace* and alternate history.

12 Given Silverberg's fondness for literary allusions of various sorts, it is possible he had Alfred Bester's short story 'The Men Who Murdered Mohammed' (1958) in mind

when writing this episode. The murder of Muhammad is a mere detail in Bester's playfully paradoxical time travel story but makes for a memorably alliterative title.

13 For a discussion of the way Kim Stanley Robinson sets puzzles for the reader who is accustomed to Eurocentric accounts of history, see Pak (2019).

14 A nineteenth-century French cartoon portrays Marx as Moses, holding tablets on which are engraved the names of his most famous works, rather than the Ten Commandments. https://www.alamy.com/stock-photo-19th-century-french-illustration-depicting-karl-marx-depicted-as-moses-57359844.html (accessed 2 March 2022). David P. Shuldiner (1999: 204) analyses a 1912 cartoon of Moses and Marx, originally published in a Yiddish satirical journal.

15 A comparison can be drawn with Niall Ferguson's (1997: 221) vision of an alternate version of history in which Marx is transformed into a 'millenarian Jewish prophet'.

1.4

What if Aristotle Had Known (Better)? Technological Counterfactuals in L. Sprague de Camp's Short Fiction 'Aristotle and the Gun'

F. Javier Campos-Daroca
University of Almería

Introduction

Any variety of alternative history, from historical counterfactuals to literary uchronies, must rely heavily on a robust idea about how things actually happened and were recorded, that is, about History with a capital H. The 'robustness' of History rests on its generally being taken for granted (*Our Time Line*), which explains the limited and recurrent nature of historical 'Jonbar hinges', but it does not prejudge the ideological inspiration of counterfactual exploration, in the sense of either confirming or destabilizing beliefs about the past.[1]

Certainly, the ways History can be written and investigated vary notably too, some of them being more hospitable to the imagination of alternatives to the accepted course of historical events. In determining how amenable a specific approach to history writing or historical research is to the idea of constructing counterfactuals, the role and range of both human agency and chance in influencing historical events is of paramount importance.[2] Also consequential are the kinds of historical facts or events we are primarily interested in. Political, economic and social history all have highly varied categorizations of what matters, arranging the relevant facts in a very different order of significance. At a more fundamental level, ideas about the nature and usefulness of counterfactual thinking depend on questions such as what should count as historical facts or events, as well as their agents, how events causally interrelate with each other, or how narratives and tropes deployed in history writing determine our understanding of them.

Today counterfactual imagination is a resource taken advantage of by writers of very different trades and for richly varied purposes,[3] but as regards its use in fiction in the mode commonly known as 'alternate history', science fiction has proved to be an extraordinary fecund genre for these sorts of inventions, by virtue of the possibilities and expectations opened up by new, scientific outlooks on space and time, that challenge the common understanding of both agency and chance.

On the same note, science fiction writing helps to broaden our outlook on the kind of facts and events that can be taken as starting points for telling diverging stories of paths not actually taken. As such, issues and figures related to knowledge and cognition, as they transform modern society beyond recognition at an increasing speed, are key to science fiction imagination.[4] There are different ways of articulating those cognitive concerns in alternate history works of fiction, but our interests are focused on those that deal with stories in which divergences are caused by 'anachronistic scientific knowledge', that is, the appearance of ideas, methods or inventions distinctive of modern science, during periods of time where it is historically assumed that there was no awareness of them. We devote this chapter to a remarkable if neglected episode in the development of this kind of alternate history fiction.[5]

At the pivotal convergence of alternate history and science fiction writing, an important part was played by L(yon) Sprague de Camp (1907–2000), an engineer by trade devoted to science fiction and fantasy writing, as well as author of one of the most successful literary uchronies in the history of the genre, *Lest Darkness Fall*, which first appeared as a short story in *Unknown* (September 1939, later expanded into a novel in 1941). Twenty years later Sprague de Camp wrote another fictional counterfactual story, 'Aristotle and the Gun' (De Camp ([1958a] 2002), from now on 'Aristotle'), before putting his science fiction production on hold with a long hiatus. In 1995 Sprague de Camp was awarded the prize for Special Achievement in the first edition of Sidewise Awards for Alternate History.[6] His last foray into alternate history was 'The Round-Eyed Barbarians' (1992), about an imaginary Chinese colonization of America, resorting to the same epistolary frame as in 'Aristotle'. In any case, 'Aristotle', although well received at the time of its first publication, has fared rather poorly in the never-ending series of anthologies of time travel and alternate history. The same applies for the whole of his science fiction production, overshadowed by the giants of the Golden Age such as Asimov, Heinlein or Hubbard.

In this chapter we will deal with de Camp's 'Aristotle', a short story that mirrors his renowned first one in many aspects, as it proceeds by reversing some of the key elements of the narrative in *Lest Darkness Fall*. Contrasting with the successful avoidance of a period of darkness effected by the intelligent and well-aimed performance of an historian accidentally landed in late antique Rome, 'Aristotle' confronts us with the colossal failure of an engineer only too ready to change history at will according to his best knowledge, who travels back in time to Greece supported by cutting-edge technological skills.[7]

Along these lines, we will focus first on de Camp's elaboration of the engineer as a stock character in science fiction writing of the Golden Age, taking into account the fact that he himself was an engineer by training and devoted an important part of his non-literary production to the history of engineering. Secondly, we will follow the (mis)adventures of the engineer Sherman Weaver as he naively attempts to manipulate the course of History as regards the pace of development of scientific knowledge together with its technological implementation. Due attention will be paid to the unexpected Jonbar point singled out by Weaver, namely Aristotle's mind, to accelerate intellectual history. At the end of the tale, the mistaken assumptions involved in the idea of a purposeful epoch-making improvement of knowledge are revealed, as the hero realizes that his seemingly well-informed plans were not up to the complexities of the task.

Engineers as Civilizing Heroes

> So, if there is any progressive, consistent movement in human history, it is neither political, nor religious, nor aesthetic. Until recent centuries it was not even scientific. It is the growth of technology, under the guidance of engineers.
>
> de Camp [1963] 1993: 26

According to Tolkien, biographical details are of little use when it comes to understanding works of artistic creation, apart from a few but important exceptions.[8] As regards de Camp, we consider that his educational background and first professional endeavours are facts of his life which should be taken into account when studying his science fiction uchronies.

Becoming an Engineer

de Camp's subject of choice was initially palaeontology, but his father's view was that an engineering school would be a much more appropriate option. In his autobiography ([1996] 2011) de Camp viewed this decision as a profoundly mistaken one, but he was not completely averse to it.

He enrolled at the California Institute of Technology in Pasadena and entered college in the fall of 1925. After graduating in 1930, he continued his studies at the Stevens Institute of Technology, where he obtained a master's degree. When he recalls the years spent at Stevens, he has surprisingly few things to say about the subjects he studied, but he gives an eloquent summary of what he learnt there: 'At MIT and Stevens I learned about efficiency engineering, the Taylor System, and time-motion studies. Ever since, I have applied these lessons, because I have more interesting things to do than I have time to do them' ([1996] 2011: 117).

Also at SIT he came to know about the technocratic ideal of social order under the guidance of experts, preached about by an 'eccentric engineer' called Howard Scott, who had been invited to present his movement to the students at the Institute. de Camp profoundly disliked the idea of 'putting the government into the hands of a kind of soviet of engineers on the doubtful assumption that engineers were more trustworthy and less self-interested than other men' (de Camp [1996] 2011: 118). Apart from his veiled attack on communist ideals, this sobering view dealing with the importance of engineering in social and political planning is particularly surprising coming from a young would-be engineer. A significant trace of both his concern with efficiency and his restrained outlook of the possibilities of his own profession can be found in his stories about premature technological improvement.

Engineers in History

de Camp's professional career as an engineer was quite short, but somehow premonitory of his future lifelong devotion to science fiction and fantasy writing. His first job was in a company founded by 'the inventor turned to philanthropy' Henry J. Gaisman, with the aim of giving advice to would-be inventors about how to develop and manage their fledgling projects successfully (de Camp [1996] 2011: 122).

de Camp, then, from his own experience, knew the complexities of inventions well, especially when considered as actions of both technical and socio-economic importance, even though his interest in technological innovation did not limit itself to those managerial issues. Throughout his wide literary career, an important part of which was devoted to popularizing science and technical advances, he carried out intensive research on the history of inventions (especially in the USA), resulting in several books, one of which deserves special attention here. Indeed, *The Ancient Engineers* ([1963] 1993) was one of his most celebrated publications on the topic.[9] Its first chapter, entitled 'The Coming of Engineers', from which a representative passage has been quoted above, reads like a manifesto for engineers as neglected agents of civilization.

According to de Camp, the first engineers in history appeared at a specific stage of social complexity, when a high level of specialization demanded a new set of skills for connecting men of power, striving for big enterprises, with a whole array of artists and craftsmen, to achieve their common goal:

> Hence arose a new class of men, the technician or engineer, who would negotiate with a king or a priesthood for building a public work, plan the details, and direct the workmen. These men combined practical experience with knowledge of general, theoretical principles. Sometimes they were inventors as well as contractors, designers, and foremen, but all men who could imagine something new and transform a mental picture into physical reality.
>
> de Camp [1963] 1993: 15

The range of abilities assigned to 'ancient engineers' is wide, but inventions feature prominently in the picture, so much so that de Camp ends up lumping together all kind of 'innovators' as 'engineers' (architects, irrigators, administrators, etc.) meaning modern distinctions are inadequate for use in ancient times.

Key though they are to technological progress in human history, engineers are *rarae aves* in any society, hence it is important to ascertain the conditions that encourage or refrain their eventual emergence. As such, de Camp points out the psychological disposition (stubbornness, courage, energy) as well as both the geographical and the cultural factors that make it possible for would-be engineers to flourish in any society. Special attention is paid to the level of development of communication networks, as the main factor in determining to what extent peoples and nations share in, and benefit from, the 'technological adventure'. However, in my view the most interesting point concerns the political side of his argument. According to de Camp, political communities such as city-states stifle invention, unlike absolute and despotic monarchies, which are able to mobilize resources both human and material, especially under certain geographical conditions (the 'Civilized Belt').[10] All in all, the history of engineering in ancient times runs parallel to the history of empires.

In de Camp's view, although engineers become figures of epic proportions, they are likely to go unnoticed because of the peculiarity of their expertise, which in a nutshell could be defined in terms of their ability to bring together social power, specialized skills and resources. Indeed, by means of their planning prowess, they bridge the gap between powerful rulers with an entrepreneurial spirit and highly skilled, specialized craftsmen, as well as theoretical principles and practical feasibility. Last but not least, they thrive in communication hubs, through which knowledge not only about particular inventions, but also inventiveness itself is spread.

Engineering the Past

Leaving aside its historical credibility, the main interest of de Camp's heroic shaping of engineers is a literary one. It provides the ideological background against which the leading role of de Camp's 'Aristotle', Sherman Weaver, stands ironically as an engineer well versed in history, who, being dissatisfied with his own time, embarks on the task of 'engineering' history with the view of producing a more hospitable present for scientific-minded people like himself.

Speaking in terms of narrative analysis, engineers belong in the long lineage of characters defined as actors by virtue of their extraordinary knowledge, as popularized in scientific romance and pulp science fiction under a variety of stereotypes, such as 'the mad scientist' or 'the young scientist in love with the professor's daughter', always inextricably linked with revolutionary inventions. However, regarding the complementary competence of power, those heroes of science usually find themselves faced with a conundrum. In de Camp's 'Aristotle', confrontations between characters representing both competences (power and knowledge) are key to the development of the plot.[11]

The Frame: a Letter from an Alternate Future

'Aristotle' is framed as a private letter that librarian Sherman Weaver addresses to consul Markos Koukidas. The date of the letter (Flower Moon 3, 3097) as well as the location of both sender and addressee let the readers know, in no uncertain terms, that the world we are about to deal with is not our world, but an alternative one.

The names of the places, although strange, do not sound completely unfamiliar to the American ear provided it has some basic historical and anthropological knowledge. Indeed, Weaver's position as a Librarian in the 'Sachimate of Lenape', as well as the name of the place he lives in (Paumanok, Sewanhaki), leaves little room for doubt as regards where the frame narrative is located and what kind of political authorities are wielding power there. It is an alternative North America, specifically, an alternative New York, where an indigenous nation (the Lenape) has consolidated its power in the area and, as will soon be revealed, is in the process of expansion over other territories and peoples (Senecas, Oneidas, Menwe). In a similar vein, consul Koukidas, who resides in the 'Moskhovian Federation', is the representative for a big political community called the 'Balkan Commonwealth'.

The main character and narrator, Sherman Weaver, presents himself as a librarian, but he soon reveals that his presence in the world of the frame story is far from a regular one. Weaver's first clarifications concern his position in his world of origin. He claims to be one of those 'natural philosophers' of his time, whose achievements he celebrates as triumphs. However, this bombastic title does in fact work as a kind of translation of his original position into a language accessible to the recipient, with whom Weaver admits communication has not been easy. 'Natural philosophers' in Weaver's original world are characteristically concerned with 'machines and discoveries', and they work on 'projects' that bring together teams of philosophers. In other words, 'natural philosopher' is actually a translation of 'engineer' for the benefit of people living in a world where scientific and technological knowledge has little if any place and prestige.

Recasting himself as an engineer of the past (aka a 'natural philosopher'), Weaver proceeds to tell consul Koukidas his own incredible story, one which has taken him to a world where he has been downgraded to the humble position of a librarian. In the embedded story, Weaver was in command of a team of 'philosophers' devoted to an ambitious project (a time machine).[12] Nevertheless, Weaver's authority was severely limited. He was at the beck and call of his superiors and had to report regularly to them about the progress and results of his project. As such, the powers that be were completely free to decide about the advisability of going on with the project, and so they did with Weaver's, to which they had paid no attention at all. After considering that other pressing interests were of higher priority, they decided to close down the project without the right of appeal, leaving Weaver in a fit of fury with no one to vent his rage against. At that moment he made up his mind to take advantage of the time travel machine, which was already finished, and use it to go on a trip to the past with the idea of accelerating the pace of civilization by means of his own advanced scientific knowledge with the intention of redressing an injustice committed against him and receiving the recognition he thought he deserved.

Aristotle's Mind as a Counterfactual Nexus

de Camp has given a twist to the travelling machine story in using it purposely with the acknowledged goal of *improving the course of history as we know it by setting it on a faster path* to a modern (techno-scientific) civilization.[13] It can be said then that, strictly speaking, Weaver intentions was not to create an alternate path of History, but to accelerate the right one, that is, a question of efficiency, as expected from an engineer. Assuredly, Weaver works on the premise that civilization has *a single* forward, progressive course, and that it can in principle be speeded up by means of a planned intervention at just the right time.[14] However, he gains some benefits from having read many 'fantastic stories about humans going back in time and overawing the natives with a display of the discoveries of his own era' (de Camp [1958a] 2002: 17). Consequently, he is not so naïf as to presume that sheer time-transportation of inventions and gadgets can bring about a momentous transformation in a society should the people there, at least some of them, not be sufficiently prepared intellectually to understand the scientific principles on which they are based. His plan, then, is to enlighten certain people by providing them with the right scientific ideas and methods.[15]

Accordingly, he thinks carefully through his plans and arrives at certain reasonable conclusions about which period in the past and, more specifically, which exact moment would be worth paying a visit to; and finally, to whom his civilizatory endeavours should be set out. As part of this delicate decision, Weaver's interest in the history of science, a trait he considers rather uncommon among engineers,[16] proves to be quite useful. Indeed, it does not take Weaver much time to take his pick. Aristotle seems to be the best option on account of both his intellectual endowment ('a key mind', de Camp [1958a] 2002: 17) and the extent to which his prejudices and mistaken convictions on scientific matters have burdened Western intellectual progression.

In so doing, de Camp fleshes out narratively a bold counterfactual hypothesis that expands on an idea implicit in most of the modern history of Western Civilization, to name, the idea that Aristotle's thought has been fateful to it and, along with Western global ambitions and expansion, for the entire world. de Camp has his main character be very clear regarding Aristotle's and generally Hellenic fateful preconceptions that pre-empted the possibilities of developing scientific and technical ideas. As such he mentions the effects of the generalized acceptance of slavery on the appreciation of work and inventions, and their only too imaginative bent to spin out theories beyond any factual basis (de Camp [1958a] 2002: 16–17).[17]

In sum, Aristotle's cast of mind, that is, his most ingrained ideas on how things are and should be, becomes the *counterfactual juncture*, the point of divergence in Weaver's peculiar counter-historical enterprise.[18] Nevertheless, the choice of the right time for this historical intervention is not so simple. It has to be a precise moment of Aristotle's intellectual life. It could not be during Aristotle's formative years under the strong influence of Plato in the ideal quarters of the first Academy, Plato's viewpoint being 'mystical and anti-scientific', to which many of Aristotle's worst intellectual vices could be traced back. It could not be the philosopher's late years either, at an age when inducing changes of mind would have few chances of success. The time passed in Macedonia in the task of tutoring the young Alexander turned out to be the most appropriate occasion for Weaver to implement his plan with any probability of success (de Camp [1958a] 2002: 18–19).

On Unsurmountable Intellectual Prejudices

Since the time travelling device engineered by Weaver has a limited effectivity, our scientific hero has only six weeks to effect this momentous change of mind upon which his own present/future depends. So, disguised as an Indian sage under the name of Zandras, well equipped with all the impedimenta he thinks useful for his task (which includes refreshing his Attic Greek),[19] he sets off to Ancient Macedonia in the spring of 340 BCE (976 according to the Algonquian reckoning) to meet a conveniently aged Aristotle. His unfortunate landing, though, right on the head of a ploughman with scarce notions of Attic Greek, is only the first of his misadventures, which will end up in an unexpected result, quite a lot far away from his expectations.

In some way Weaver succeeded in his original determination. Indeed, he managed to change Aristotle's ideas regarding both the sense it makes devoting efforts to doing intensive research on nature, as well as the importance of technological inventions. However, he fails miserably as per the effects of this change on Aristotle's mind and his reaction to Weaver's powerful exhibition of knowledge. In his original scheme, only Aristotle's mind needed to be changed, while the subsequent course of History should have remained *essentially* the same with respect to scientific and technological advancement. It is assumed that a powerful mind already on the right track will only go faster when intellectual obstacles are removed. Nevertheless, things prove to be much more complicated. Instead of accelerating *the* process, Weaver's intervention gives rise to an alternate history, in which science and technology are all but ignored.

The unexpected results of Weaver's attempts at historical engineering are registered in an alternative version of Diogenes Laertius' *Lives of Eminent Philosophers*, which Weaver came to know later on, when he was back in the 'other' America, trying to get to the bottom of what went wrong with his schemes.[20] In that alternative Laertius, Aristotle's biography reads as follows: 'Now Aristotle, during his sojourn at Mytilene, had been an assiduous student of natural sciences. (...) But after he had removed to Macedonia and busied himself with the education of Alexander, there one day appeared before him a traveler, Sandos of Palibothra, a mighty philosopher of India' (de Camp [1958a] 2002: 53)

The effect of the visit, 'Diogenes' went on, was catastrophic. Sandos (i.e. Zandras), poked fun at Hellenic attempts at scientific research so heavily that he managed to discourage the philosopher, to the point of making him abandon any further endeavours in this field. It is implied that Aristotle's authority regarding natural scientific research led the following centuries to remain barren of any achievement in the field, not because of the philosopher's mistaken ideas on nature and methods of scientific enquiry, but as a result of his principled withdrawal from any activity of such kind.[21] Aristotle's reasons were detailed as follows:

> ... as he (sc. Aristotle) explains in his celebrated treatise *On the Folly of Natural Science*, there are three reasons why no good Hellene should trouble his mind with such matters.
>
> One is the number of facts which must be mastered before sound theories become possible is so vast that if all Hellenes did nothing else for centuries, they would still not gather the amount of data required. The task is therefore futile.
>
> Secondly, experiments and mechanical inventions are necessary to progress in science, and such work, though all very well for slavish Asiatics, who have a natural bent on it, is beneath the dignity of a Hellenic gentleman.
>
> And, lastly, some of the barbarians have already surpassed the Hellenes in this activity, wherefore it ill becomes the Hellenes to compete with their inferiors in skills at which the latter have an inborn advantage. They should rather cultivate personal rectitude, patriotic valor, political rationality, and aesthetic sensitivity, leaving to barbarians such artificial aids to the good and virtuous life as are provided by scientific discoveries.
>
> de Camp [1958a] 2002: 54–5

Even in his poor estimation of them, Aristotle seems to have been utterly convinced of the significance of three mainstays of modern Western technologically oriented science, namely, collecting facts, doing experiments and being competitive. To that extent, Weaver's enterprise was certainly successful. However, 'the Master of those who know' got the wrong end of the stick about Weaver/Sandos' lessons, with a devastating effect on human history and, ironically, on the time traveller's own life.

We should remind ourselves that Aristotle in de Camp's story was a kind, civil fellow, and had shown both genuine sympathy towards Sandos and a keen interest in his display of knowledge. What went wrong, then, in this apparently promising coming together of masterminds that, on the face of it, should have given a tremendous boost to the development of civilization, already launched (if modestly) by the young Aristotle with his auspiciously critical spirit and enquiries on nature?

There are two sides to the answer. On the one hand there is the psychological factor regarding both the opportunity and the pace of scientific learning. Aristotle's prejudices are deep-seated. Certainly, Aristotle's gripping exchanges with Zandras whetted his appetite for knowledge, to the point of admitting that much valuable knowledge could be expected from a barbarian (de Camp [1958a] 2002: 47). Nevertheless, there are limits to what an individual on their own can intellectually achieve, and stretching these limits can be counterproductive. Since Weaver/Zandras firmly insisted on the most arduous part of the scientific activity (experiments, inventions, checking theories against facts, de Camp [1958a] 2002: 31), the effect of his learning was to announce the long road to be taken, with deterring results.

On the other hand, there is also a socio-historical side to the issue. In the obstinate political entourage of a court like that of Macedonia, an ill-advised attempt at scientific enlightenment pushed Aristotle back onto the well-trodden path of his xenophobic convictions, to the extreme of condemning any kind of scientific activity as improper for Hellenes but perfectly suited to barbarian nations.

Similar thoughts about the socio-historical conditioning of knowledge and, consequently, the limits of scientific and technological progress, again illustrated in the figure of an imaginary Aristotle, can be gleaned from Sprague de Camp's ([1958b] 2013) historical novel *An Elephant for Aristotle*, which came out the same year as 'Aristotle', inaugurating a series of historical novels set in antiquity, in which philosophers, artists, technicians and craftsmen were cast in leading roles.[22] In this novel we are invited to imagine what would result from exposing the philosopher's preconceptions about this animal to a direct experience of it. As a matter of fact, in *History of Animals* Aristotle collects a good deal of (for the most part) sound information about elephants, so much so that the possibility is there that he actually based his description on direct observations (by him or some other reliable source). However, since de Camp remained unconvinced of this very possibility, the title could be enticingly reworded as a counterfactual hypothesis of cultural significance, as follows: what if Aristotle had seen a real elephant for once?[23]

de Camp fantasizes about an expedition dispatched by Alexander from India to Greece, bearing gifts for his beloved teacher, amongst which was King Poros' war elephant. The former student, well aware of his master's zoological inquisitiveness, sends him this huge animal (named 'Aias') with all the personnel and impedimenta required for its maintenance, trusting an officer of proven courage and integrity, namely, the Thessalian Leon of Atrax, with the task of leading the convoy back to Greece and delivering the present alive to the philosopher, at that point teaching in Athens in his school at the Lyceum.

Nevertheless, the highly anticipated delivery of the huge royal present to Aristotle ends up being a considerable disappointment. The size of the animal obviously made a big impression on him, and the bones of its legs roused his curiosity, but his first reaction after recovering and reading the letter Alexander addressed to him was to wonder how he could possibly afford to feed this gigantic beast. He vaguely recalls having said to Alexander something about his desire to see an elephant, but only in jest. In the end, he takes it all as a practical joke by the king and, without giving it a second thought, goes back to his lessons at the exact point he was interrupted by the elephant's arrival. Apart from keeping the elephant strictly under control, his main concern is with his own school and teaching, which remains as chauvinistic and self-centred as before.

At the end of the day, both in the novel and the short story, Aristotle's prejudices carry the day, although the significance of the failure differs widely in each case. In the former nothing results from the failed enlightening of this fatally benighted mastermind. In the short story, on the contrary, it is precisely the success in changing Aristotle's mind regarding the modern idea of scientific research methods that, far from accelerating the advance of scientific knowledge, jumping as it were over whole periods of history plagued with ignorance, brings about a world where science is all but nonexistent. Ironically enough, while trying to spare history some time by means of early enlightenment, as expected from a decent engineer who aims exclusively at efficiency, Weaver discovers that it is precisely time that is needed, and a bit of blissful ignorance too.

Conclusions: The Closing of a Mastermind

de Camp's humorous story of the misfortunes of an engineer at odds with his own time reveals, after close reading, a narrative of certain complexity which entails a moral almost in the vein of a fable. An epistolary frame embeds a story told by the correspondent as a character-bound narrator, expressly, a talented

American engineer who tasks himself with altering history, in line with his wishes and convictions about progress and civilization. The juncture targeted in his scheme involves no other than Aristotle's mind, assuming that giving it a gentle push in the right direction at just the right point in time would naturally result in a momentous change of far-reaching effects in the history of human progress, certainly to his own satisfaction, but implicitly for humankind's sake too.

Weaver actually succeeds, and history diverges at the point of his choice, but not exactly as he expected. The resulting alternative world turns out to be, from the point of view of our own (Western) history line, a technologically regressive one, literally a 'brave' new world, where courageous warriors wield power with a spear. The reasons for this anomalous divergence can be found in a mistaken idea about how minds, even masterminds, work, as well as in the naive conviction that history can be accelerated at will. Aristotle's mind works slowly, much like anyone else's. It is not enough to put facts about nature and adequate methods of scientific research in front of him. Good science and practical knowledge built on top of it take time as well as collaborative efforts, and in the long and laborious process of acquiring them, some mistaken ideas and 'glittering theories' may prove to be progressive.[24]

Without taking into account the psychological and socio-historical conditioning involved in any process of cultural progress, the sheer exhibition of factual knowledge ultimately proves to be counterproductive, resulting in the confirmation of stereotypes already in force.[25] A premature, ill-targeted enlightenment, coupled with an oppressive entourage, leads the mastermind of ancient times to a kind of closure that caused a darkness darker than the Early Middle Ages, and left a poor engineer marooned in a sort of historical prison.

Notes

1 Gallagher offers a precise formulation of the counterfactual 'mode', its varieties of expression, best established *loci*, and 'basic perennial issues' (2018: 2–20). Prendergast (2019: 49) points out that the term itself exhibits a parasitical dependence on facts, while Rodiek (1997: 25–31) underlines the implicit 'cultural knowledge' in uchronies. On *Our Time Line* (OTL) see Gallagher (2018: 51–2). There is a useful list of recurrent nexus in Henriet (2011: 113).

2 Shippey (1973) distinguishes between a 'Malthusian' view of history (impersonal, technical, and hard to manipulate in any purposeful direction) and a whiggish one

(mythopoetic, hero-making, and progressive). On the relevance of human agency and contingency, see Black (2015).

3 A fairly complete overview of the range of usages and interests of counterfactual thinking can be found in Deuermoth and Singaravélou (2016), with special attention paid to the remarkably diverse reception of counterfactual thinking in different countries around Europe.

4 On how this cognitive factor works in some authoritative definition of science fiction, see Roberts (2016: 1–4).

5 The relationship between alternate history and science fiction is far from being a settled question, but it is common practice to consider the fictional side of the former as a subgenre of the latter, see Suvin (1983: 149). On the contrary, Rodiek (1997: 41–3) considers that alternate history science fiction is not 'faktenorienterte' enough to be considered on a par with Uchronies. The short story 'Sidewise in Time', by Murray Leinster (1934) is frequently mentioned as pioneering the use of alternate history in science fiction writing.

6 de Camp ([1996] 2011: 224). *Lest Darkness Fall* (1939), 'The Wheels of If' (1940), and 'Aristotle' were the pieces winning him the award. 'Aristotle' has been reprinted many times since its first appearance in *Astounding Science Fiction Stories*, September 1958. In this paper we will quote the text from the last edition available of a collection of de Camp's most renowned short stories ([1958a] 2002).

7 Shippey (1973: 9) has described 'Aristotle' as a 'pointed parable of the downfall of one misguided interpretation of history'. The contrast with *Lest Darkness Fall* is clearly delineated by Shippey, who focuses on the crucial differences between the archaeologist Martin Padway, who accidentally becomes a time traveller by 'sideslip', and the more 'whiggish' (see n. 2), overconfident engineer Sherman Weaver, who purposely travels to the past with a well-rounded plan. The differences account for the success or failure of their respective endeavours.

8 See letter 'To Deborah Webster on 25 October 1958', in Carpenter (1981: 288).

9 de Camp ([1996] 2011: 282), which was welcomed by Asimov in a laudatory review in *Times Literary Books Review* (14 May 1963).

10 de Camp (([1963] 1993): 19) takes up the idea of a belt stretching from the Mediterranean lands through the Middle East to China, as a space of speeded-up spread of technology resulting in a high level of civilization. This idea resonates today with current much debated 'Belt and Road' initiatives.

11 On the 'Engineer Paradigm' and the engineer as a 'cultural hero' in science fiction and pulp fiction, see Luckhurst (2006: 50–75). On the evolution of 'the scientist' as a stock character in science fiction, see Attebury (2003: 38–9), who refers to the engineer featuring in Heinlein (1940) as an early example of the kind. de Camp deals ironically with scientists as stock science fiction characters in a nonfiction article,

1951. The literary evolution and the persistence of stereotypes in this figure are clearly delineated in Stableford (2006: 469–72). As for knowledge as a kind of actors' competence, see Bal (2017: 172–3).

12 Time machines in imaginative fiction can be considered both as literary devices (in keeping with strategies of 'literalizing', at the level of the fable, the classical mechanisms of temporal discontinuity operating at the level of the story, see Wittenberg 2013: 1–25), and as sophisticated fictional contraptions, assessed according to current scientific ideas of what is possible and technically feasible (see Broderick 2019). By the time of 'Aristotle', time travel machines have become a trite trope of the genre, as de Camp has Weaver comment, but he elaborates briefly on the science supporting Weaver's invention in terms that will prove relevant in the course of the story.

13 This key point has been acutely made by Winthrop-Young (2009: 113) regarding *Lest Darkness Fall.*

14 Sheer historical or personal curiosity is usually the main motivation for travelling to the past in the first works of the genre. Counterfactual effects of backwards time travel assume that history can actually be changed, an idea still unfamiliar in the 1930s (Winthrop-Young 2009: 108). Representative exemplars of backwards time travel-cum-time-machine alternate history narratives in the pulps are Schachner (1933) and Sell (1938), in which resulting divergences in history are accidental. Hale (1881) is the earliest example of a counterfactual historical narrative with the intentional (and catastrophic) intervention of the narrator in the historical events, although it is not clear in which sense of the word he is travelling. On the religious inspiration and purposes of Hale's story as well as its possible precedents, see Pinkerton (1979). Closest to de Camp's 'Aristotle' is Słonimski (1924), in which a well-intentioned planned intervention in the French Revolution ends up in paradoxical results. Time travel for hunting purposes, whose chaotic effects are told in Bradbury (1952), is the topic of a lengthy series by de Camp (1993), featuring Reginald Rivers, who makes a living out of hunting tours in prehistoric periods.

15 A precedent close to Weaver's idea that anachronistically enlightening the Greeks can bring about a great improvement in history can be found in Asimov (1949). As pointed out in the previous section, de Camp was well aware of both the historical and psychological conditioning of progress. More importantly, he was sensitive to the fact that progress is a 'fractured notion', to put it in Schiavone's terms, which means that scientific and technological advances do not go hand in hand with civil and political rationality, see Schiavone (2021: 32). Interestingly, Schiavone's ideas concerning the causes of the primitive state of ancient technology (as well as the role Aristotle's plays in it) are very much the same as de Camp's, see Schiavone (2021: 47–50).

16 Weaver says proudly that he belongs to the *History of Science Society* and that some papers of his have been published in the prestigious journal *Isis* (de Camp [1958a] 2002: 16). de Camp and his character share the same interest in the discipline and was also very proud of his contributions to the same publication, cf. de Camp ([1996] 2011: 264).
17 Weaver says expressly that his choice of Aristotle as the 'mastermind' to be influenced, as well as his ideas about the limits of Greek scientific research, are taken from Sarton ([1952] 1993) and other historians of science. de Camp, whose interest in languages is well known (see n. 19), has Aristotle speak with his characteristic lisp (Diogenes Laertius, 5.1).
18 On 'nexus stories', see Hellekson (2001: 11–13).
19 de Camp's pioneering interest in language issues, more specifically in the communicative interferences arising from time travel, is reflected in a nonfiction piece of writing that came out in *Astounding* 1938. In his first short story to be published, 'The Isolinguals' (1937), an increasing number of people experience a reactivation of an atavist sort of 'ancestral memory', that makes them speak in dead languages, Latin and ancient Greek among them.
20 Diogenes Laertius (in *Our Time Line*, see n. 1) devotes book 5 of his work to Aristotle and his successors at the Lyceum in Athens.
21 The main stages of the alternate history of Western Civilization caused by Aristotle's categorical condemnation of scientific research are summarized by Weaver in 'Aristotle' as follows: 'It is after the fall of the Roman Empire that profound differences appear. In my world there was a revival of learning that began about 900 years ago, followed by a scientific revolution beginning for centuries after. In your history, the revival of learning was centuries later, and the scientific revolution has hardly begun. Failure to develop the compass and the full-rigged ship resulted in North America being discovered and settled via the northern route, by way of Iceland, and more slowly than in my world. Failure to invent the gun meant that the natives of Hesperia were not swept aside by the invading Europeans, but held their arts of ironworking, weaving, cereal growing and alike. Now most of the European settlements have been assimilated, though the ruling families of the Abnakis and Mohegans frequently have blue eyes and still call themselves by names like Sven and Eric' (de Camp [1958a] 2002: 52–3).
22 *The Bronze God of Rhodes* (1960), *The Arrows of Hercules* (1965), and *The Golden Wind* (1969), his preferred one.
23 Details regarding the inspiration of this novel can be found in de Camp ([1996] 2011: 245–6). Aristotle's books on what today may be considered as zoology and biology have been the most positively appreciated in modern times. That Alexander was keen to assist Aristotle in his scientific undertakings, especially with information

about new specimens from distant countries, had already been pointed out by Pliny (*Natural History* 8.17.44). On this contested issue, see Bigwood (1993).

24 This idea resonates with 'postmodern' reflections about science and scientific research, see e.g. Roberts (2016: 5–15).

25 On this prominent idea regarding Martin Padway's strategy (in *Lest Darkness Fall*) see Shippey (1973), who brings to comparison the anachronic presence of technological advances in the Middle Ages and the Roman Empire in Kipling (1926) and Golding (1956), respectively.

Section 2

Narratives of Power in Uchronias: Between 'Big Men' and Underrepresented Voices

2.1

The Triumph of Greek Civilization? Projecting Ancient Greece into an Alternate Future

Anastasia Bakogianni
Massey University

Power tends to corrupt, and absolute power corrupts absolutely. Great men are almost always bad men.

Lord Acton in his letter to Bishop Mandell Creighton
(Dalberg-Acton [1887] 1907: 504)

Introduction

Anxieties over the corrupting influence of power on political leaders were widely discussed in the nineteenth century and were closely connected to the Great Powers' oppressive imperialist and colonial projects. John Emerich Edward Dalberg-Acton's famous saying pithily captures this contemporary concern about the negative effects of having power concentrated in the hands of one man. The British historian was specifically criticizing the Catholic popes who spearheaded the persecution of perceived heretics in the thirteenth and fourteenth centuries, but he was also concerned with creating a set of general moral principles by which all the great men of history could be judged, especially those in whose hands was concentrated great authority. Pericles and Alexander the Great could be characterized as 'great men' as well, as they both were deeply implicated in imperialist projects and wielded enormous personal, political and military power in their respective states; indeed, they are probably two of the most famous ancient Greek leaders who have continued to fascinate us down the centuries to the present day. Pericles was Athens' pre-eminent democratic leader from around 461 BCE directing its imperialist agenda against the Persians in the Mediterranean and nurturing the city's desire to become the first city of Greece.

This desire brought Athens into conflict with Sparta in what is known as the Peloponnesian War, which was recounted by the ancient historian Thucydides (*Peloponnesian War*). King Alexander's successful conquest of the Persian empire and territories took him into modern-day Afghanistan, Pakistan and India; his exploits recounted by the ancient historians Arrian (*Anabasis*), Diodorus Siculus (*Library*), and the biographer Plutarch (*Alexander*). Both men died before they fully realized their political and military objectives, Pericles of the plague in 429 BCE (aged around sixty-five or sixty-six) and Alexander of an illness in 324 BCE (aged around thirty-two). But what if they had not perished, but were able to fulfil their plans in an alternative version of ancient Greek history?

Counterfactual narratives of ancient Greece are rarer than Roman ones, on par with the trend for popular culture receptions of the two classical civilizations, where the latter tends to outnumber the former.[1] There are, however, some distinctive, highly imaginative examples of alternative versions of ancient Greek history and culture that echo contemporary aspirations and fears, while simultaneously allowing us to reflect on the reception process itself and our own role within it.

This chapter examines two case studies that construct post-classical futures in which Greek civilization has triumphed and become a Mediterranean and even a galactic power. *A Choice of Destinies* (1986) offers an alternative history of Alexander's campaigns, in which the Macedonian king survives and goes on to found a stable empire that allows humankind to bypass the Middle Ages and conquer the stars. In 'Pericles the Tyrant' (2005), the Persians conquer Greece, but Athenian refugees found a new 'Athens' in Sicily at Panormos (modern-day Palermo) that becomes the centre of a new Greek League (the counterpart of the Delian League) that brings them wealth and power in the western Mediterranean. Both my case studies were published and marketed as science fiction stories, but as this chapter argues they rightfully belong to the counterfactual history genre. Both authors demonstrate a close engagement with ancient Greek history, but also provide readers with enough information to follow the story, even if they are largely unfamiliar with these ancient names and events.[2]

It is these bold 'what if' scenarios that Melissa Scott (born 1960; see Clute 2022 and ISFDB) and Lois Tilton (born 1946; see ISFDB) creatively addressed in their works. In Scott's novel *A Choice of Destinies* and Tilton's short story 'Pericles the Tyrant' Alexander and Pericles' lives took radically different paths, creating distinctive alternative pasts and futures for both democratic Athens and Alexander's empire. At first glance, they appear to offer readers narratives of Greek triumph and success, but underlying anxieties over the nature of power and its corrupting influence are never far from the surface, especially in Tilton's short story. Scott in the 1980s and Tilton in the mid-1990s reflected contemporary concerns about power and its abuse, the human cost of military ambition and the corruptive influence of sole rule. Comparing these two narratives about famous ancient Greek men, written by women and published nearly twenty years apart, offers readers the opportunity to reflect on the changing nature of our relationship with ancient Greek history in this period and in our own time.

This chapter explores questions of theory and methodology and my case studies' specific ancient and modern contexts, before focusing on how these two authors have responded to ancient politics (including using them to indirectly critique their own times), alongside the interlinked theme of leadership and the inherent dangers of great power, before touching upon gender issues. These theoretical and thematic preoccupations are filtered through the prism of two distinctive and engaging examples of counterfactual histories of Alexander and Pericles.

Theoretical Frameworks

In my work for this chapter, I found Catherine Gallagher's (2018: 3) definition of 'alternate history' as 'works that describe one continuous sequence of departures from the historical record, thereby inventing a long counterfactual narrative with a correspondingly divergent fictional world' particularly helpful.[3] Both Scott and Tilton have constructed a vivid alternative world that is firmly based on what we know about ancient Greek history (and in the case of the former also of Roman Republican history). The *Histories* of Herodotus, and Thucydides, as well as of Arrian and Diodorus Siculus, in combination with Plutarch's biographies, form the bedrock of modern interpretations of ancient Greek history. Scott and Tilton use this foundation to imagine what might have happened had key events turned out differently. Counterfactual narratives thus tap into historical personages' and states' unrealized potential to work through alternate outcomes (Gallagher 2018: 13–14), not just as a historical thought experiment but also as a means of working through contemporary anxieties and problems.

The practice of imagining different versions of history dates back to antiquity. The popularity of alternative history, as we conceptualize it today, has increased steadily since the 1970s,[4] but its roots can be found in the speculations of ancient Greek historians like Herodotus and Thucydides, and even further back in the

Iliad's poetic 'what ifs'.[5] The Roman historian Livy proposed a 'what if' scenario in his *History of Rome* (9.17–19) that is particularly relevant for the present discussion. In his ancient thought experiment, he considered an alternative history where Alexander went to war against Rome and lost. Unlike Scott's novel that imagines a Greek victory, Livy is convinced that 'A thousand battle-arrays more formidable than those of Alexander and the Macedonians have the Romans beaten off' (Livy, *History of Rome* 9.19). Although he devotes space to an assessment of the troops and weaponry on both sides, ultimately, Livy based his judgement on Alexander's leadership skills, which he believed to be inferior to those of the Roman consuls he would have faced on the battlefield.

Livy is dismissive of the Persians and other Eastern peoples that Alexander defeated on his campaigns, who he views as easily conquered. He also condemns Alexander for adopting their style of living and trappings of power. He thus echoes the critique of Alexander's behaviour after his defeat of the Persian Empire found in other ancient sources, such as Arrian, Plutarch and Diodorus Siculus, that highlight the corrupting influence of too much power and wealth. For Livy this short digression is nothing more than a rhetorical exercise that he can use to highlight Roman military virtue and tenacity. As a Roman author he cannot (or will not) imagine a scenario where the Greeks win. Although Scott also negatively reflects on some of Alexander's leadership decisions in the later chapters of the alternative future she imagines for him, her creative response to her thought experiment has a different outcome in which Alexander succeeds politically. The Greek empire he built continues, whereas Rome never gets the chance to become one, with the city and its allies becoming instead subsumed into the Greek empire Alexander and his descendants founded and consolidated.

Ancient and Modern Contexts

Melissa Scott and Lois Tilton thus offer their readers two detailed counterfactual narratives of ancient Greece (in long and short formats respectively) that are designed to appeal to both a knowledgeable and non-knowledgeable readership. For classicists their carefully worked out scenarios challenge us to spot the points of divergence from the history we are familiar with from our ancient sources. In Scott's case 328 BCE is the main point of divergence, although the changes she introduced go back even further to 335 BCE. In her narrative, Alexander shows mercy to Thebes' Sacred Band (Scott 1986: 37, 40–1). This stands in sharp contrast to the ancient authors who paint a vivid picture of how, enraged by the Thebans' revolt, Alexander made an example of them by destroying their city and selling the majority of its population into slavery (Arrian, *Anabasis* 1.8–9; Diodorus Siculus, *Library* 17.13–14; Plutarch, *Alexander* 11.4). But the main change involves Alexander's decision to turn back to Greece rather than embarking on the Indian campaign (Scott 1986: 62), a choice that brings him into conflict with a resurgent Greek League (Scott 1986: 80–1), and eventually Rome (Scott 1986: 127–8) and even Carthage (Scott 1986: 242).

In Tilton's short story the point of divergence is a key moment in the Graeco-Persian Wars, when a small alliance of Greek city states that resisted Xerxes in Herodotus' famous account of the Graeco-Persian Wars fell apart when the Spartans deserted it. The popularity of counterfactual scenarios and speculations about a different outcome for the Persian Wars in 480 BCE demonstrate the importance of this turning-point.[6] In Tilton's version of history, the Athenians were forced to abandon the Greek mainland for Sicily where they re-established their city (Tilton 2005: 90) and over time became the leaders of the Free Hellene League (Tilton 2005: 95). Their foreign policy brings them into conflict with Carthage, the other main power in the region. Eventually Sicilian Athens' oppression of its allies led to unrest and revolts, as happened with its historical counterpart, the Delian League. In both the historical and alternative version of Athenian history Athens becomes increasingly imperialist and oppressive towards its allies.

Scott and Tilton's close engagement with the classical world was not a one-off occurrence. There are classical resonances in Scott's early work, dating back to her first novel *The Game Beyond* (1984), which like Isaac Asimov's early *Foundation* novels, drew on Edward Gibbon's popular narrative model of the decline and fall of the Roman Empire. Scott also turned to Greek tragedy for inspiration in her novel *The Kindly Ones* (1987), whose title directly ties it to *The Eumenides*, the third play in Aeschylus' *Oresteia* trilogy. Questions of power and politics are also raised in this novel, which imagines a planet called Orestes, where dissidents are ostracized by the other members of this strict society. In the turbulent decade of the 1980s, which culminated in 1989 in the fall of the Berlin Wall, Scott drew on ancient Greek and Roman history and literature to reflect on the major political shifts that were radically transforming our world in this period. Tilton's *The Gladiator's War: A Dialog* (2004) offered readers an alternative history of Spartacus and was nominated for the Nebula Award for Best Novelette the previous year, another story exploring a famous revolt against oppression in the ancient world.

Both authors won the acknowledgement of their peers, but also faced the challenge of making their mark in the male-dominated world of sci-fi (with some notable exceptions such as Octavia E. Butler, Anne McCaffrey and Ursula K. Le Guin).[7] Both authors have, however, been much less active of late than in their heyday when they wrote their fascinating counterfactual stories about ancient Greece.[8] The field continues to prove challenging for female authors, but as my two case studies and their nuanced discussions of masculinities and gender roles demonstrate (analysed in detail below), female authors can add fresh perspectives on older narratives about famous men of the past. Scott and Tilton's work thus exemplifies the increased presence of underrepresented voices in science fiction.

Power, Politics and Questions of Leadership, Then and Now

Intellectuals, historians and artists have long debated what qualities a good leader should possess and how they should behave. They also critiqued and even outrightly condemned bad behaviour, as we saw in the opening quotation of this chapter. In their search for both good and bad models, many have turned to the past. The Graeco-Roman world with its big personalities (exemplified in this case by Alexander and Pericles) has inspired many debates about leadership, power and politics.[9] But is this perennial search for good leaders itself inherently biased, weighted in favour of concentrating power in the hands of the few, or even just one person (usually a man)? The past is often viewed through the distorting lenses of nostalgia or moral disapproval, but a more nuanced approach is needed to do justice to the complexities of the issues involved.

This nuanced approach entails exploring in greater detail some of the key issues that Scott and Tilton address. I begin by investigating the impact of the historical context on their narratives, especially how it informed the design of the plot. Then I analyse several key facets (the deployment of the military and rhetorical power of the protagonists; the role of prophecies; leadership skills; and the receptions' reframing of the politics of Pericles and Alexander's own time), which ultimately leads me to address two questions with wider implications. How have Pericles and Alexander been re-imagined as leaders and to what extent can their re-presentations be analysed as an illustration of our evolving understanding of the concept of 'big men'?

On the surface, both Scott and Tilton's narratives offer aspirational alternative histories in which Greek civilization lives on and even comes to dominate these alternative realities. But there are darker undertones that destabilize any easy conclusions that the triumph of ancient Greece (or even democratic Athens) is an inherently desirable alternate future. To consolidate his empire, Scott's version of Alexander is forced to become more like his father Philip II (Scott 1986: 207, 246 and 275), a cunning and ruthless diplomat and strategist for whom the end justified the means. Most disturbingly of all, Tilton's Pericles oversees the new Athens' transformation from democratic city of refugees, fleeing the destruction of their *polis* by an invading force, to a corrupt and tyrannical regional power that in turn oppresses and mercilessly exploits its neighbours.

The narratives serve as an exploration of contemporary political concerns, and the authors use these historical characters to reflect on power dynamics in their own time. Scott wrote her novel under the long shadow of the Cold War. This is reflected in the alternative realities she created, where the world is still divided into two opposing camps, a binary model of world politics, where two superpowers fight each other for dominance. Ultimately, however, Scott offers a hopeful message for the alternative reality she created where Alexander's unified empire brings prosperity. Tilton's warning of the dangers of democracy and corrupt leadership in a post 9/11 world, where extreme political narratives have flourished, feels disturbingly familiar. In the early 1990s public debates in the United States and Europe and their allies centred on America's decision to invade first Afghanistan and then Iraq. Tilton's portrayal of an increasingly imperialist, tyrannical Athens that is a democracy in name only had some disturbing real-life resonances that became even sharper a decade later, when conservative politics took a turn towards more extreme ideological positions that undermined not only young but also more established democratic governments, for example Jair Bolsonaro in Brazil and Donald Trump in the United States respectively.

Rhetoric (the art of oratory, or how to persuade people of your point of view) was taught in fifth- and fourth-century BCE democratic Athens as a powerful tool in the arsenal of its politicians. For the ancient Greeks the ability to persuade people in the assembly and/or the battlefield was one of the characteristics of a strong leader and was greatly admired. But it was also a source of anxiety as people could be swayed by rhetoric to make bad decisions. Scott and Tilton interrogate charismatic leaders and how they employ their powers of persuasion (*peitho* in Ancient Greek) in the public sphere. Pericles and Alexander were famous in antiquity for their rhetorical skills,[10] and this is preserved as an essential character trait in Scott and Tilton's alternate versions (e.g. Scott 1986: 55, 63–4 and Tilton 2005: 90). Pericles is seen entirely through the eyes of the narrator (Sophocles) who is absent from the city during the period in which the famous Athenian statesman becomes a fully realized tyrant, while continuing to pay lip service to democratic ideals. Scott (1986: 64) demonstrates how Alexander persuades his troops and commanders to follow his lead even against their own better judgement, but ultimately Pericles fails to persuade his old friend that he and by extension Athens are treating their allies fairly (Tilton 2005: 100–1). As Thucydides has the historical Pericles say in his final speech, gaining an empire might be wrong but having gained one letting it go is more dangerous than holding onto it by any means necessary (Thucydides, *Peloponnesian War* 2.61–63). In both Scott's and Tilton's counterfactual narratives we encounter examples of this 'Periclean' way of thinking. Once in positions of sole authority, their protagonists grow ever more ruthless in order to hold onto their power.

Alexander's leadership skills, his strategic planning, and military successes are vividly on show in Scott's novel in Alexander's unbroken succession of victories over the Greek League (Scott 1986: 90–6), Neapolis (Scott 1986: 140–63), Rome (Scott 1986: 187–206), and finally Carthage (Scott 1986: 260–310). Scott not only demonstrates her extensive knowledge of ancient Greek and Roman warfare but puts it to effective use in her novel. An exciting military episode involves Alexander's battle against the Roman legions (Scott 1986: 187–202). The Greeks and their allies attack a position at the fording of a river that the Romans have hastily fortified. Eventually, they prevail, driving their opponents to flee to the city of Rome. A telling detail in the heat of battle involves a Roman pilum spear that gets stuck on a Greek shield and cannot be dislodged because it was designed to bend (Scott 1986: 195), a well-known technological advantage of the Roman spear. The siege of Carthage gives Scott the opportunity to imagine Alexander engaged in the lengthy business of besieging an ancient city (Alexander's siege of Tyre is the famous example from the historical record: Arrian, *Anabasis* 2.18–24; Diodorus Siculus, *Library* 17.40–46; Plutarch *Alexander* 24.3–25.2). Scott moves up the timeline by bringing forward the Punic Wars and the destruction of Carthage that we are familiar with from Livy (*History of Rome*, book 30 for the third and final war) and Polybius' accounts (fragments of books 38–39 on the fall of the city). In the male-dominated field of historical novels that focus on military aspects, Scott's creative use of her research into ancient warfare is one of her novel's strongest elements.

Scott also encourages her readership to pronounce judgement on Alexander's career and to imagine a very different future. She uses her counterfactual scenario to argue that Alexander's decision to invade India was a bad choice. At several key points in her alternative timeline Scott has added a series of short vignettes from the alternate future of Alexander's empire that she interspaces throughout the length of her novel about Alexander's counterfactual life (Scott 1986: 1–4; 73–6; 129–31; 251–5; 311–14). In one of these she explicitly argues that turning back at Bactria gave Alexander the chance to consolidate his empire (Scott 1986: 73–6) rather than exhausting his energies in continuing to expand in the East. Scott thus passes judgement on the historical Alexander's life and career. She proposes an alternative scenario where he consolidated his conquests; as a result, he ensured the longevity of his empire and changed world history even more radically than the historical Alexander did. In her epilogue, set in 1591 CE, Scott imagines a descendant of Alexander preparing to lead an expedition into space on the anniversary of the empire's foundation (Scott 1986: 311–14).

Prophecy and omens play a decisive role in the two counterfactual receptions of Greek history analysed in this chapter, as they did in ancient Greek politics. They remind knowledgeable readers of the history that Scott alters in her novel and the political and military opportunities she creates for her Alexander. At the beginning of the story Alexander receives a warning from the gods via the Syrian seeress Pasithea that he is in danger, his life 'balanced on the sword's point between one fate and another' (Scott 1986: 10). Her prophecy turns out to be true: the path not taken (the Indian campaign) is the main fork in the road that alters Alexander's destiny and leads to the alternative reality where he makes war on Rome and Carthage and founds an empire that outlasts him (instead of an early death followed by the collapse of his empire). In contrast, Tilton's short story demonstrates the unreliability of human conduits. Once the Panhellenic sanctuary at Delphi falls under Persian control, its prophecies offer no hope to the Athenians, but the oracles at Cuma in Italy do (Tilton 2005: 91). Tilton's more cynical portrayal of the role of prophecy thus makes for an interesting contrast with Scott's greater acceptance of ancient Greek religious beliefs.

Dreams and visions play a guiding role in the life of Scott's Alexander, as they do in the ancient accounts of the life of Alexander that survive, written centuries later by Arrian, Diodorus Siculus, Plutarch and others, which comprise receptions of the legend of Alexander illustrating the distorting perspective of hindsight. During his illness Alexander is visited by the ghost of King Darius and imagines he can see his mother back at Pella. The god Ammon, whom he believes to be his true father, also appears to him (Scott 1986: 225–7). The god throws a pair of dice across the king's bed, but Alexander cannot read their message before they disappear. These ambiguous dream visions are left open-ended, for the reader to interpret as they see fit, but Alexander begins his long road to recovery that very night. The appearance of two past antagonists he defeated (Darius and Olympias) and the dual choice/paths that the dice arguably represent are resolved in that

Alexander passes through this time of danger and emerges victorious and alive at the other end. But both he and his empire are forever changed by virtue of the alternative path Scott imagines him taking.

Tilton's Sophocles becomes disillusioned with his city's trajectory towards empire-building and its exploitation of its allies for profit. This version of Sophocles travels extensively for a decade and learns how to view events through a non-Atheno-centric lens. Tilton emphasizes the importance of travel in facilitating intercultural exchanges and the greater acceptance of diverse points of view. These formative experiences make it possible for this Sophocles to creatively respond to the criticism levelled at his dramas: 'It's clear you know nothing of Carthage and only listen to the evil rumors spread by our enemies' (Tilton 2005: 97). Unlike the ancient view of Sophocles as a proud Athenian citizen, Tilton's version of the ancient tragedian reconsiders his long-held political and civic beliefs and adopts a more questioning attitude towards the new Sicilian Athens. Although not expressly mentioned in the short story, Sophocles' experience of the trauma of losing the original city of his birth and becoming a refugee is another factor in shaping his character in this alternative version of Greek history. He becomes more open to different ideas and cultural perspectives and (non-Athenian) ways of seeing the world. These experiences bring him into direct conflict with Tilton's version of Pericles who, having learned the opposite lesson from his experiences as a refugee, has become a de facto tyrant (foreshadowed in Tilton's choice of title) that holds an intractable belief in the superiority of Athens over other cities and peoples.[11]

At the end of the story Sophocles is ostracized for daring to write plays that criticize Pericles' rule and Sicilian Athens. This Pericles (like the philosopher Plato who famously banished it from his ideal state) views drama as dangerous and exiles his former friend to stop him putting on plays like *The Ransom of Chryseis*, *The Fall of Minos*, and *Pericles the Tyrant*, that were but thinly veiled criticism of his tyrannical rule and of Athens' imperialist, irridentist policies. The historical Sophocles was a proud Athenian who, as well as being a successful playwright, served his city in both administrative (for example, in 442 BCE he was a treasurer for the Delian League) and military roles (in 440 BCE he was elected one of the ten commander of Athens' forces). As far as we know, he never wavered in his support of his city and its democratic leaders (Lefkowitz 2014: 1291). The alternate Sophocles' theatre career thus starts with pro-Athenian plays (e.g. *Betrayal at Salamis*, *The Chaining of Typhon*, and *The Mothers of Carthage*) that supported Pericles' agenda but ends challenging his policies and rule of Sicilian Athens. At the early stages of his career Sophocles is guilty of writing populist and sycophantic dramas. Aeschylus' inditement is telling, 'you pander to politicians and promote their wars on stage', rather than producing plays that 'honor the gods' (Tilton 2005: 96).

But Tilton's Sophocles is capable of both personal and political growth. In her short story, art stings the tyrant like a Socratic gadfly but cannot change the new world order. A similar sense of frustration was felt when numerous protests against the war in Iraq did not alter the political and military decisions of the US and its allies.[12] For example, several productions of Euripides' *The Trojan Women* were staged around the world,[13] because of this particular Greek tragedy's long association with the anti-war movement.[14] In Tilton's story art can only challenge the status quo and ultimately either cease to create (Aeschylus' choice) or find free expression elsewhere (Sophocles' choice). Tilton's Sophocles ends up living in Cuma, in mainland Italy (the seat of the Sibylline oracle previously mentioned in the story), where no constraints are put on his creative powers. Tilton (2005: 103) concludes her short story on a hopeful note with Sophocles' dreams of bringing theatre to his new home and honouring the gods by freely practising his art.

In both these counterfactual receptions of ancient Greek history, ultimately, it is the perennial problem of Greek disunity that alters the course of history. In Scott's novel the revolt of the Greek League cities forces Alexander to return to Greece, while in Tilton's short story the Greek alliance of cities falls apart and the Spartans desert their fellow-Hellenes forcing the Athenians to abandon their city (to which they are never able to return). The authors thus creatively play on a well-known historical Hellenic trait to justify the alternative histories and futures they created. Scott even pointedly reminds knowledgeable readers familiar with ancient Greek history of the historical consequences of Alexander's early death. Wounded by a javelin in the aftermath of his first encounter in battle with the Romans (Scott 1986: 157–61), her version of Alexander succumbs to a fever and his staff fear he will perish (Scott 1986: 211). The jealousies, quarrels and jockeying for power Scott describes once Alexander's powerful personality no longer supresses them (1986: 222–5) are but a taster of the historical Wars of the Diadochi that his successors fought after his death (323–279 BCE) that led to the fragmentation of the empire he built. Thus, while on the personal and creative levels hope is possible, on the larger political stage both Scott and Tilton are less sanguine that the alternative paths they imagined Greek history taking would prove any better than what took place. Concentrated in the hands of just one such 'big man', absolute power is dangerous, whatever their qualities as leaders.

Masculinities, Ancient and Modern

A distinctive feature of my Greek case studies is that they were both written by women, but reflect ancient history's focus on 'big men', wars of conquest and complex international politics that centre around male protagonists.[15] Their points of divergence, the points in time where these stories break away from what we know about ancient Greek history, take place during the lives of famous ancient figures like Alexander and Pericles, and well-known large scale historical events like Alexander's campaigns and the Graeco-Persian Wars. Scott and Tilton thus seek to offer their readers entertaining alternative versions of famous historical men from ancient Greek history and speculate on the impact that changes in their lives might have made on the course of history, thus creating alternate future timelines. The authors might utilize modern story patterns and characterizations, reflecting contemporary worldviews and issues back into this alternate past, but their focus remains on narratives of 'big men'.

Male friendship lies at the core of both counterfactual narratives. The friendship between Pericles and Sophocles is broken by the end of Tilton's short story, but it forms the core relationship around which the narrative is built. Its gradual disintegration mirrors the moral degeneration of Sicilian Athens itself, as the city and its leader are corrupted by power and wealth. Upon his return from his travels Sophocles is appalled by his fellow citizens' change in outlook: 'Athens had grown arrogant, and the slave trade was so lucrative' (Tilton 2005: 100). He quarrels with Pericles, now first general on the city council, over his tacit condoning of the selling of rowing places on Athenian triremes. Sophocles sees this as profiteering and unworthy of Athenian men, who should be fighting to defend their own city rather than hiring slaves to row in their place. He is disenchanted that 'under Pericles they didn't have to lift a hand to earn it, or pay for it with their own sweat and blood' (Tilton 2005: 101).

A noteworthy feature of Scott's novel is its LGBTQ subtext, although Alexander's relationships with men are never directly addressed in her novel.[16] Alexander's close bond with Hephaestion is highlighted on several occasions when the Macedonian king turns to his companion for advice and/or for consolation.[17] Their close, affectionate relationship is but the most prominent of several same-sex partnerships between men, including among the members of the Theban Sacred Band (famously made up of one hundred and fifty pairs of male lovers), a unit that plays a key role in the novel when they prove their royalty to Alexander even against their own city. In response to the king's personal appeal to Theagenes, commander of the Sacred Band, the Theban begs for his unit to be allowed to serve Alexander 'Even – especially against Thebes' (Scott 1986: 49). Honour among men and loyalty trump even allegiance to a city, a point Scott emphasizes by changing history to have the unit fight in Alexander's campaigns.

These core relationships thus shape the male-centred worlds these two female authors have created where high-status women are confined to the traditional roles of daughters, wives and mothers, while slave and poor women are cast in the roles of mistresses and prostitutes. Women live on the side lines of male lives in these worlds. A representative example is Cassia, the tribune Cassius' sister who becomes Alexander's Roman wife, and who meekly accepts male control over her life (Scott 1986: 230–2). As Scott (1986: 231–2) succinctly puts it Cassia 'had never expected to be consulted in the matter' and thinks 'to ask what Alexander was like' only as an afterthought. She is content to simply acquiesce with her brother's choice of husband, dictated by Roman politics that favour an alliance with the Macedonian king. Cassia is thus a pawn in alliances made by men in furtherance of larger political goals. In Tilton's narrative, women are even more peripheral, for example Pericles' justification for why the Greeks need a strong leader is delivered in a brothel at Cuma but Sophocles is its intended recipient. In Tilton's counterfactual world women form part of the background of male lives. These two receptions thus illustrate the embedded misogyny of ancient narratives centred on 'big men' that served to reinforce women's traditional roles as wives, mothers and sexual partners.

The only exception is Olympias (Alexander's mother), whom Scott portrays negatively as a stereotypically meddling woman. She attempts to control men by pitting them against each other, thus disrupting the male bonds that in Scott's story are responsible for Macedonian/Greek success. Upon Alexander's triumphant return to Pella, he realizes that his mother has been trying to turn his son and heir, Philip Alexander (son of his deceased first wife, Euridice), against him, just like she had previously done with her husband Philip and her own son (Scott 1986: 111). Olympias also meddles in politics and military matters by undermining Alexander's regent, Antipater, thus damaging not only his standing, but also her son's imperialist plans (Scott 1986: 106). Like other stereotypical interfering mothers,[18] Olympias' gender makes it impossible for her to have direct access to power, so she is forced to work through men, the cause of a great deal of personal resentment. Her interference does have one important positive outcome in Scott's (1986: 128) alternative version of history and that is that Alexander is forced to stay in the West.[19] Scott makes it clear to her readers that Olympias' desire to punish her son by frustrating his plans to conquer India result in an unintended 'happy ending' for the Macedonian king. Alexander is forced to realize that he cannot continue to expand his empire but must stop to ensure that it outlasts his (now longer) lifespan. This does not in any way mitigate Olympias' negative portrayal in Scott's novel: she is but a plot device to ensure Alexander remains committed to the alternative path the novelist imagined for him.

Conclusion

Melissa Scott's novel and Lois Tilton's short story focus on major ancient historical events with important political consequences based on what-if scenarios. This creative strategy also allows them to refract contemporary concerns about politics, power, masculinity and leadership. As Weiss (2013: 1) argues 'literature emphatically creates an *alternative* to history, be it the history of an individual, or of a community or nation', but in the genre of alternative history this transformation takes centre stage and allows us to reflect on the overlapping intersections between history and literature.[20] Moreover, as Gallagher (2018: 10) argues, the dynamism of counterfactual narratives means that they can be adapted to meet contemporary needs. In the twentieth and twenty-first centuries, the focus on politics and questions of leadership remains ever relevant and a major source of communal fears. In 'Pericles the Tyrant' Tilton's counterfactual short story engages with the 'consequences in democratic politics' (Gallagher 2018: 4–5) of a leader who promotes irridentist and imperialist policies amongst the people. Alexander's wars of conquests and the different directions they might have taken are explored in Scott's novel, as is the corrupting influence of sole power concentrated in the hands of one man. These two counterfactual histories thus exhibit many commonalities because at heart they deal with the nature of politics and of power.

Passing judgement on history from a modern perspective, forcibly reminds us of the key role played by the artist/author/creative practitioner as well as the audience member/reader/receiver in the reception process itself. Our modern perspective colours our view of these famous ancient Greek leaders and our interpretation of the ancient evidence. The example of democratic Athens in the fifth century BCE is symbolic of this phenomenon.[21] Long viewed as the world's first democracy, ancient Athens' darker aspects, its imperialist ambition and warmongering, have been highlighted in recent modern scholarship and have in turn inspired creative outputs that explore these facets of its history. The two-directionality of the reception process highlights that such modern interpretations, engendered by a modern outlook and values (see Hardwick 2003: 3–4), can also help focus scholarly criticism on the importance of problematizing ancient politics. The reception of counterfactual histories thus adds further layers to our engagement with the classical world. Looking back from a contemporary perspective is helpful because: 'When we study the past . . . we can benefit from our distance – our alienation, if you will – from the actors and their beliefs . . . if we make use of this alienation to better understand the past, we can also improve our purchase on the present' (Lamoreaux 2011: 50)

In a 2004 essay, Bunzl is sceptical about the value of counterfactual thinking for the historian, but more recently Gallagher (2018: 15) argues for the benefits of engaging with counterfactuals because 'alternate worlds strip our own of its neutral, inert givenness and open it to our judgment'.[22] Counterfactuals encourage us to be more critical not only of the outcome of major wars that shaped the history of large regions and peoples (like the Graeco-Persian Wars and Alexander's campaigns), a long-established practice in military history (Gallagher 2018: 27; see also Schmid 2009), but also of the political and military motives that drove the participants involved. Tilton offers her readers a timely warning from history about how fragile democracy is, while Scott gives us an imaginative demonstration of how absolute power corrupts.

'What if' scenarios can also serve as useful pedagogical tools that encourage students to reflect on the history they have studied. Inspired by my work for this chapter, I have added an alternative history elective component to the assessment for my *Greek History* course at Massey University. After students complete their work on the historical section of the module, they can write a short reflective five-hundred-word 'what if' piece for extra credit. This has proven a popular writing activity with students, who often identify the Graeco-Persian Wars and Alexander the Great's campaigns as key turning points. Student feedback on this activity is overwhelmingly positive with students commenting on the intellectual fun to be had in thinking up of alternative historical scenarios. But it is also a way for them to become more active in both their learning and in their reception of the ancient world.

Ultimately, at the heart of this investigation lies an interesting paradox. Both Scott's novel and Tilton's short story are categorized as popular receptions of the ancient world, and yet neither is particularly well-known (especially the former). The term 'popular' has long been used in a derogative way to dismiss modern receptions of the classics. But both Scott's and Tilton's works reward closer attention, especially in their exploration of the themes of power, politics, masculinity and leadership. Their exploration of these themes are why Scott's and Tilton's alternative history narratives remain relevant. They continue to strike a timely note of warning in the second decade of the new millennium, with extremism on the ascendant and the very concept of democracy under sustained attack. Their stories offer us a useful refracting lens through which we can continue to engage with ancient Greek history and the richness and variety of its reception in popular culture, as well as with the burning question of whether art can ever effectively challenge the structures of power.

Acknowledgements

Many thanks are due to the editors of this volume for their collegiality and helpful suggestions. Also, many thanks to my friend Sue Raven for helping source a copy of Scott's novel.

Notes

1 Gideon Nisbet (2008: 7–8) explains ancient Greece's lesser appeal in film (compared to the popularity of Rome), and in popular culture more generally, as the result of Victorian prejudices against same-sex love and modern anti-intellectualism, both qualities associated with ancient Greek culture.
2 Reader reviews, however, suggest that even non-knowledgeable readers enjoy the ancient settings and famous characters and view these stories as a way of engaging with the classical past. An Amazon reviewer specifically mentions that they purchased Scott's novel because of their fascination with Alexander the Great which led them to 'eagerly devouring anything to do with the subject' (K. Gilligan 2007, accessed 22 November 2022).
3 See also http://www.uchronia.net/intro.html (accessed 17 November 2022).
4 Gallagher (2018: 1), Rosenfeld (2022: 515). For a longer history of counterfactuals see Weiss (2013) and Wohl (2014: 1–14) on how the ancient Greeks conceptualized alternative history.
5 On Thucydides' use of counterfactuals, see Tordoff (2014); on *The Iliad*, see Slatkin (2019).
6 For example, Harry Turtledove's short story 'Counting Potsherds' (1989) in which Athens lost the Persian Wars and Athens was destroyed. For further information see: http://www.uchronia.net/bib.cgi/diverge.html (accessed 17 November 2022) and Hanson (2000) in an essay imagining the impact of an alternative outcome for the Persian Wars in which the Greeks lost.

7 Scott won the John W. Campbell Award for Best New Writer in Science Fiction in 1986, the same year that *A Choice of Destinies* was published. Tilton's short story 'Pericles the Tyrant' first appeared in the October/November 2005 issue of Asimov's *Science Fiction* magazine and won that year's Sidewise Award for best short-form alternative history (Langford 2013, accessed 20 November 2022).

8 Later in their careers both authors contributed entries to popular television series novel tie-ins. In recent times they diversified their output, Scott by contributing to issues in an e-magazine and Tilton by writing essays.

9 For one such recent discussion, see Cooke (2022). For an example of this type of interpretation of Alexander on the internet, see Bullari (2020).

10 Thucydides both admired Pericles' rhetorical skills and feared the power they gave him over the democratic assembly. For more on this, see Makridis (2011) and Crick (2014). Arrian praised Alexander's powers of persuasion in his epitaph for the Macedonian king (Arrian, *Anabasis* 7.28.2) especially his ability to raise their spirits and expectations by his own example of fearlessness which helped them overcome their own fears.

11 Pericles' single-minded belief is reminiscent of contemporary 'certainties' like NATO's mission to eradicate Islamic extremism in Afghanistan and the existence of Weapons of Mass Destruction that the United States used to justify its invasion of Iraq in 2003. For an interesting comparison between Alexander's successful campaigns in Afghanistan and the failure of NATO's mission see Warren (2018).

12 For more details of classically inspired protests against the war (including performances of ancient war plays, readings, think pieces, etc.), see Bakogianni (2015a: 2).

13 A notable example was Katie Mitchell's production titled *Women of Troy* at the National Theatre (London) for the 2007–2008 season.

14 For the tragedy's anti-war pedigree, see Bakogianni (2015b: 300).

15 Two examples of novels told from the point of view of ancient women involved in Alexander and Pericles' lives respectively are: Stephanie Thornton's *The Conqueror's Wife* (2015) and Elise Garrison's *The Milesian Mistress: The Autobiography of Aspasia of Miletus* (2011). These two examples form part of a wider trend of novels written in the new millennium and set in the ancient world that centre the female perspective, such as Margaret Atwood's *Penelopiad* (2005), Pat Barker's *The Women of Troy* (2021) and Jennifer Saint's *Ariadne* (2021), to name but a few prominent examples.

16 Cf. Mary Renault's famous Alexander trilogy: *Fire from Heaven* (1969), *The Persian Boy* (1972), and *Funeral Games* (1981). See Baynham and Terry (2018) on the key figure of Bagoas, Alexander's Persian slave.

17 For example, the tender scene between the two men when Hephaestion comforts Alexander after the king is forced to abandon his plans for the Indian campaign

(Scott 1986: 62) and again when they discuss Alexander's plans in bed together (Scott 1986: 246–9).

18 The ancient goddess Demeter is another famous example from antiquity for her interference in the life of her daughter Persephone. Mrs Bennet in Jane Austen's novel *Pride and Prejudice* (1813) and Livia Soprano in the television series *The Sopranos* (1999–2007) are two famous fictional interfering mothers.

19 Alexander suspects that his mother uses her kinsman Mentor as a pawn in her schemes to frustrate his plans to return to the East. Mentor is a vocal member of an embassy sent to Alexander from the Italiote League to beg for his help against the aggressive Samnite tribes (Scott 1986: 124–6).

20 'All historical arguments by their very nature imply that history would have turned out differently if the events or factors singled out for emphasis did not occur' (Lamoreaux 2011: 39).

21 Tordoff (2014: 119) argues that 'we find historical counterfactuals at the very heart of the democratic deliberation' in post-Peloponnesian War Athens, too.

22 On the debate about the usefulness of counterfactuals see also Evans (2014). For another useful perspective see Maar (2014).

2.2

Emperor Julian's American Dream

Alberto J. Quiroga Puertas
University of Granada
Elia Otranto
University of Granada

Introduction

On 6 January 2021, the Capitol Building in Washington DC was attacked and vandalized by a mob of far-right extremist groups. Most of them were supporters of Donald Trump, who had just lost the 2020 presidential election and claimed that the result was not valid as Joe Biden had allegedly won due to electoral fraud. This violent episode left us a good number of shocking and striking images. In one of those images Jake Angeli, a white supremacist and one of the leaders of the rioters who stormed into the Capitol, appears dressed up as a Native American. He was not alone in this, as other rioters also resorted to using elements of the stereotyped attire associated with Native Americans. This misappropriation is a characteristic feature of some of the anti-government groups involved in the Capitol attack that fashion themselves by claiming elements from Native American cultures as constitutive of their identity (Trudelle Schwarz 2013: 15–43). The strong symbolism of these images immediately echoed Gibbonian approaches, as public debates in the aftermath of the attack revolved around the continuous decline and fall of democracy in the USA. Public figures and contemporary historians could not help but draw parallels between the decline of political life caused by Trumpism and the worst days of the Roman Republic and the Roman Empire, with Catiline, Nero and Commodus as the main figures with whom Trump was compared (Bowman 2021; Brockell 2020).

In no way do we wish to minimize the political implications and the gravity of this historical episode. However, it would also be hard to disagree that the images from this event are extremely symbolic. The Capitol, a neoclassical building and the centre of the USA democratic system founded on perceived values from the classical past, made the front pages around the world, showing rioters using adulterated symbols of Native American cultures. Such images led to a bizarre scene reminiscent of the flabbergasting effect produced by some uchronias and alternate histories. In this sense, some similarities concerning politics and the (re)creation of the Graeco-Roman past can be found between the images from the Capitol attack and some essential elements in the plot of the alternate history stories *Imperium Solis* (2009) and *Gladius Imperii* (2012) composed by the Italian journalist and writer Mario Farneti. In these two uchronias full of sci-fi tropes, Farneti fictionalizes the history of the Roman emperor Julian.[1] The Italian writer presents Julian escaping death in the year 363 CE, going to America and civilizing its technologically underdeveloped population. After that, Julian comes back to Europe with a multi-ethnic army in order to create the first alliance of civilizations.

Even though considered through considered through the lens of uchronia and science fiction, aspects of the influence of the Graeco-Roman cultural legacy in Pre-Columbian America are dealt with by Farneti. The analysis of these aspects will be at the core of this contribution. First, an outline of the role of the emperor Julian in fiction and a summary of the novels *Imperium Solis* and *Gladius Imperii* will be given. Second, we will deal with how Julian's presence in America is explored by Farneti by paying particular attention to the author's approach based on an exercise of *interpretatio romana*. Third, we focus on the notion of progress and technology applied by Farneti in his description of the invention of different contrivances (from planes to submarines). In doing so, we intend to suggest that in Farneti's stories Julian is characterized as a modern Prometheus who represented the paradigm of the technological superiority of the Western civilization over Native Americans. Finally, we will compare *Imperium Solis* and *Gladius Imperii* with other novels composed by Farneti (the uchronic trilogy *Occidente*) and by other Italian writers in order to ascertain whether Farneti's novels hide a political agenda. Our analysis is motivated by the criticism that has been levelled against the author on the grounds that *Occidente* is philofascist propaganda in the guise of fiction.

Julian the Chrononaut

The emperor Julian (331–363 CE) is perhaps one of the most ambiguous and puzzling figures from the Ancient Mediterranean. Nicknamed 'the Apostate' because of his efforts to reverse the process of the Christianization of the Roman

Empire in the mid-fourth century, he did not enjoy a good reputation after his early death. Julian was denigrated by Christian tradition for centuries, although this attitude towards his works and thought started to find some opposition in the Renaissance and, especially, in the Enlightenment. During the fifteenth to the eighteenth centuries, the focus on Julian's religious beliefs was less intense since intellectuals grew more interested in the emperor's philosophical and literary achievements (Braun and Richer 1978).[2] These two opposing views on Julian have determined the nature of his fictionalization in literature, even though his main traits have rarely changed: Julian is consistently portrayed in fiction as a bookish emperor obsessed with mysticism, philosophy and religious transcendence. For instance, Ibsen's play *Emperor and Galilean* ([1873] 1986), Merezhkovsky's novel *The Death of Gods* ([1895] 1901), and the set of poems by Kazantzakis on Julian delineated the profile of an emperor tormented by a continuous spiritual crisis as he was dissatisfied with the futility of philosophy in his attempts to attain the knowledge of the sacred. At the other end of the spectrum, Gore Vidal's *Julian* (1964) presented a more nuanced figure. Julian rarely experiences moments of doubt and pain, but he is sketched as a bona fide philosopher as well as a political figure who is greatly concerned by the power dynamics of his times.

The presence of the emperor Julian in science fiction or speculative fiction, however, is scarce. Robert C. Wilson's *Julian Comstock: A Story of the 22nd Century America* (2009) is one of the few examples. Wilson masterfully illustrates a dystopic future in which Julian Comstock, whose biographical episodes replicate those of the historical emperor Julian, lives in a world in which nature is trying to recover from the damage caused by climate change, Darwinism is forbidden, and political institutions are corrupt. Julian also features in *Fireball* (1981), a science fiction novel for young adults written by John Christopher in which two teenagers travel back in time and find themselves in an empire in which Julian had survived the Persian campaign in which he died in 363 CE and had managed to implement some of his political and religious reforms (see Fowler in this volume).

The plot of Farneti's *Imperium Solis* and *Gladius Imperii* unfolds along the same uchronic lines. In these two works, the Italian writer combines historical facts with sci-fi elements in order to develop a counterfactual plot: what would have happened if the emperor Julian had not died near Ctesiphon during the Persian campaign he launched? What if he had survived after what would come upon him had been foretold? The first novel begins with Julian's visit to the ancient site of Troy.[3] While there, he approached the sanctuary built in honour of the Trojan prince Hector. That night, Julian had an epiphanic vision in which Hector himself appeared to him and told him that the Roman Empire was about to fall. Nevertheless, Hector revealed a way to save the empire: after faking his own death during his military campaign against the Persians, Julian should set off on a long journey, hide in a faraway land, and create a new empire. Then, he should return to Rome and integrate this new empire into the Roman one. When the time of the Persian military campaign arrived, Julian did as he had been told and faked his own death, which is the point of divergence from real history, as Julian was actually killed by an arrow during the Battle of Samarra, a location nor far from Ctesiphon – the capital of the Sasanian Empire. In Farneti's novel, though, he escaped death disguised as a merchant. It is at this point that uchronia merges with constituents of fantasy and science fiction. Having escaped his fate, Julian began a journey in the company of some loyal soldiers and a civilian retinue composed of Romans, Greeks and Celts. During their journey from Persia to North America, they stopped at Thule, a land mentioned in classical sources – especially by the fourth-century BCE geographer Pytheas of Massalia.[4] Julian and his entourage continued their journey and reached Meropis, an imaginary land invented by the historian Theopompus.[5] Finally, they arrived in North America, where the encounter between the Romans and the Natives was fruitful. Both cultures started to cooperate thanks, to a great extent, to the fact that the Hisat'sinom, one of the first peoples the Romans met, spoke Etruscan. Both cultures were also bonded because the Natives worshipped Taoiwa, a solar divinity analogous to Helios, the Greek god fervently revered by Julian. His project of conquering the territory was compromised by a plot to kill him by some radicalized Christians that had come with him to America, yet the loyalty of most members of his army, together with the help of the force of local tribes, placated the insurrection. The success of this collaboration between Native Americans and Romans is epitomized in the novel by the foundation of big cities such as *Novum Eboracrum* (New York) and the change in the Roman signature from SPQR into SPQA: *Senatus Populusque Americanus*.

The narration of the second book, *Gladius Imperii*, begins with a new epiphanic vision. On this occasion, the Genius Publicus showed himself to an old yet wise and still vigorous Julian and announced that the time had come for him to come back to Rome, reconquer it and save the empire from disappearing. Following the divinity's instructions, Julian started to call his people to arms. The original army that had arrived in North America had grown in number thanks to alliances with peoples from North and Central America. In addition to the increase in size, Julian's army was now weaponized with planes, submarines and automata developed by the Roman technology (see below, 'From Brick to Marble: Technology at the Service of the Empire'). Upon his arrival on the *old continent*, Julian found the Roman Empire on the brink of disappearing because of the barbarian invasions (the sack of Rome by Alaric in 410 CE had happened recently), Christian persecution of the pagans and religious conflicts between the different Christian creeds. Julian dealt with these problems by promoting tolerant religious edicts and cunningly making use of his military superiority that easily crushed the barbarian forces. As a result, at the end of the novel the Roman Empire is a religiously tolerant territory that has been enlarged by Julian's conquests and which faces a bright future thanks to technological knowledge. Julian, hence, is portrayed as the emperor who saved Western civilization and rerouted its destiny.

At the crossroads of uchronic sword-and-sandal and pulp science fiction novel, *Imperium Solis* and *Gladius Imperii* are uchronias with no aspirations to literary merit other than exploiting the allure of the figure of an emperor-philosopher transformed by Farneti into a Columbus *avant la lettre*. This appraisal can also be applied to most of the works of this genre for, as G. Feeley (2004) put it, 'alternate histories lend themselves almost uniquely well to what publishers call "high concept". The central idea behind most alternate histories is as straightforward as being iconic – sometimes conveyed in the title, but often reducible to a single image, which publishers have been happy to employ'. In the case of Farneti's novels, that central idea subscribes to the commonplace that the Western civilization has always spearheaded technological progress and that this type of progress has made societies advance in a teleologically predetermined world.

Ubi Iulianus, ibi patria: Julian as a Foundational Hero

Novels dealing with the history of the United States of America have become a literary genre of their own, one in which major historical events like the War of Independence, the Civil War, the Cold War and the role of USA in the Second World War have been incessantly fictionalized (Gallagher 2018: 97–189; Hugill 2010; Morley 2010: 6–8; Schneider-Mayerson 2009). Yet not all novels centre around the USA's military involvement in conflicts. In popular and media culture, somehow the USA has come to symbolize the land of opportunities and the crucible of civilizations that welcomes all those willing to work hard in order to live (and fulfil) the American Dream. The revisitation of these historical episodes and the idea of America as a tabula rasa where people from any part of the world can start afresh have been approached from a variety of angles, including historical speculations. These constitute a subgenre in which what-if scenarios involving characters from the Ancient World have taken centre-stage. In these novels, past events take a different turn from what actually happened and end up creating societies onto which authors project their hopes and concerns. In these instances, imagination runs wild and anachronisms are added to the what-if core of the novels, resulting in historical figures visiting America. In *The plot to save Socrates* (Levinson 2006), for example, Bar Kokhba time-travels from the second century CE Roman Empire to the New York of the mid-twenty-first century.[6]

Although the plots of these speculative fictions are far-fetched and conceived as literary entertainment, they also provide us with insights into how the history of Ancient Mediterranean civilizations has been reshaped for different purposes in alternate history stories. In this context, drawing parallels and making connections between Rome (in both its Republican and Imperial incarnations) and the USA stand out, given their recurrence in literature and journalism. But what is the reason for this time-honoured tendency to look back to Rome in search of answers to current problems? Historian and classicist Neville Morley (2017) has warned of the dangers of overusing the comparison between Rome and the USA. His caveat was expressed at the peak of the comparisons drawn between Donald Trump and several Roman emperors traditionally known for their eccentric behaviour, but its applicability still stands:

> We risk deluding ourselves, or at least limiting our perspective by our choice of historical analogies. Perhaps through mere force of habit, we resort to antiquated conceptions of autocrats and their power; the inherited belief that these inherited images can help us make sense of the world. This enables us to depict the tyrant in lurid anecdotes, with the effect of magnifying his power and disguising its true nature.
>
> Morley 2017

Historian Sarah E. Bond contextualizes some of the numerous comparisons drawn between Rome and the USA after Donald Trump was elected president in 2017. Bond (2019) has commented on concerns about the public perception of the decline of the Roman Empire as a mirror of the state of USA politics during the Trump administration.

Bond's interests are shared by Ed Watts (2021: 234–42), who has recently explored the manipulation of the decline and fall of Rome in different political contexts concerning the USA, especially when the analogy with Rome is not particularly cogent or it is simply preposterous – e.g. homosexuality, feminism, and AIDS as possible causes of the collapse of the empire according to some leading public figures in the USA.[7]

These ideas about the analogy between Rome and USA are related to the rationale of *Imperium Solis* and *Gladius Imperii*. The emperor Julian is portrayed in anecdotes that give us a glimpse of his historical stature, but Farneti's portrayal of Julian barely contextualizes or hints at historical causes for the emperor's actions. It is obvious that historiography and fiction work according to different criteria and purposes, but Farneti's narrative is teleologically inspired to such an extent that readers know in advance that at every turn of Julian's adventures the emperor will easily fulfil Hector's prophecy and create a new empire. The narrative of power, therefore, is anchored to Julian's predestined future, a literary strategy that, as Morley states (see above), limits our critical appraisal of the nature of politics and emperorship.

On the other hand, the alliance between Native Americans and Romans is Farneti's solution to the 'perceived flaws', as Bond puts it, that Farneti saw in the first decade of our century: the inappropriate management of globalization in the post 9/11 world and the political imbalance in Western civilization could cause its collapse, just as the barbarian invasions did to the Roman Empire.[8] In order to deal with these topics, Farneti accommodates the widespread narrative of the *discovery* of America by Columbus and of the legends surrounding El Dorado to his purposes: the richness of America is wisely and justly exploited by the Romans, who do not exert the violence used by the conquistadores from fifteenth and sixteenth centuries on the Natives. Farneti bypasses everything that may seem problematic for the union of Natives and Romans by, for example, coming up with the use of Etruscan as a common language and the worship of a very similar deity (Taoiwa–Helios).

Farneti's opinions are presented in fiction, but they are actually held by some political groups in the contemporary USA. In his 2007 book exploring the similarities between Rome and the USA, journalist and author Cullen Murphy (2007: 9-10) has divided and labelled these groups according to their political and religious tenets. It is noteworthy that two of these groups (the Augustinians and the Ambrosians) share the vision of Farneti's Julian as they hope to reach a *pax Americana* under the protection of Christianity.[9] Thus, in *Gladius Imperii* (Farneti 2012: 398–9; 504–6), Julian similarly expresses his longing for a peaceful empire comprising Western peoples. Although they do not need to be Christians, Julian's speech is clear about the relevance of religion in the SPQA as a uniting force that intersects with politics.

From Brick to Marble: Technology at the Service of the Empire

According to the Roman historian Suetonius (*Lives of the Caesars* 2.28), the emperor Augustus felt so proud of the results of the urban reformation and architectural programme that he had planned for Rome that he claimed that he had transformed a city built of brick into a city built of marble and had made it safe for generations to come. The essence of this anecdote echoes Farneti's persistent recourse to technological innovations in both his novels in which Julian can be likened to a late antique Augustus who promoted the invention of machines and artefacts with the intention of making America great for the first time. Certainly, Farneti designs his vision of the fourth century CE upon Peter Brown's understanding of that period. The Irish historian spearheaded a historiographical trend that argued that Late Antiquity was not a period of decadence dissociated from the intellectual achievements of the classical past, but one that thrived with innovation thanks, to a great extent, to the combination of classical legacy with Christian culture (Brown 1971). It seems that not only has Farneti gone along with Brown's views, but he has hyperbolized them in his depiction of the innovations designed by Romans. In this way, in *Imperium Solis* and *Gladius Imperii*, Romans – with the occasional help of Native Americans – invent the train, flying machines and submarines. They also perfect warfare and build highways. As a result of these inventions and improvements, Julian's army was furnished with a state-of-the-art equipment that guaranteed its victories.

Surely Farneti let his imagination go too far even for the standards of an alternate history, but some of the machines and inventions were inspired by actual sources contemporary to Julian's times. Take, for instance, *On the things of war* (*De rebus bellicis*), an anonymous treatise that dates from the fourth/fifth centuries and deals with how the implementation of technological innovations could help improve the Roman army in a time of intense war activity against external peoples.[10] *On the things of war* included illustrations of what the new contrivances would look like if completed, and those depictions are preserved in several manuscripts. Among other issues, this treatise addresses the perfection of minting of coins by adopting new sizes and styles in order to avoid fraud and reduce the expenses in different areas (ch. 3–5). In *Imperium Solis*, Farneti explains that Julian introduces the coin in America in order to replace barter as the main trading system. The coin is originally called *talaurium*, which means 'similar to gold', due to its resemblance to gold despite its low-alloy composition (Farneti 2009: 375). In fact, the *talaurium* was originally made of copper and zinc but, as a symbol of the growing economic power of the new Rome, the low-alloy composition of the coin is later replaced by gold, thanks to the discovery of massive gold mines in the West of America (Farneti 2009: 547). Finally, the *talaurium* acquires a new name too due to the Natives' pronunciation of Latin: the *dollarium*.

When it comes to military machines, it is in chapters 6–19 from *On the things of war* where innovations can be found. The author describes chariots (*currodrepani*) equipped with offensive weapons and scythes that can be extended or lifted above the axles of the chariot depending on the needs of the battle (ch. 12–14). This weaponization is similar to that applied to the naval ships described in *Gladius Imperii* (Farneti 2012: 193–5). Improvements in the soldiers' armour (*thoramachus*) were also taken into account in *On the things of war* (ch. 15), an issue that also features in *Gladius Imperii* (Farneti 2012: 98) where Farneti describes the armours as Roman in style but adorned with Native American elements with ornamental functions, such as feathers and geometrical drawings.

Apart from their role as literary props in the novels, Farneti used these technological innovations for his ethopoeia of the emperor Julian and of the Romans in general during their time on the American continent. As an Augustus-like figure, Julian embodies the civilizing spirit traditionally attributed to the Romans. In this sense, Farneti's Julian is less intellectual and much more industrious than Ibsen's or Vidal's Julian. In *Imperium Solis* and *Gladius Imperii* the emperor does not only rule, but also encourages research and advancement. Relatedly, then, the Romans are portrayed as superior to the well-intentioned but technologically underdeveloped Native Americans.

It is worth contrasting the way in which Farneti used Roman technological superiority with Wu Ming's *Manituana* (2007), a historical novel about the political situation of a group of Native Americans known as Mohawks during the American Revolution. The interest in comparing Farneti's and Wu Ming's works is justified by their different approaches to the same topic – namely, the impact of machines and weapons in America – as will be dealt with in the next section. Farneti's oeuvre has been labelled as conservative and nostalgic about the Italy of the first half of the twentieth century.[11] Wu Ming, in turn, can be located at the other end of the political spectrum. Wu Ming, which means 'anonymous' in Chinese, is a group of Italian writers committed to the free circulation of artistic and cultural productions (De Pascale 2009). Although they have not explicitly positioned themselves in political terms, Wu Ming's members come from Luther Blissett, a name used by a group of artists from Europe and the USA with connections to Marxist groups. The plots of Wu Ming's novels like *Manituana* revolve around recent historical episodes, but also revisit important past events by taking us through 'the ambiguities surrounding utopia today and illustrate the danger of utopia's potential duality' (De Donno 2014: 268). The novels of Farneti and Wu Ming deploy anachronisms involving technology for different purposes. The former resorts to technological advances applied to war as instruments for political stability and peace, which would eventually allow Julian to found a new and improved Roman Empire. Therefore, Farneti's use of technology acts as a kind of harmonizing element by which the Romans civilized and grouped Native Americans. In Wu Ming's *Manituana*, however, colonialist policies against Native Americans are represented by the constant use of cannons and guns that forced them to leave their homelands in search of new and peaceful ones. The different approach to the use of military technology in relation to Native Americans could be interpreted as a reflection of the political agendas of Farneti and Wu Ming.

The introduction of advanced technology as a narratological device in the relationship between Romans and Native Americans also appears in Alan Smale's *Clash of Eagles* (2015), the first book of a trilogy in which the Roman army arrives in America in the year 1218 CE only to be defeated by the Natives. The plot, unequivocally indebted to modern Westerns (the story of the protagonist, Gaius Marcellinus, strongly resembles the film *Dances with Wolves*), features the Cahokiani – one of the North American peoples that crushed the Roman army – flying, thanks to the Thunderbirds, a rudimentary wooden prototype of modern planes. The use of Thunderbirds is connected not only with the plot of the trilogy, but also with the characterization of Gaius Marcellinus as he changes from being a boastful Roman to an admirer of the Cahokiani's technology.

Therefore, Farneti's deployment of the notion of progress in the Julianic uchronias is developed in the context of wars leading to fuse different peoples under the aegis of one empire. As will be shown in the next section, Farneti's doctrine of progress seems to be reminiscent of the conservative and colonizing views that make Western civilization inherently superior to other cultures.

Is Farneti's Julian a Fascist?

It is important to stress from the outset that the purpose of this section is neither to confirm nor to deny whether Farneti has sympathies for fascist figures, neither are we interested in questioning the political tenets he holds. However, the way in which some literary elements (especially those relating to the notions of political power and technological progress) have been dealt with in *Imperium Solis* and *Gladus Imperii* closely resemble the approach taken by Farneti and by other Italian uchronias from the Fantafascismo movement that have been criticized for romanticizing fascism. Although we will not engage in an extended discussion of other fictional works written by him, we believe that comparing *Imperium Solis* and *Gladus Imperii* with his *Occidente* (2001–6) may help us interpret some underlying issues in the plot of Julian's epic journey.

Occidente is an uchronic trilogy (*Occidente*; *Attacco all' Occidente*; *Nuovo impero di Occidente*) in which Italy managed to remain neutral in the Second World War, but, after making an alliance with the United States, emerged as one of the greatest political world powers in the face of threats to Western civilization. As a result, in this alternate history Italy became a buffer-zone to repel a Muslim invasion and immigration into the vast empire over which Italy reigned. This trilogy has been linked to Fantafascismo, a literary trend that gained a certain level of popularity in Italy at the beginning of this century. Fantafascist literature found its main form of expression in science fiction and uchronias, two genres that allowed authors to revisit the first decades of twentieth century Italy and to imagine alternate scenarios in which fascism survived (Brioni 2015: 306–11; Marra 2014: 6–9). Although focused exclusively on Italian history, Fantafascismo is a trend that shares in what Gallagher (2018: 148) has called 'historical activism', that is, a movement that seeks to revisit the past as its proponents understand 'history as a reparable continuous process in which we might consciously and actively intervene to undo or reverse some regretted course of events'.

In this context, Farneti's portrayal of what Italy would have achieved if fascism had not come to an end in the Second World War has granted the writer a reputation for being a 'nostalgic for the immutable and unchangeable "values" of fascism' (Brioni 2015: 316; also Malvestio 2018: 98–100). Within the same framework, *Occidente* has been interpreted by some critics as a reaction to the 9/11 attacks by al-Qaeda (Comberiati 2019: 171), whilst it has been read by other scholars as an attempt to iron out the controversies that emerged after the collaboration of far-right politicians in Silvio Berlusconi's government (Marra 2014: 13–15). Farneti has defended himself from the accusations of sympathizing with fascism by stating that his reinterpretation of this ideology in *Occidente* was exclusively motivated by literary purposes. He rejected the accusations by arguing that his approach resembled the way in which Philip K. Dick had used Nazism in *The Man in the High Castle* (1962), a work unanimously acclaimed by connoisseurs of the uchronia genre. Concerning his political views, Farneti showed that he is willing to speak calmly about Mussolini without caricaturizing him, and also without trying to satisfy the common views held about this historical figure (Marra 2014: 12).

Most of those literary elements in the plots of Fantafascist novels were itemized in 'Ur-Fascism' (1995), a short essay by Umberto Eco in which the Italian polymath compiled and briefly analysed the most important characteristics of fascism. According to Eco (1995), fascist ideologies tend to practise the cult of tradition and to believe in revelations. These two features make up the principle that substantiates Farneti's novels on Julian: when the emperor and his army arrived in America, they anchored the territory to traditional Roman mores. This process of acculturation derived from Hector's revelation in which the Trojan hero warned Julian that his own destiny and that of the Roman Empire rested on the emperor's shoulders. This is a feature frequently deployed in the 'the big man narrative' that characterizes novels based on historical figures.[12] Another frequent trait of fascism, according to Eco's essay, is the syncretism of various beliefs. In order to contain the contradictions that may arise from this syncretism, Eco considers that there is a 'primeval truth' that holds these different beliefs together. In *Imperium Solis*, the cultural syncretism resulting from the encounter between the American Natives and Romans is represented by the belief in the same primeval force: the solar god Taoiwa–Helios. The cult of this deity contributed to rendering the syncretism of both cultures possible and, ultimately, to the creation of the SPQA. Another characteristic that Eco mentions in fascist ideology and that appears in Fantafascist novels is the prevalence of technology, action and warfare over critical thinking and reflection. In the case of Farneti's Julian, something that is definitely not missing in the account of how he conquered and united the different peoples of America is battles and action.[13] As mentioned above, Farneti's Julian is less bookish than other fictional Julians and much keener on action, a characteristic that dovetails with fascism's penchant for the cult of heroic and bellicose figures. Eco continues his essay by underlining the importance of the avoidance of disagreement in fascist societies, as it is perceived as a form of treason and diversity. 'The People', Eco states (1995: 7), 'is conceived as a quality, a monolithic entity expressing the Common Will'. In Farneti's novels, Julian is credited with the creation of an ecumene free from internal dissensions rightly governed by his ability to interpret the common will of its people.

In addition to the features that Eco listed as being inherent in fascist societies, we believe that other criticisms concerning philofascist views received by Farneti's *Occident* can help us get a better grasp on *Imperium Solis* and *Gladius Imperii*. Marra (2014: 12–13) has highlighted Farneti's tendency to produce flattering and hagiographic descriptions of Benito Mussolini in *Occidente*. In a similar way, the same can be argued about Julian since the emperor is portrayed as an almost completely flawless figure in Farneti's uchronias. Brioni (2015), who is particularly harsh on Farneti in his analysis of *Occidente*, underlines the similarities between the ideology of the fictional and the historical Mussolini. According to Brioni (2015: 314–15), Farneti's conception of 'the immortal spirit of Rome' replicated Mussolini's to the point that in *Nuovo impero di occidente* 'Farneti's ideal of romanità [Roman-ness] mirrors Benito Mussolini's definition of the term that he gave in a public speech in Trieste on 20 September 1920'. Brioni (2015: 316) also notes that *Occidente* focuses only on 'Western civilization, which is nonetheless separated from the rest of the world'. These two aspects of Brioni's assessment could also be applied to Julian's novels. For example, in *Gladius Imperii*, the emperor delivers a speech on the greatness of Rome and its superiority (e.g. Farneti 2012: 62; 398–9) that mirrors Mussolini's. Moreover, the *Senatus Populusque Americanus* created by Julian was geographically vast, yet, as pointed out by Brioni in his judgement of *Occidente's* Italy, it was completely isolated from the rest of the world. Indeed, in the two novels little is said about non-Western peoples that were not eventually absorbed by Rome, with the exception of two brief references (one to China and another to India in Farneti 2012: 390 and 555 respectively).

Finally, Malvestio (2018: 95–8; also Marra 2014: 16) has explained that the introduction of esoteric scenes and issues in *Occidente* was due to the influence of Julius Evola, one of the leading figures in the creation of fascist ideology in the twentieth century. Evola wrote on the essence and the spirit of fascism as the combination of mystic and esoteric traditions from ancient civilizations.[14] In the case of *Imperium Solis*, it was the combination of Roman and Native American traditions that represented the mystic and esoteric element that is so important in Evola's ideology. In the novel, Farneti (2009: 377–80) portrays Julian following an eagle across one of the vast plains of America. When he was surprised by a storm, the emperor tried to look for shelter but he tripped and lost consciousness after hitting his head on a stone. While unconscious, he sensed that he was in front of an androgynous figure that symbolized a city Julian had founded. In this vision, this figure told him that he would become its 'Pontifex Maximus'. This mystical experience continued with Julian ascending to heaven, where he saw 'la vera Luce' (the true Light) and 'la vera Sapienza' (the true Wisdom). It was only after that mystical encounter that Julian came to really understand the true meaning of two religious and political concepts: 'il Culto' (the cult) and 'il Verbo' (the Verb).

This scene epitomizes Farneti's use of some of the elements listed in Eco's 'Ur-Fascism' (1995): the dreamlike atmosphere of the episode is related to the taste for revelations and the search of a primeval truth that, in turn, are meant to legitimize the power of a figure under whose rulership the syncretism of cultures will be completed.

Conclusion

In this chapter we have read Mario Farneti's *Imperium Solis* and *Gladius Imperii* as an allegory of global political and cultural issues at the beginning of the twenty-first century. Farneti does not seem interested in exploring more historically realistic scenarios that could have unfolded if Julian had survived the Persian campaign. Instead, his interest lies in turning an uchronic Julian into a utopian Julian by displaying the unfulfilled potential that Farneti thinks the emperor had. At first, both novels may give the impression of being two apolitical exercises of *ars gratia artis*. However, underneath this surface of entertainment there is a vision of history and progress that relates to contemporary issues. Farneti unhooks his exposition of a dream of unity and peace from the 'postmodern dystopia' to which all fiction genres had succumbed after the 9/11 attacks (Sicher and Skradol 2006: 165–9) and fantasizes about a Western world enlightened by technological advancements and a historically misunderstood 'big man'. In Farneti's novels, technological progress is intimately related to warfare, which is presented as the epitome of modernization. Julian's political agenda is, hence, carried out exclusively with innovations for warfare, limiting the impact and importance of other potential uses of technology for the purposes of this narrative.

The comparison between ideological features of fascism and literary motifs in Farneti's novels has shown that it is hard to refute allegations that the works by the Italian writer share similarities with Fantafascist novels. In the *Occidente* trilogy, Farneti idealized the counterfactual past of a dominating Italy that safeguarded the Western civilization from external enemies – mainly communism and Islam – by exploiting characteristics of fascism, as noted by Umberto Eco (1995). The same strategy can be perceived in *Imperium Solis* and *Gladius Imperii*, although in the case of these two novels the mixture of elements of science fiction combined with uchronia partially obscures those characteristics. However, it is evident that technological advancement and the idea of an empire led by a heroic figure ruling the Western world dominates Julian's narrative.

Acknowledgements

The authors would like to thank Dr Leire Olabarria for her comments, observations and help on idiomatic and methodological issues. All remaining errors are our own.

Notes

1 On the connection between science fiction and counterfactual history, see Schneider-Mayerson (2009: 64–5).
2 Hitler was also attracted to Julian both by his religious tenets and his philosophical acumen; see Trevor-Roper's (2000: 76, 87–8, 254) edition and translation of Hitler's informal conversation.
3 The actual version of Julian's visit to Troy in 353 CE is narrated by Julian himself in his *Ep.* 79.
4 The information about Thule that was given by Pytheas has reached us in Strabo *Geographica* 2.5.8. The exact location of Thule remains unknown, and the attempts to identify it have resulted in interpretations as varied as Scotland, Norway, Iceland, Ireland and Estonia. More information on this issue can be found in Scott's translation (2022) of Pytheas.
5 Theopompus' information about Meropis that has come down to us is scanty and fragmentary (*Fragments of Greek Historians* 115 FF 74–5). On the purposes that Theopompus had for this invention, see Zaccaria (2016: 54–7).
6 The same pattern can also be found in the field of historiography since antiquity; see Fernández-Camacho (2022).
7 Although the Roman Empire is the recurrent mirror with which civilizations are compared when their collapse is discussed, it should be borne in mind that other civilizations experienced the same process: see the essays edited by Schwartz and Nichols (2006).

8 On the impact of the 9/11 attacks and Islamic terrorism on Italian science-fiction and on the Fantafascism movement, see Comberiati (2019: 171–3). Also, in his uchronic trilogy *Occidente* Farneti develops a plot in which fascism acts as 'the resistance to the barbaric Muslim invasion of Europe in 1992' (Brioni 2015: 314).
9 Interestingly, Murphy (2007: 10) also mentions the expansionists, an ironical group that aims for the creation of the 'United States of the West' by enforcing a new Edict of Caracalla in order to grant citizenship to several countries to resist 'the coming Islamist and Confucianist onslaught'.
10 Farneti notes in the appendix to *Imperium Solis* (2009: 572) that he used *De rebus bellicis* to gain knowledge on naval technology.
11 On science fiction and political conservatism, see Huntington (1975: 350–2).
12 The 'big man narrative' occupies a central place in the plot of numerous historical novels. See Fowler and Campos-Daroca in this volume.
13 On the narratological relevance of war and battles in counterfactual novels, see Schneider-Mayerson (2009: 72–4).
14 On the role of mysticism and esoterism in fascism (and also in Evola's ideology), see Senholt (2013).

2.3

Alternat(iv)e Fiction in T. S. Chaudhry's *The Queen of Sparta*: Unrepresented Voices and Counterfactuality

Lynn S. Fotheringham
University of Nottingham

Introduction

This chapter explores the issue of genre-classification in relation to T. S. Chaudhry's 2014 novel, *The Queen of Sparta* (*TQoS*), which focuses primarily on the Persian invasion of Greece of 480–479 BCE and its aftermath. On the website of the publisher, John Hunt Publishing (JHP), *TQoS* is described as 'Alternative history' (see Figure 2.3.1); this phrase has been used for the genre under scrutiny in this volume but also has other meanings. A publisher's website, unlike an academic analysis, is under no obligation to define its terms; academics who have written on our genre disagree on how to define it and what to call it. My goal here is not to decide which definition/name is the best, whether *TQoS* belongs to our genre or even whether the JHP website claims that it does, but rather to lean into the ambiguities of language and disagreements about genre, inside and outside the academy, in order to explore different ways in which the novel *might* be understood.

The multiplicity of possible reader-responses to any cultural artefact is key to this analysis. In the next section I explain how I will eke out the minimal evidence for actual responses with hypotheses and how I will be using the labels 'alternate/ alternative history'. I then discuss various academic approaches to our genre, highlighting areas of disagreement which will be relevant to the analysis of *TQoS*. After an outline of the novel, my exploration of its relationships with both alternate history and alternative history will gradually be extended by bringing in the evidence of the paratext and promotional materials, which tends to confirm the existence of ambiguity and misunderstanding. Finally I will explore the reader-reviews and focus on the question of reader-knowledge, extending previous scholars' observations about the importance of this knowledge in order to explain the potential difficulties in deciding whether or not to classify a work as alternate fiction.

Readers and Labels

I begin with a hypothesis about possible reader-responses to the label 'Alternative history' on the JHP website: even if whoever chose this label for *TQoS* had a different meaning in mind, it is possible that some readers of the website will interpret the term as referring to our genre – usually considered to involve some kind of counterfactuality, but see further below – and therefore have that genre in mind as they begin to read *TQoS*. How might starting from this point affect their understanding of the novel? I suggest that this will depend, among other things, on each individual's concept of the genre (for if academics have different definitions, so will others), knowledge of the historical period covered by the novel, and state of mind while reading. Some will forget about the genre-label they started with, when none of the features they associate with the genre (as they understand it) appear; others will keep an eye open for features that match their conception of the genre – and given the variety of conceptions to choose from, they may find them; a third group will be surprised, disappointed or even annoyed, when the novel does not meet their expectations.

My exploration of reader-response here relies as much on hypothesis – with the likelihood of different readers responding in different ways being a key premiss – as on direct evidence. If my argument reads at times like a thought-experiment, exploring possible rather than clearly evidenced readings, I hope this will seem appropriate in a volume whose main theme is counterfactual speculation. Evidence for how the novel was conceived by its author and has been understood by promoters and readers can be found in the paratext, the publisher's and booksellers' websites and a handful of on-line reader-reviews. Some of the reviews include elements that *may* point to our genre, but neither they nor the paratext explicitly address the question of classification. The websites provide evidence for how the book has been marketed and some include a label suggesting classification, but no clear definition or explanation. This relative lack of precision and consequent openness to multiple possible interpretations may be generally typical of extra-academic discourse – a suggestion not intended as a criticism. Those of us who study popular culture need to take account of this aspect of popular discourse about culture; if we fail to do so, our analyses of public perceptions, whether of genre, the ancient world or anything else, are likely to be oversimplified.

Another way in which readers of the JHP website might understand the label 'Alternative history' is as indicating that *TQoS* will present a surprising new take on historical events, perhaps specifically that it will give voice to people relatively under-represented in traditional history, such as women, non-Europeans and lower-status groups. *TQoS* does both; unrepresented voices are also relevant to the novel because Chaudhry is from Pakistan, a nationality/geographical origin not well represented in the corpus of historical novels set in ancient Greece.

While researching for this chapter, my impression has been that 'alternative history' is widely used *both* for history/historical fiction involving novel interpretations/perspectives *and* for our genre, while the twin term 'alternate history' usually refers to our genre; the latter is the most popular term for the genre in recent academic work and in non-academic websites.[1] It would be possible to avoid 'alternat(iv)e history' altogether in discussing our genre; among many other names given to it in English are '"what-if" story', 'allohistory', 'uchronia' (listed with others at Singles 2013: 16) and 'counterfactual historical fiction' (used by e.g. Raghunath 2020). The first of these is as vague as 'alternative history' (see further below); the next two are somewhat opaque coinages; the last, while relatively comprehensible and appropriately descriptive, is perhaps too narrow for the purposes of this exercise (see below on definitions) – although I will argue that even the term 'counterfactual' can be ambiguous.

Given my focus on multiple meanings and interpretations, using twin adjectives with shared ambiguities like 'alternate/alternative' can be seen as symbolic. Distinguishing between them allows me to be precise when speaking in my own voice, while the repeated need to query how the same terms are being used by others will provide a useful reminder of their general *im*precision. I will therefore use 'alternate history' for our genre and 'alternative history' not for a genre but for the unorthodox approach to the past that stops short of creating a new hypothetical imagined world. Alternate history is a kind of fiction; alternative history can be expressed in fiction or in non-fictional historical analysis. The two categories are not mutually exclusive; an alternate history can *also* be alternative history. I reserve 'counterfactual history' for non-fictional historical analysis.

Readers both actual and hypothetical are central to this analysis. The above discussion, of how *TQoS* might come across to readers who had seen the label on the JHP website, anticipates the importance of reader-knowledge: these readers know how that website categorizes the novel and may therefore think they know what kind of novel it is. The question of what readers are in a position to know when will come up in later discussions of the paratext and promotional materials; the question of readers' *historical* knowledge will also gradually become more important.

Academic Definitions and Disagreements

One of the narrowest (and most elaborately worked out) academic definitions of alternate history is that of Singles (2013: 6); the following points can be taken as key: 'The fictional world of an alternate history diverges at a specified point from the normalized narrative of the real past. This divergence is most typically permanent, i.e. there is no point of convergence. . . . The world of the alternate history is actual within the fiction. Alternate histories are works of fiction, counterfactual histories are not'. Contrast the following: 'An alternate history is . . . work of fiction in which history as we know it is changed for dramatic and often ironic effect' (Duncan 2003: 209). In line with this much less precise definition, Duncan's discussion of the genre includes works that Singles does not accept as alternate history, including some – such as the films *Groundhog Day* (1993) and *Sliding Doors* (1998) – without any real focus on 'history'; for Singles (2013: 121–4), these are 'forking-paths narratives', a separate category from alternate history although the two are not mutually exclusive. Hellekson (2001) covers a range at least as broad as Duncan's in a book-length analysis; Gallagher (2018) and Raghunath (2020) are among those whose narrower definition of 'the alternative history novel'/'counterfactual historical fiction' is closer to Singles'. Most writers treat alternate history as a form of fiction: Singles, above, emphasizes its difference from non-fictional counterfactual history; Gallagher (2018: 3 *et passim*) has a more elaborate typology distinguishing 'counterfactual history' (non-narrative texts), 'alternate history' (hypothetical sequences of events) and the 'alternate history novel' (works with fictional characters); Hellekson (2001: 14–18) seems to encompass both fiction and non-fiction in her broad definition of 'alternate history'.

Several specific disagreements in the academic literature are relevant to my analysis, e.g. the question of whether any alternate history is by definition science fiction because it is set in a world different to our own. Hellekson (2001: 3) states that 'alternate history is a subgenre of the genre of science fiction, which is itself a subgenre of fantastic (that is, not realistic) literature'; Raghunath (2020: 4–5), however, argues that to be classified as science fiction, an alternate history must *also* contain more specific markers of that generic identity such as time-travel or the ability to move between parallel universes. For my purposes, it is not important to decide who is right but to note the possibility of associating alternate history with science fiction, which will come up in relation to the way *TQoS* is labelled on booksellers' websites.

Two potentially linked issues are the status of 'secret histories' and the question of whether convergence with the 'normalized narrative of the real past'/'history as we know it' is permissible in alternate history. The term 'secret history' is applied to (re)interpretations of the historical record revealing previously hidden patterns of control, motivation or connection; many historical fictions fall into this category, one of the most famous being Graves (1934). Singles (2013: 73–81) argues against a number of scholars who consider the secret history a subgenre of alternate history (e.g. Dannenberg 2008: 202). Some of the works discussed could be understood as filling in gaps in the historical record rather than changing it; Singles (2013: 78), however, argues that even those including clearly counterfactual episodes are not alternate history if the limited time-frame of the revelatory narrative means that divergence is not permanent. This claim that 'convergence' and alternate history are incompatible causes her some trouble in relation to Roth (2004), which she is compelled to describe as a '"flawed" alternate history' (Singles 2013: 169).

In contrast, Hellekson (2001: 2–10, 97–107) includes a whole chapter on works involving convergence, specifically 'time-policing' stories in which the historical timeline is temporarily 'altered' but then 'corrected' by a supervisory body. Some of her terminology – 'true alternate history' for a work taking place in a world permanently changed; 'anti-alternate history' for Poul Anderson's Time Patrol stories and 'meta-alternate historian' for their author (Hellekson 2001: 9–10, 97–9) – suggests common ground with Singles: whereas Singles excludes convergence stories altogether, Hellekson uses a centre-periphery model with time-policing stories on the periphery. Again, it is not important to decide whether secret histories, stories involving divergence followed by convergence, or time-policing stories always/necessarily count as alternate history, but rather to note the possibility of associating these categories with our genre. If some academics, following serious reflection, make these associations, it is likely that some general readers will also. Since – as covered in the next section – *TQoS* qualifies as secret history and one aspect of the narrative echoes the divergence–convergence pattern of the time-policing story, the possibility of some readers associating *TQoS* with alternate history is difficult to exclude.

Outline of *The Queen of Sparta*

This section describes some formal features of the novel, summarizes its plot and comments on its relationship with the ancient sources, noting features that could be aligned with either alternative or alternate history. I will begin to speculate about possible reader-responses, suggesting reasons both for categorizing *TQoS* as alternate history and for not doing so.

The structure of *TQoS* is complex. A main narrative running from autumn 480 BCE to late summer 477 BCE, repeatedly interrupted by flashbacks (and with a postscript dated to 457 BCE), is framed by a prologue and epilogue set in 327 BCE. The geographical setting also varies: the main narrative alternates at first between Sparta and Plataea, while flashbacks and later narrative encompass locations as varied as Persia, northern Europe and the Italian peninsula; the frame narrative takes place in the Indus Valley (modern Pakistan). Although the title focuses on only one, the novel has two protagonists: the Spartan queen Gorgo and the Indo-Scythian prince Sherzada. Individual chapters tend to focus on the actions of one or the other and most of the third person narration is focalized through them; some flashbacks are in the first person.

Gorgo is a historically attested figure (Herodotus 5.48–51, 7.239) while Sherzada is fictional, although belonging to a group of people who must have existed: the native leaders of the Scythian (= Saka) and Indian contingents in the Persian army (Herodotus 7.64–65, 184; 9.31, 71). Many other figures from the historical record, primarily Greek but also Persian and Italian, make an appearance in the story. The frame narrative focuses on Alexander the Great but includes Indian historical figures: the future emperor Chandragupta Maurya and his teacher-adviser, Kautilya. The Indian setting and characters in the frame narrative and the identity of the protagonists in the main narrative – one female and the other non-European – already qualify *TQoS* as alterna*tive* history.

Gorgo and Sherzada are brought together after Sherzada is captured by the victorious Greeks at the battle of Plataea; they recognize in each other a courage, intelligence and humanity that marks them out from their peers in both the Greek cities and the Persian Empire. As they remember/narrate episodes from their past, a 'secret history'-style interpretation of events is gradually revealed: it was Gorgo's behind-the-scenes actions, pursuing policies established by her father Cleomenes, that brought about many aspects of the Greek defence most salient to the eventual defeat of the Persian invasion. Whereas Gorgo's plans show remarkable political foresight, Sherzada – a man, leading a life of public action – is able to travel widely and thus has knowledge of multiple cultures; he also gets to participate in a wide range of events both historically attested and newly invented. This linking of multiple and far-flung events through a single character also evokes secret history. These secret history elements of the narrative could lead some readers who, like Dannenberg rather than Singles, equate or at least associate the two genres, to understand *TQoS* as *alternate* history.

Because Gorgo's responsibility for the Greek victory over the Persians is secret, she gets no credit for it and faces opposition at Sparta after the end of the war, including from those who object in principle to any participation in politics by a woman. Her friendship with the 'barbarian' Sherzada is viewed as suspect and her attempts to improve the lot of the helots (the Spartan serf-class) are considered treasonous by her less enlightened compatriots. Sherzada, on the other hand, shares Gorgo's opposition to rigid social classifications, supporting the Plebs in Rome and attempting to work against the caste-system in his homeland. The protagonists' consciousness of the ill-treatment of these lower-status groups, despite their own positions as royalty, gives the novel another claim to be alternat*ive* history – albeit a less striking one than the identity of the protagonists themselves. Gorgo and Sherzada themselves could be described as having a non-traditional or 'alternative' outlook on the world or even a desire to build an 'alternative' world.

When her opponents in Sparta plot to kill both Gorgo and her son, they flee with Sherzada to his homeland in the upper Indus Valley; in the prologue and epilogue, Alexander the Great encounters and apparently exterminates their descendants. He also insists that all copies of a text telling their story must be destroyed; he wishes to suppress, among other ideas, the possibility of giving 'political credit' to a woman and the protagonists' positive attitude towards the helots and other oppressed groups (Chaudhry 2014: 359). The suggestion that a previously unsuspected Sparto-Scythian culture developed in the Indus Valley between 477 and 327 BCE only to be wiped out by Alexander has the potential to evoke the time-policing narrative; this could trigger the concept of *alternate* history in the minds of readers who, like Hellekson rather than Singles, associate time-policing narratives with this genre. As the 'normalised narrative of the real past' does not include Gorgo and Pleistarchus' departure from Sparta, such readers could see that as the 'point of divergence' and the resulting hybrid culture as counterfactual.

On the other hand, it could be argued that *TQoS* is *not* alternate history because the major political and military events narrated conform to the historical record, that the invented elements are of the kind expected in any historical fiction: dialogue; the motivations and personal feelings of historically attested figures; the invention of characters to fill roles in the narrative that must or may have existed – in sum, the filling in of gaps in the historical record rather than contradictions of that record. As the final fate of Gorgo and Pleistarchus is not recorded and our knowledge of the Indus Valley in the fifth and fourth centuries BCE is relatively limited, *TQoS*'s account, however boldly imaginative, could be seen as filling in a particularly large gap. For readers familiar with the ancient sources, an interpretation of this as possible may be backed up by noting places where the novel sticks closely particular passages: the fiasco of Mashistiyun/Masistius' attack on the Greeks during the first skirmishes at Plataea (see chapter 3) is an interesting reworking of Herodotus 9.20–24 through Sherzada's eyes, creating sympathy for Sherzada but a negative impression of the Persian high command; Alexander's encounter with a Greek-speaking woman named Cleophis after taking Aornos (see Prologue) combines two episodes from Quintus Curtius (*History of Alexander* 8.10–11). Even the European-Amazon tribe Sherzada spends time with have an origin echoing the story told at Herodotus 4.110–117.

Especially in the case of this final example, however, some readers might simultaneously note the echo of the ancient sources – an observation – *and* find the adaptation of it to *TQoS*'s narrative implausible – a judgement. A third group of readers, in this vein, rather than justifying surprising aspects of the narrative as possible history or interpreting them as markers of alternate history might reject them as simply implausible. The narrative may come across as trying too hard to squeeze in as many historically attested figures as possible, to credit Gorgo with the ability to foresee and control so much or Sherzada with such extensive multicultural experience; the 'alternative' attitudes of the two protagonists may strike some as anachronistically modern.

A slightly different argument against viewing the Sparto-Scythian culture in *TQoS* as the core of an *alternate* history narrative is that so little of the narrative is spent with this culture; the book is less interested in it than in the inter- and intra-city politics of the historically attested Greek world. This question of what the book/author is interested in will come up again in the next section, which explores some limitations on *TQoS*'s alternat*ive*-history credentials in terms of unrepresented voices.

The Queen of Sparta and Alternative History: Unrepresented Voices

As de Groot has pointed out (2010: 3, 139–82), the licence to fill in gaps in the historical record which is granted to historical fiction in general can make it a congenial home for authors wishing to give a voice to previously unrepresented groups. Other novels focusing on the Persian Wars have attempted to give voices to women, lower-status groups or non-European characters. For example, Gorgo has a prominent role in Schrader (2010b, 2011, 2012), and Pressfield (1998) creates important roles for invented Spartan women. Helot characters are prominent in Pressfield (1998), Schrader (2010a, 2011, 2012), and Manfredi (2002). Pressfield's narrative, narrated by a Greek, is framed by the notes of the Great King's historian; Davis (1907) and especially Vidal ([1981] 2002) include historically attested Persians as characters. In the field of Alexander-novels, Renault (1972) is famously narrated by a Persian character. As helots are only minor characters in *TQoS*, this section will focus primarily on the handling of female and non-European characters.

The existence of other novels that try to give voices to the unrepresented, including women, does not itself undermine *TQoS*'s credentials in this respect. Many recent female-authored historical and mythistorical novels (e.g. Haynes 2017, Barker 2018, Miller 2018) re-focus the narrative on domestic life and/or emphasize the oppression of women in the past. Schrader's six Sparta novels (2006–12), for example, although far from neglecting politico-military affairs, emphasize domestic life in an attempt to counter the clichés about Sparta's brutality; the first two expose the suffering of some (mainly non-Spartiate) women, some poorer Spartiates and some helots. At the same time, inspired by the unusually high status of Spartan women evidenced in the historical record, Schrader gives some of them – including Gorgo – political views and influence on the men close to them.[2]

In contrast, *TQoS* contains only a handful of domestic scenes, mainly concerned with Gorgo's relationship with her helots, but goes much further than Schrader in challenging familiar androcentric assumptions about political and even military control. Chaudhry's picture of Gorgo may build on the intelligence and strength of character attributed to her by Herodotus, but the amount of credit he grants her for the course of the war might be surprising even in the case of a male character; in the case of an ancient Greek woman, it is extraordinary. The desire to give women more representation and more of a voice in both history and historical fiction can embrace both the valorization of the traditionally female domestic sphere *and* the creation of female characters who are successful in the traditionally male politico-military sphere. That this success must be behind the scenes and unacknowledged may be justified as reflecting historical reality.

TQoS nods towards the approach that emphasizes the historical oppression of women and other groups by making a significant plot-point out of the opposition Gorgo faces due to the misogyny, xenophobia and classism of other Spartans. Alexander's suppression of Gorgo and Sherzada's story is motivated by similar misogyny and classism, also shared by Kautilya. The alterna*tive* history aspects of the novel are thematized here, with Alexander representing a traditional or establishment attitude in contrast to that of Gorgo and Sherzada – and the triumph of this traditional attitude. Although the figure of Cleophis suggests the women may have had more equality in the Sparto-Scythian society destroyed by Alexander, Kautilya's comments on Sherzada's failure to eliminate the caste system, like the narrative representation of Gorgo's failure to eliminate helotage, hints at a still more *alternate* historical culture that could have arisen from their story, but did not. There is an interesting potential convergence of alternative and alternate here.

The representation of non-European characters, events and viewpoints could be seen as less developed. While Sherzada does talk about his homeland and his people's past, we never see him there and his compatriots are largely absent from the narrative. Like the hypothetical Sparto-Scythian culture he and Gorgo create, the Indo-Scythian culture he grew up in appears to be less interesting to the narrative than Greek culture. The novel's picture of non-European people more broadly is highly variable: as hinted above in relation to the Mashistiyun/Masistius episode at Plataea, the presentation of the Persian high command is not always positive. Although military competence is attributed to some Persian individuals and some of the army's troops, and Persian military competence is said to have declined, Orientalist clichés about softness, luxury, corruption and nepotism are evident in the narrative. In the Prologue, Alexander is described as encountering no real opposition anywhere in Persia until he reaches the land of Sherzada and Gorgo's descendants: 'Unlike most Asiatic foes Alexander's force had faced before, these warriors fought with skill and discipline' (Chaudhry 2014: 1).

Although this skill and discipline might be attributed to Spartan influence once the narrative reveals these warriors' ancestry, the main narrative sets up a different explanation: the Sakas/Scythians were always the Spartans' equals, 'a great warrior nation' (Chaudhry 2014: 179). This is evident from both the military discipline of Sherzada and his troops at Plataea and the fact that Gorgo and Sherzada find common ground so easily. The plot of *TQoS*, rather than presenting an alternative view of the Persian invasion that gives all contributors an equal point of view, posits a culture in the Indus Valley that is as exceptional among the Persian-dominated nations as Sparta is among the Greek city-states; the two merge into the Sparto-Scythian culture that gives Alexander so much trouble.

As it happens, a novel published before *TQoS* presents a more extensive attempt at exploring the Persian, Indian and even a variety of Chinese perspectives: Gore Vidal's *Creation* ([1981] 2002), whose (invented) narrator-protagonist, Cyrus Spitama, is the half-Greek, half-Chaldaean grandson of Zoroaster, brought up at the Persian court with Xerxes. *Creation* is explicitly flagged as alterna*tive* history in the sense that Spitama's memories of his life are framed as a response to Herodotus' account of the Persian Wars, deliberately giving an anti-Greek point of view that contrasts strongly with that in *TQoS*. But the focus on Greek–Persian interaction is not maintained; instead, Spitama recounts his experiences as Persian ambassador to other lands far to the east, where he meets Buddha, Mahavira, Lao Tzu and Confucius – as he meets Socrates in Athens – exploring a wide variety of perspectives on religion and especially 'creation'. Chaudhry's Sherzada, who travels far to the west from the eastern edge of the Persian Empire, is in this respect a mirror of Vidal's Spitama, who travels far to the east from a relatively western point in that empire. It would be unsurprising if Iranian, Indian or Chinese readers of *Creation*, written by a wealthy white man, were to find Orientalist attitudes in the narrative, but the novel could be described as trying harder than *TQoS* to present an Eastern point of view; at the very least, a much larger proportion of it is spent outside Greece, including in (Gangetic) India.

What the two novels share is an interest in depicting a more multicultural ancient world than is sometimes imagined. While the 'Acknowledgements' and 'Author's Note' in *TQoS* (Chaudhry 2014: 371–6), like the narrative itself, focus far more on the Greek than on the Indo-Scythian aspects of the novel (see below), Chaudhry does comment on his creation of Sherzada as a protagonist: 'Such a person could well have existed. In a world when time and again, the notion of a clash of civilizations has almost become a foregone conclusion, this novel tries to challenge many notions that continue to dog our political thinking' (Chaudhry 2014: 373). This implies concern that readers may find Sherzada's existence implausible because they do not believe that historical figures from Eastern and Western civilizations interacted on friendly terms. Later Chaudhry

(2014: 374) again mentions evidence for 'far more inter-cultural interactions across a wider area of the globe than is generally accepted'.

The Author's Note is a widespread and often revealing inclusion in the historical novel (see de Groot 2010: 6–9, 63); several aspects of Chaudhry's paratext may provide a clue to his motivation. He demonstrates his wide reading by acknowledging thirteen Greek historians and two military historians, a relatively high number that perhaps suggest an anxiety about demonstrating his qualifications for writing about this period. The number of fictional works he names, although smaller, is also unusual; it even includes the film *300* and its sequel, widely panned for their inaccurate or even fantastical approach to the material, 'in spite of my reservations about their portrayals of events and personalities' (Chaudhry 2014: 372). Although he does not mention Vidal or the graphic novel *300* (Miller and Varley 1998), Chaudhry does here demonstrate that he has engaged with most of the recent fictionalized treatments of the Persian invasion in English. All these references make it clear that he is writing this novel in a Western, Hellenocentric tradition. Concern for what a Hellenocentric audience might accept may have been a factor, conscious or otherwise, in his reducing the amount of space given to Sherzada's homeland and people; the similarity to Sparta and the Spartans may make their presence easier for this audience to accept.

As I have noted elsewhere (Fotheringham 2020: 20), not all readers bother to read authorial paratext of this kind, although they may assume that it will demonstrate the research he has done. The hypothesis above is only about the audience's possible reactions inasmuch as it is about the author's possible concerns vis-à-vis those reactions. In the next section, I speculate more directly about the audience and introduce other paratextual elements which overlap with the on-line promotional materials.

Ambiguity in the Promotional Materials

Potential readers browsing in a bookshop, on picking up *TQoS*, see the title, the author's name and a photograph of a woman dressed in plausibly pre-modern clothes, with architecture evocative of the ancient world in the background. If they turn the book over, they will see a synopsis which includes the following seven 'what if . . .?' questions focusing primarily on Gorgo:

> Though history has relegated her [= Gorgo's] role to that of a bystander, what if she played a central role in the Greek resistance to the Persian invasion? What if

> she kept her true role a secret in order to play it more effectively? What if she was hiding other secrets too – dark secrets of murder and vengeance? What if the only person who truly appreciated her genius was an enemy prisoner whom she has vowed to kill? What if after their victory, the Greeks started to turn on each other? What if, eventually, Gorgo had to choose between the security of Sparta and safety of her son? And what if the only one who could find a way out is the same prisoner who had once fought against the Spartans?

The conditional questions may turn readers' thoughts to the *alternate* history genre, which along with counterfactual history, its non-fictional equivalent, is strongly associated with the phrase 'what if?' (see e.g. the titles of Cowley 2000 and 2002). The focus on Gorgo chimes with the woman on the front cover and the word 'Queen' in the title; the references to 'an enemy prisoner whom . . .'/ 'the same prisoner who . . .' suggest that an individual who was part of the Persian army plays a significant role in the plot, but does not indicate the extent of his importance as a second protagonist. This raises the possibility that readers may feel that the novel itself does not match the expectations created by the paratext. The synopsis does provide advance notice of Gorgo's politico-military role, but not of the fact that Sherzada takes up slightly more of the text. One reader-review, to be discussed further below, points in this direction: 'I was hopeful when I begun [*sic*] the reading of this book that I had found a worthwhile read about Gorgo and her life as Queen of Sparta. Unfortunately, the book isn't really about her, but instead about the Persian prince invented by the author' (Barre 2015).

Almost all readers will see the title and the cover-image before beginning to read *TQoS*; many of them will also have read the synopsis in order to get a sense of what the novel is about. The e-book does not include the synopsis, but readers of this format too are likely to have seen it on the website of whichever bookseller they purchased it from, on many of which it appears word-for-word (see Table 2.3.1). It is likely that these booksellers' web-pages are based on information that the publisher sends out, which corresponds to the information on both the paperback's cover and the JHP web-page advertising the novel (Figure 2.3.1). Those booksellers who do not include the synopsis provide instead, again word-for-word, the shorter summary given at the top of that same web-page: a single 'what if . . .?' question focusing on Gorgo.

Do the 'what if . . .?' questions evoke an association with alternate history? If strict counterfactuality is a requirement of the genre, as opposed to Duncan's more vague 'change' to 'history as we know it', both a grammarian and a historian could provide an argument against the association. The grammarian could point

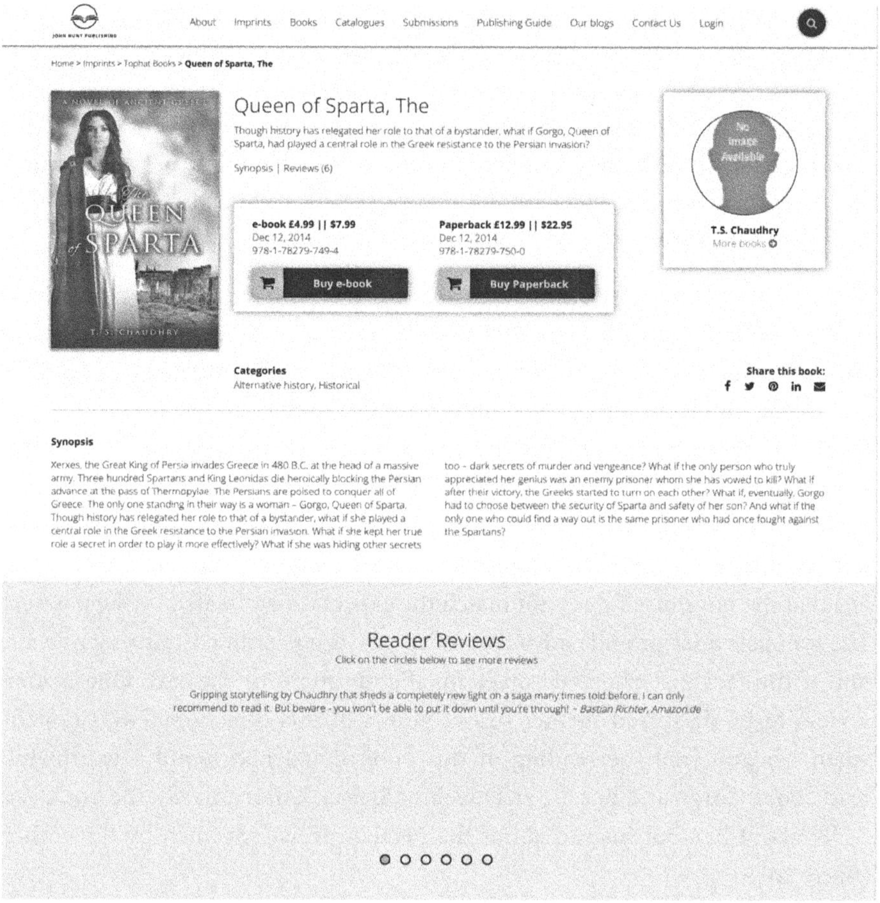

Figure 2.3.1 John Hunt Publishing web-page advertising *The Queen of Sparta* (image captured 10 August 2022).

out that the simple past tenses in the questions do not signal a definitely counterfactual condition, for which the past perfect/pluperfect is required, e.g. 'what if the Persian invasion had succeeded?'[3] The historian could point out that while some of the questions are, if not counterfactual, at least speculative ('What if, eventually, Gorgo had to choose between the security of Sparta and safety of her son?'), the fifth expresses a generally accepted historical fact: 'What if after their victory, the Greeks started to turn on each other?' But not all readers will recognize the historicality of the Greeks' turning on each other, and few are likely to pause to consider the grammatical issue. For at least some, the mere accumulation of 'what if . . .?' clauses may be enough to evoke the idea of speculation and therefore of alternate history – especially when, as on the JHP page, these clauses appear beside the label 'alternative history'.

If a user were to click on the link under Chaudhry's name on the *TQoS* webpage, they would find the following sentence, which is more expansive than the corresponding one on the back of the book and echoes some of Chaudhry's statements in his Author's Note: 'He has a passion for history and a fondness of [*sic*] offering alternative explanations for well-known stories without changing the essential facts'. Here 'alternative' clearly does *not* suggest counterfactuality, and on this basis it could be argued that 'alternative history' was not intended to refer to our genre. The categorization of *TQoS* on the booksellers' websites, however, provides evidence that it has been read in this way. This categorization is the one element that is not always taken word-for-word from the publisher's materials (see Table 2.3.1), suggesting that that information had to be interpreted to make it fit with the categories each bookseller happened to use. The fact that four websites categorize the book as 'science fiction' strongly suggests that the label 'alternative history' was taken as referring to our genre, as there are no other

Table 2.3.1 Comparison of information provided on the back of the paperback and on bookseller websites/the Apple Books app

Location	Synopsis	Summary	Author info	Classification
paperback	x		x	–
e-book				–
Bookseller websites				
Amazon	x		x	*with publication information (paperback):* • Historical Fiction (books) • Science Fiction Alternate History *with publication information (e-book):* • Alternative History • Science Fiction Alternate History • Historical Fantasy Fiction
Apple Books		x		*above book information:* • Fiction and Literature
Barnes & Noble	x			*above book-information:* • Books

Table 2.3.1 *Continued.*

Location	Synopsis	Summary	Author info	Classification
Blackwells	x			*above book-information:* • Fiction > Fiction & Related items > Historical fiction
Books etc.		x		*immediately below title:* • Science fiction • Historical fiction
ebooks.com	x		x	*in right-hand column:* • Fiction > Historical
Foyles	x			*right of the synopsis:* • Fiction & Poetry > Historical Fiction • Fiction & Poetry > Science Fiction
Google Play	x		x	*after clicking 'About this eBook':* • Fiction / Alternative History • Fiction / Historical / General
hive.co.uk	x			*below synopsis, with publication information:* • Science fiction • Historical fiction
Rakuten Kobo	x		x	*above book-information:* • eBooks / Fiction and Literature
Waterstones	x			*above book-information:* • Fiction > Historical fiction
Bookshop.org, W H Smith Wordery	no results from a search for *TQoS*, now out of print			

elements that suggest science fiction in *TQoS* and certainly none in the publisher's information. The multiple 'what if?' questions in the synopsis may have influenced this interpretation. But it is interesting that three of the four provide dual categorization, with 'historical fiction' as the other option – perhaps hedging their bets; Amazon offers four separate possibilities.

Three booksellers give only 'historical fiction', possibly indicating a different interpretation of the publisher's label; three more present only very vague labels ('fiction and literature' or just 'books'), suggesting lack of interest. Only Amazon and Google Play use the ambiguous term 'alternative history' itself, as one of two or more options; Amazon's four options appear to aim at covering as many angles on the novels as possible; both science fiction and fantasy, both 'alternate' and 'alternative' are included. Google Play have not made it possible to click the label to find other books in the same genre; anyone who clicks on the Amazon categories, seeking the current bestsellers in each, will find nearly identical lists for 'science fiction alternate history' and 'alternative history', containing works that would not normally be considered either alternate history or in any other way science fiction. Both also show considerable overlap with 'historical fiction (books)' list, as does the 'historical fantasy fiction' list. Although the categories appear precise, they have not been applied with precision.

If the booksellers' websites in general confirm the ambiguity of the publisher's label by appearing to interpret it in different ways, exploring the Amazon site confirms the ambiguity of one bookseller's labels. If potential readers notice a categorization label at all, they too can be expected to interpret it in different ways, confirming the possibility of the scenario with which this chapter opened.

Reader-Reviews and Reader-Knowledge

In this final section I turn to the implications of actual reader-responses to which the internet now gives us access. Fourteen reviews of *TQoS* can be found across Amazon websites from the UK, US, Canada and Germany, all posted in 2014–15, eight awarding five stars. The comparatively small number reflects the relative obscurity of the novel, but still provides some interesting material. The closest the *TQoS* reviewers come to discussing alternate history is in using the phrase 'what if': 'We will never know what really, truly happened and so exploring the what-ifs is a clever device to capture the reader's interest' (Mrs K. 2015). Another example is: 'What if she had a much bigger role to play than was ever documented or ever known?' (Oh My Bookness 2016).

The first comment is too vague to tell us much about the writer's understanding of 'the what-ifs'; the second use appears focused on the possible rather than the counterfactual, since Gorgo's substantial role is contrasted not with 'what really, truly happened' but with what was 'documented/known'. This implies an understanding of the existence of gaps in the evidence – also shown by Mrs K. – that make invention unavoidable for a historical novelist. Invention, even if not counterfactual, could be viewed as change to 'history as we know it'; if they share one of the looser definitions of alternate history, it is possible that these readers would place *TQoS* in that genre.

Much more common in the reviews are comments on historicity, expressed in terms of accuracy/inaccuracy, authenticity/inauthenticity, or praise/criticism of the author's knowledge or research. In the case of novels with hundreds of reviews, some of them responding directly to others, we can see a debate on these issues; more detailed study of the insights this material gives us into the minds of readers than there is room for here would be very useful. The most critical review of *TQoS* (Barre 2015) provides food for thought. It is characterized by phrases such as 'complete and utter *fallacy* on historicity', '*inaccuracies* or downright *inventions*', 'pale, *unrealistic* shadow of what she *truly* was' (emphases added). Where Barre provides a specific example, it is revealing: '... Kleomenes, Gorgo's father ... is shown as ... a perfect figure worthy of every praise who brought to Athens democracy and freedom (and, contrary to historical facts, was not a warmongering despot who tried to support a specific Athenian tyrant rather than any notion of democracy)' (Barre 2015).

Barre views it is a 'historical fact' that Cleomenes was 'a warmongering despot ...'. Although this could be seen as a reasonable summary of (parts of) Herodotus' account, in contemporary historiography there is considerable debate over Cleomenes, partly because that account contains numerous inconsistencies; the negative features of Cleomenes' treatment are often taken to be heavily influenced by Spartan informants inimical to the king (see, e.g. Cartledge 2002: 124–32, 136–7 with further references). Individual historians might feel that 'warmongering despot' is the most plausible way to understand Cleomenes; they might critique an account involving a different interpretation as implausible or in some other way unsatisfactory, but awareness of scholarly debate might make them stop short of describing it as 'contrary to historical facts'.

Chaudhry (2014: 373) in his Author's Note shows he is aware of the issue, providing a brief explanation of his alternative to Herodotus' interpretation of Cleomenes that both invokes the importance of a good story and offers a historical explanation for other, negative views: 'That she [organized the Greek resistance] by following her father's apparently mad policies was too compelling a story for me to resist telling. Rather than seeing him as a mad king, I see him as a visionary and a great practitioner of *realpolitik*, something very few Greeks of that era understood'. Barre knows Herodotus, or a narrative derived from his; he either does not know or rejects the academic criticisms of Herodotus' reliability, just as he either has not read or rejects Chaudhry's argument here. There is no reason why any particular reader should be expected to know about these, although writers of historical fiction may hope that their readers will have a more open mind about what is fact and what is interpretation than Barre seems to.

Previous scholars who require counterfactuality for our genre (e.g. Singles 2013: 110) have observed that a reader without historical knowledge may fail to recognize the counterfactual 'point of divergence' from 'the normalized narrative of the real past'; the point has been elaborated by Raghunath (2020), using a version of Possible Worlds theory, to create a cognitive-narratological model for how readers process our genre, which she calls counterfactual historical fiction. Here I argue that Barre's narrow understanding of what constitutes historical 'knowledge' leads him to consider factually inaccurate something that others would consider an allowable interpretation of the evidence. In my final thought-experiment, I ask: what response to *TQoS* can be imagined from a reader who also views Cleomenes' warmongering despotism as a 'historical fact', but who for whatever reason is less invested than Barre in condemning historical fiction that does not conform precisely to this 'fact' – perhaps enjoys the surprise experienced on encountering Chaudhry's boldness of imagination rather than being irritated by it? Might such a reader conclude not that the work is '*fact*ually inaccurate' but that it involves 'counter*fact*ual' speculation – that it is alternate history? This way of understanding *TQoS* is not dependent on the reader's having seen it labelled as 'alternat(iv)e history' or 'science fiction' on some website, though the two things could reinforce one another.

Conclusion

In this chapter I have argued not necessarily for adopting a flexible definition of alternate history, but for at least acknowledging that, among a plural readership, different definitions of the genre are possible; one result of this will be disagreements over how to classify an individual work. Someone who wanted to argue that *TQoS* is *not* alternate history might contrast the various historical issues raised here as possible points of debate – the plausibility or otherwise of a woman's wielding politico-military power, the character of Cleomenes – with a statement that most people would agree was not factual: the Persians defeated the Greeks in 480–479 BCE. Discussion of the counterfactual conditional question, 'what would have happened if the Persians had defeated the Greeks?', goes back at least as far as Meyer (1901: 446); a recent debate on the question by historians – counterfactual history – is represented by Hanson and Strauss' contributions to Tetlock, Lebow and Parker (2006). Fictional accounts – alternate history – include Harry Turtledove's 'Counting Potsherds' (1989) and Lois Tilton's 'Pericles the Tyrant' (2005).[4] There are many besides Singles who, setting *TQoS* next to these works, would acknowledge that there is a difference between them.

Where individuals might differ is on the question of whether the difference is one of kind or only one of degree. Those with a broader understanding of what constitutes alternate history might not require that anything in *TQoS* be shown to be untrue/counterfactual; those with a narrow understanding of historical fact might decide that the story *is* counterfactual, although to a different degree from the one where the Persians win the war. More than the readers' knowledge is at stake here; understanding, belief and attitude also play a role: how do they understand historical evidence to work? What do they believe constitutes a fact? Faced with something they believe is not a fact, will they adopt a positive attitude, viewing it as an interesting hypothesis (potentially an alternate history), or a negative one, viewing it simply as an error? Others may not consider the novel as a whole to be alternate history, but interpret the novel's hints at the unattested culture Sherzada and Gorgo are depicted as creating, and the still more radically alternat*ive* one(s) they wished to create, as gestures towards our genre that would at least justify the inclusion of an analysis of this novel in the current volume.

The exploration of these issues has also brought up a number of points where the counterfactual and the alternative, as the latter term is defined here, appear to be connected. Barre's response shows that an alternative interpretation in the sense of new one (or one new to Barre) may be rejected; his negative response to the portrayal of Gorgo and the invention of Sherzada suggests – although he does not express his complaint in these terms – that Chaudhry's attempt to create more of a historical role and voice for a woman and a non-European character has not succeeded *with this reader*. I have also suggested that the desire to pay more attention to previously un(der)represented groups may be constrained by fear of the audience's reaction. Perhaps alternative historical fiction can do much the same work as alternate history/counterfactual historical fiction in challenging readers to think about the way 'history' works.

Notes

1 For academic works, see the titles of Hellekson (2001), Rosenfeld (2005), Spedo (2009), Singles (2013); for websites, see Schmunk (1991–2022), Jones (2005), Alternate Historian (2013–), Anon. (n.d.).

2 For a recent review of the evidence for Spartan women, see Millender (2018).

3 For the disagreements on how to categorize conditionals in English, see Berry (2021: 51–2, 63–6); cf. *ODEG s.vv.* 'condition', 'conditional'.

4 For publication details and further examples of both counterfactual and alternate histories centring on a Persian victory, see the 'Divergence' catalogue at Schmunk (1991–2022) under the dates 490 and 480 BCE.

Section 3

Art, Culture and the Poetics of Counterfactuals

3.1

'A Picture That Can Only Ever Come in Parts': Alternate Histories of Film in Catherynne M. Valente's *Radiance*

Benjamin Eldon Stevens
Howard University

Introduction

This chapter explores how alternate histories often deploy art, including counterfactual versions of both real and fictional art, to help defamiliarize setting: a fiction's mooted difference from the world of fact may be signified in changes to known works of art and by the inclusion of wholly invented works. The mode of signification varies, with artworks serving as symbols, indices and/or icons. In general, however, in a genre that is by definition self-conscious about its status as 'fiction', alternate-historical works of art may be read as concrete microcosms for the fictions' more abstract ideas about time, change and causality. Works of art, therefore, are re-imagined as vivid images for divergent theories of history.

On this reading, depictions of art in counterfactual stories are emblematic of how alternate history centres metalepsis and *mise en abyme*. Alternate history involves metalepsis, or representations of movement between separate realities, as when a real-world work of art crosses into the fiction's imagined world or *vice versa*. In turn, such metalepsis may be read as *mise en abyme*, a kind of recursion in which a work of art is represented in another work of art. For example, in the 1991 film *Star Trek VI: The Undiscovered Country* (dir. Nicholas Meyer), hanging in Spock's starship quarters is a framed print of part of Marc Chagall's 1961 painting *Adam and Eve Expelled from Paradise* (*Adam et Eve chassés du paradis*). Spock describes the painting as 'a depiction from ancient Earth mythology' and explains that he keeps it as 'a reminder . . . that all things end'.

The painting is thus an example of metalepsis in the form of *mise en abyme*: a real work of art, Chagall's painting appears in the fictive world of a different work of art, Meyer's film. Further, and for our purposes most importantly, the real painting is a sign – a symbol – of an unreal character's idea about time: 'all things end'. Beyond defamiliarizing setting, then, such alternate-historical depictions of the arts can do in miniature what the genre does writ large: embody ideas and theories about history (see Ferguson 1997; cf. Dolezel 1998). Indeed, in their combination of vividness and unfamiliarity, nearly 'the uncanny', such descriptions of alternate-historical works of art emphasize how all historical 'fact' is a matter of discursive 'fictions' – and, so, suggest how all historiography may productively be approached as 'alternate history'.

To explore that possibility in this chapter, I draw on alternate histories that involve classical receptions, or transformations of stories from ancient Greece and Rome. My modern examples include a constellation formed by the 1968 film *Planet of the Apes* (dir. Franklin J. Schaffner), its source, Pierre Boulle's 1963 novel *La planète des singes*, and a sort of alternate history of that film's ending in the 1997 film *Alien: Resurrection* (dir. Jean-Pierre Jeunet). My main example is Catherynne M. Valente's 2015 novel *Radiance* (summarized below). Beyond the concepts of metalepsis and *mise en abyme* as mentioned above, my exploration builds on approaches to alternate history and related genres as 'transmedia phenomena' and – therefore – as being open to study via 'media archaeology'. As technologies of representation in which the fictional becomes the factual, alternate histories form part of a long tradition of arts replacing 'historical accuracy' with 'authenticity' or 'cogency'. In ancient rhetorical terms, alternate histories work like *ekphrasis*, or 'representation of representation', to produce *phantasia*, or 'vivid unreal image in the mind('s eye)'. As such they bear comparison not only with any ancient materials they represent but also – and more essentially – with ancient materials that already depict counterfactual pasts: for example, the paradigmatic *ekphrasis* of the Shield of Achilles in Homer's *Iliad*.

Radiance's 'Radiant Car': Ancient Microcosms of Alternate Cosmologies; or, Sappho's Cinematic Science Fiction?

My main example of the use of *ekphrasis* and *phantasia* in alternate narratives is Catherynne M. Valente's 2015 science-fiction novel *Radiance*, which pairs classical receptions with a cosmos whose (meta)physics allowed humankind to colonize the solar system starting in the late nineteenth century. Against a backdrop of changed twentieth-century history and culture, *Radiance* foregrounds an alternate history of film, focusing on differences from our Hollywood's 'silent' and 'Golden' ages: 'talkies' were written off as an unsuccessful aesthetic experiment, silent melodrama has stayed in the mainstream – its epicentre is moved, to the moon – and directors aiming at *avant garde* make documentaries.[1] The plot centres on attempts by several parties to recover or, failing that, to document the loss of one such documentary, most of whose footage and crew disappeared in 1944 during filming of the mysteriously abandoned settlement of Adonis on the planet Venus. The director, among those who disappeared, is Severin Unck. Other characters to feature below include Erasmo St. John, Severin's lover and a lone survivor from the crew, and Anchises St. John, orphaned by whatever befell the settlement, unofficially 'adopted' by Severin and Erasmo before the crew's disappearance, and now in adulthood – in the novel's present, the 1960s – a private investigator.

That set-up – what Valente herself has described as 'a decopunk alt-history Hollywood space opera mystery thriller. With space whales' – is closely linked to classical receptions via the lost documentary in question, entitled *The Radiant Car Thy Sparrows Drew* (see Scalzi 2015). The overlapping titles of real novel and fictional film point to *mise en abyme*, as characters in *Radiance* seek and find parts of *Radiant Car*, a kind of pun as they find '*Radiants*'.[2] The titles also suggest how the novel links its alternate history, grounded in alternate cosmology à la pulp science fiction, to early film and classical reception. Abstract and pervasive 'radiance', which as we will see is a characteristic feature of the novel's imagined cosmos, takes more particular form in the film *Radiant Car* – or rather it would have, if only the film existed still. In an overarching metapoetic gesture, what exists is rather the novel *Radiance*, a story which is likewise told in parts of divergent types. All of this together forms a first example of how alternate history trucks in *mise en abyme* and/via metalepsis, interaction between separate and incommensurable realities.

In context of that preliminary understanding of alternate history, the lost fictional film, *Radiant Car*, is a microcosm of the novel's, *Radiance*'s, mixture of science fiction and classical reception *insofar* as it is fragmentary and therefore richly evocative.[3] On one hand, 'radiance' is a metonym for film, evoking the 'ray(s) of light' required for photography or 'writing in light'; on the other hand, the 'radiant car' loops in antiquity by coming from a description of Aphrodite's chariot by the ancient Greek poet Sappho. Furthering metapoetics, that part of Sappho's poem appears in the novel as paratext, as an epigraph for the fifth and final section: 'The radiant car your sparrows drew / You gave the word and swift they flew, / Through liquid air they wing'd their way, / I saw their quivering pinions play; / To my plain roof they bore their queen, / Of aspect mild, and look serene' (Valente 2015: 413).[4]

Adapting Sappho's lines 7–12 in three rhyming couplets in iambic tetrameter, this description of the 'car' in heavenly motion is iconic for – it formally resembles – an alternate cosmos in which travel through 'space' is possible. Indeed, rendered more literally, Sappho's description of 'space' is if anything more vivid, referring to '[starry] firmament', 'upper air / element above the air', and 'black Earth' (γᾶς μελαίνας . . . ἀπ' ὠράνωἴθε-/ρος διὰ μέσσω).[5] Building on those qualities, in Valente the radiant universe is set in sharp contrast with our own unilluminated cosmos; a description of the latter is worth quoting to illustrate the novel's frequent use of film-script formatting to evoke emotive visuality in connection with cosmology

> [The camera shows a solar system without electric lights-save on one glowing world. Dark Mars, Neptune, Venus, the Moon, all many, many miles further apart than we know them to be. No Orient Express, no Grand Central Station, no bright cannons firing into the black. All those worlds, dead and empty, with no air, no oceans, no rivers, no trees. SEVERIN covers her mouth with her hands]
>
> Valente 2015: 425–6

In contrast to our impoverished universe, Valente's imagined cosmos is a rich combination of spaces literal – between the planets – and more figurative, i.e. notional space between stories and modes of storytelling. The particular mode of cinema notwithstanding, in general this combination is characteristic of Valente, many of whose works imagine travel into fictional story-worlds: in her 2011–16 *Fairyland* series of novels, travel into fairyland is modelled on Dorothy going to Oz (as well as on ancient myths of Underworld journey or *katabasis*); and in her 2017 novel *The Glass Town Game*, the Brontë sisters enter a world of their own invention. Described in fantasy scholarship as 'portal quests', such stories depend, again, on metalepsis, a movement across boundaries between fictions (esp. Mendelsohn 2008: 1–58). By centring that rhetorical device, these stories overlap with the functioning of cinema as a transmedia phenomenon: in parallel to how film realizes verbal script on visual screen (see further below), such overtly metapoetic literary fictions emphasize how all storytelling is multimodal, representing in a given form what is not present in its own – often different – original medium.

A 'Dream of the Solar System': Mental Moving Images and Other Metaleptic *Phantasiai* of Fictive Worlds

An alternate history like *Radiance* thus draws attention to how the intrinsic multimodality of storytelling applies with special force to historiography, as the past, by definition not present, may only be re-presented in a form that is necessarily different from the past as such. *Radiance* emphasizes narration's need for metalepsis by linking metalepsis to *mise en abyme*. As the real present novel collapses into representation of the fictional lost past film, so too is the narrative present itself a fiction, constituted by semiotic codes for time. If such temporal coding is characteristic of narrative, it is emphasized in a narrative like *Radiance* by classical receptions.

The allusion to Sappho is only one of *Radiance*'s many classical receptions. They range from paratextual quotations of other ancient literary texts (e.g. epigraph from Ovid's *Metamorphoses* for Part One, Valente 2015: 31, discussed below), through diegetic allusions and retellings of many ancient myths (e.g. the myth of the Graeae, Valente 2015: 391), to echoes of *katabasis* and related encounters with the dead or *nekyia* (as in a lost human settlement on Pluto named Proserpine, Valente 2015: *passim*).[6] The possibility of reading that complex mixture as a story about history and metalepsis is raised by Valente (2015: 431) herself, who in the Acknowledgments alludes to 'all the classic science-fiction writers who envisioned the worlds of our solar system as they were not but might be'. Valente singles out Roger Zelazny, perhaps alluding to his 1965 novel ... *And Call Me Conrad*, whose plot also links classical receptions and film: the Greek god Pan is involved in filming the Great Pyramids of Egypt being torn down, ultimately to simulate their construction by playing the film in reverse.

That possible allusion aside, *Radiance* figures movement into versions of the cosmos as imagined in earlier science fictions partly by developing images drawn from the cinema. An important related storytelling tradition is therefore the 'cinematic epic tradition', which has been interpreted as furthering ancient epic's figurative visuality, a matter of verbal art, in the literal visuals of film.[7] In particular, film can depict what a verbal art may only describe: in terms from ancient rhetorical theory, film replaces verbal *ekphrasis*, 'description', and consequent 'image in the mind', *phantasia*, with literal – actually visual – images.[8] If film as a medium thus performs what speculative fictions premise as genres, the two modes are profoundly linked as 'knowledge fictions', i.e. fictions that centre problems in epistemology (Rogers and Stevens 2015: 6 n.8, 11–20).

A central such problem is in knowledge of the past or 'theories of history' which, once again, are treated to metaleptic literalization: the 'looking' implicit in the etymology of 'theory', deriving from ancient Greek *theoria* (θεωρία), 'an act of looking', is made real in the medium of film. This real-ization combines metaleptic movement between separate realities, including metaphor and other figures of speech made literal, with concrete mediation of abstract problems in epistemology. In *Radiance*, that combination takes shape in metapoetic signals of participation in genre traditions and in the story's subject-matter of classical receptions, altered cosmos, and alternate-historical film. One such signal is deepened metalepsis, as when, in a programmatic example, the real Valente's (2015: 57) love of 'envisioning the worlds of our solar system' is unwittingly (?) echoed by the fictional Severin: 'I used to look up at night and dream of the solar system.'[9]

Also deepened here is *mise en abyme*, as the quotation reaches us at secondhand: the reader's stand-in, Anchises, recalls Severin recorded speaking the quoted sentence in a film, in fact 'the first words of her first movie'. That filmic voiceover has haunted Anchises and in parallel haunts the novel, recurring later, when in Severin's ongoing absence it 'spool[s] out of the dusk' (Valente 2015: 329), a time of (in)visible transitions that is well-suited both to cinema-going and to the supernatural. Indeed, recalled here is a tradition of interpreting film as a 'haunted medium' that transmits ghostly presence: insofar as Severin has disappeared and, from a perspective like Anchises', may well be dead, the recording of her voice comes as if from beyond the grave.[10] All these overlaps together sketch something like concentric circles – orbits? reels? – of feeling ('reel-ing'?): the plot is structured partly around Anchises' recollection of Severin's recorded voice, a *mise en abyme* (a memory of a voice in a film, reported in a novel about a – different, lost – film), which in turn is metalepsis, crossing from our reality into fiction to echo there Valente's real expression of feeling.

An Alternate Ancient Source for Modern Science-Fictional Cosmologies: Valente's *Radiance* as Shooting Script for Ovid's *Metamorphoses*

Radiance may thus be read as a kind of narrative labyrinth, a structure of concentric and overlapping circles that offer only partial views of themselves, each other, and the centre. At the centre of this labyrinth, a 'Minotaur' or hybrid 'monster' and so by definition a 'revealing' mixture ('monster' from Latin *monstrare*, 'to demonstrate, show, reveal'), is classical reception in science fiction.[11] A subset of Valente's beloved science fiction thus draws on, and consciously departs from, cosmologies from various ancient cultures. To name only a few examples: in Michael Bishop's 1987 story 'For Thus Do I Remember Carthage', a traveller challenges St Augustine's world-view with modern-physical understandings of collapsing stars and other astronomical phenomena; in Richard Garfinkle's 1996 novel *Celestial Matters*, space travel occurs in context of divergent ancient metaphysics and traditions of science, with, especially, Athenian and Spartan world-views ranged against classical Chinese; in Michael Swanwick's 2007 story 'Urdumheim', the Tower of Babel is retconned as a human solution to the problem posed by Sumerian demons, who otherwise could have possessed all of humankind through its previously sole language; and in Jo Walton's 2015–16 *Thessaly* trilogy of novels, a similar explanation is retrojected onto Plato's mythical Atlantis, whose founding and culture are attributed to Olympian gods and other divine figures travelling through space and time.

Such examples show how, while alternate history is often associated with events changed as if per 'great man' theories of history, many works centre other kinds of explanation, including metaphysics. Indeed, perhaps the most characteristic feature of speculative fiction is divergent metaphysics and with it altered causality, temporality and related narrative tropes. That is, events in genre fictions are rightly interpreted in context of the fictional worlds' particular 'rules'. For example, when in horror a character *must* go into an unlit basement (vel sim.), the obligation is not psychological but metaphysical, 'caused' by the narrative constraints of the imagined world. Many 'knowledge fictions' emphasize this metaphysical shift in metapoetry, making problems in knowledge an overt theme. The combination of altered cosmos and artistic self-consciousness or irony, characteristic of modern genre fictions, is ancient: e.g. Lucian's *True Story* parodies traditional claims about knowledge in a genre-fictional way, marking its tale of ludicrous sailing-trip to the moon as a 'true falsehood' by placing it in the tradition of fantastical 'literary horseplay' that was, paradoxically, established as authoritative by the status of Homeric epic.[12]

Radiance fits into this ancient tradition of alternate history as parody and play, enacted partly in mooted changes in metaphysics, by developing images of metalepsis as image-making or, equivalently, of adaptation as a transmedia phenomenon.[13] This metapoetic emphasis on transmediation can bring us back to Sappho, the transmission of whose poetry from antiquity has depended on testimonia in other works, partial quotations and many – but not very many novel – papyrus fragments.[14] As if it has come along with the borrowed line, that real, historical situation is reflected in the (verbal) novel *Radiance* in the fragmentary state of the unreal (audiovisual) film *Radiant Car*. As suggested above, the novel further captures the complex materiality of such transmedia traditions in its use of formatting to imply the book's – the physical object's – composition or collage as if from different types of media, including diaries and historical documents like the chronology as well as screenplays or shooting scripts.[15]

The ekphrastic physicality of Valente's novel, with description of disparate media that are composited to compose a whole, recalls the multifaceted productions of modern film. It also recalls the ancient author whose poetry is arguably both the most cinematic and centred on storytelling of, precisely, composite physicality: Ovid, in his epic *Metamorphoses*. Reception of Sappho aside, *Radiance* proceeds under an Ovidian metamorphic sign: Part One has as epigraph the beginning of Ovid's poem, 'My soul burns to speak of strange bodies transformed! / O gods in heaven, you ardent lovers of mutation, / become the breath inside me / and draw up my song, untroubled, unbroken, / from the first beginnings of the world / to this very moment and this very day' (Valente 2015: unnumbered 31).[16] Composite physicality in an Ovidian tradition of metamorphic bodies forms another of *Radiance*'s labyrinthine concentric circles or ring-structures. Recalling that early epigraph, the penultimate chapter figures the reader's accumulated knowledge of all the novel's scenes as a kind of cinematic viewing of Severin's body *post mortem*: 'What you have seen in this shadowed room ... is the body of Severin Unck. All her pieces, laid out for viewing. It does not live – we are not Victor Frankenstein, nor do we wish to be – but it looks like a woman we once knew. Look at her' (Valente 2015: 420–1).[17]

Thus invited to see Ovidian shapes all through the story, we might link Ovid's 'strange bodies transformed ... in heaven' to Severin's 'dream of the solar system' – and, as noted above, thereby and metaleptically to Valente's feeling for 'envision[ing] the worlds of our solar system as they were not but might be': Ovid's 'heavenly bodies', including the planets or as Valente calls them 'the worlds of our solar system', are made 'strange' in science fiction's alternate cosmologies. The same page links such composite metamorphoses to traditions of personhood transformed into *persona* in film: the second epigraph to Part One is from the American actress Ethel Barrymore, claiming that in the Hollywood studio system a successful actress 'must have the face of Venus, the brains of Minerva, the grace of Terpsichore, the memory of Macaulay, the figure of Juno, and the hide of a rhinoceros' (Valente 2015: unnumbered 31). Although we might quibble over some of the attributes, at work here is composite personhood recalling certain ancient myths, perhaps especially that of Pandora, and evoking metamorphosis in a ludic mode.[18]

As with its trope of fragments of Sappho, then, *Radiance* echoes Ovid's playful retelling of earlier stories. Beyond its transformations of earlier science fiction, the novel's alternate cosmos retains features of real historical traditions of astronomy including receptions of Greek and Roman myths, many to be found in the *Metamorphoses*.[19] Thus filming for *Radiant Car* was on the planet Venus in a village called Adonis after the goddess' mortal beloved (Ovid, *Metamorphoses* 10.503–739). *Nomen erat omen* ('the name was a sign'), for like the man, the village is doomed by 'divine' action, beset by supernatural phenomena and left in ruins shortly after the crew's arrival (description of the mysterious event is scattered across various recollections, e.g. Valente 2015: 245–59). Redoubling doublets as in Ovid's narratology, this recalls the unexplained destruction of a colony on Pluto called Proserpine, after the woman abducted by him (Ovid, *Metamorphoses* 5.332–571). In such allusions the novel varies a running theme in myth, death due to close association with gods.

Tightening the weave here is a related thematic ring-structure: Severin, the documentary's director, was born in a lunar colony called Tithonus, after the human beloved of Aurora / the goddess of the Dawn (e.g. Ovid, *Metamorphoses* 9.418–438), and so appears and disappears in connection with doomed 'beloveds' of the gods. In such points of contact, ancient myth is not inert but a matter – rather literally, an elemental substance – of possibility in *Radiance*'s cosmos. This dreamed-real possibility, the novel's imagined multiverse, is ultimately revealed to be like film: as a being with cosmic perception tells Severin, '[t]here are a million million frames . . . Each frame is a world; a universe . . . and there are ever so many more than twenty-four per second' (Valente 2015: 426–7; cf. 406). If each universe is a frame, then all the frames together make a cinematic multiverse of infinite and endlessly moving images.

Like the explicit comparison discussed above between the novel's radiant universe and our dark one – the former lit as if for photography, the latter a *camera obscura*, allowing only inverted dreams or photo-negatives of alternate worlds? – the premise of a properly 'cinematic' multiverse invites comparison with examples of alternate history in real-world films. Those in turn will illustrate tropes for alternate history and historical antiquity, especially 'ruins' and 'ruined icons' as indices of fuzzy boundaries between the different claims to realism made in terms of 'accuracy', a matter of art's perceived fidelity to alleged historical fact, and 'authenticity', in which by contrast art is judged compelling when its depictions match a modern audience's cultural expectations about historical fiction. Although all, again, is metalepsis linked to *mise en abyme*, the spiral is not necessarily downwards: the abyss looks back, circling back to theories of alternate history, what is 'looked at' including alternate – changed, invented – arts.

'Always Already Ruined' Icons for Alternate Histories: The 'Statue of Liberty' and the Shield of Achilles

To take perhaps the best-known or 'classic' modern example of alternate-historical art in film: the final scene of *Planet of the Apes* (dir. Franklin J. Schaffner 1968) reveals that said planet, until that point presumed to be an 'alien' world, is in fact our future Earth. The revelation is via ruined icon: the 'Statue of Liberty', no longer standing whole but nearly buried at the shore. This climactic epiphany changes how the planet must be understood: seemingly 'alien' in a sense typical of science fiction, i.e. 'extraterrestrial', the planet is rather 'other' or 'alternative'. That is, the ruined icon above all requires the film's main character, and through him viewers, to revise their prior theory of the film-world's fictive history: we must replace a provisional image of what might have been, a different course of hominid evolution, with what is instead imagined as our own history's farther future.[20]

Like *Radiance*, *Planet* as 'knowledge fiction' thematizes the unsettled search for historical fact, in its case centring our view of ape society on scientists who debate competing theories about human evolution. Although their sciences are biological and/or behavioural, 'anthropology' in the strict sense, they are also 'archaeological' in the sense of comprising scientific storytelling about origins. *Planet* thus fits into a tradition of popular-cultural depictions of archaeology (esp. Moshenka 2017). Most importantly for our purposes, archaeology is often depicted as an exploration of counterfactuality, especially of secret histories in which human civilization has been affected by forces supernatural and/or extraterrestrial. In turn, those secret-historical forces are often linked to antiquity. Arguably the most influential modern formulation of the idea, Erich von Däniken's 1969 book *Chariots of the Gods?*, proposes that ancient civilizations were inspired by such 'alien astronauts': otherwise, runs the counterfactual and racist logic, how could 'primitive' humankind have built 'wonders of the ancient world'? Although the 'Statue of Liberty' is rather a modern marvel (dedicated 26 October 1886), its appearance in *Planet* thus fits into a mythology that has been applied to modern re-imaginings of 'ancient worlds' and what counts as 'classical antiquity'.[21]

Indeed, the historical more generally is often represented as the 'archaeological', i.e. via a shorthand of material remains that are fragmentary but recognizable. As signs, such imag(in)ed remains are icons, since their own ruin is parsed as resembling the 'always already ruined' past.[22] The trope of objects taken as signifying other – alternate – times has roots in antiquity, stretching back to epic poetic objects that reflect the genre's preoccupation with temporality. From luxury goods beloved of aristocracy, including imported foodstuffs, through tokens of guest-host relationships (*xenia*) like household objects made of precious metals (e.g. Homer *Odyssey* 4.128–135), to items of divine manufacture (like the Shield of Achilles, below), such objects point beyond the limits of human life.[23] As such, they embody the epic-heroic aspiration to immortality or, failing that, immortality in culture, 'undying glory' in the form of representation in works of art (κλέος ἄφθιτον). Quite like counterfactual works of art as vivid images for theories of history, these objects are both icons of immortality – formally resembling it by lasting longer than human life – and displacements of the possibility: they are simulacra of immortality's endless precession away from what is possible in ordinary historiography.

From this perspective, we may read such objects as representing alternate histories already in epic.[24] To take the paradigmatic example, the Shield of Achilles' depiction of the world includes scenes of daily life, including weddings, a busy marketplace, festivals and agriculture, that are in sharp contrast with the *Iliad*'s setting of seemingly endless war. Although the divine Shield also shows a city at war, by depicting peacetime it images a counterfactuality that could not be sounded by the characters' ordinary modes of human knowledge including lived experience.[25] Emphasizing that difference is the fact that the Shield's recipient, Achilles, knows alternatives to the present and possibilities for the future by extraordinary means: his mother Thetis, a goddess, has told him of his 'two fates', on one hand a long peaceful life in domestic obscurity, on the other hand the heroic paradox, an early violent death that should lead to undying glory (e.g. Homer, *Iliad* 9; cf. Homer, *Odyssey* 11, where Achilles' *psyche* regrets his heroic choice).

Here is an example, then, of 'alien astronaut' theory à la von Däniken *avant la lettre*: the Shield as an object is beyond human making, made by higher powers; and as an image it is beyond human understanding, a 'knowledge fiction' that cannot be withstood, such that Achilles' troops, the Myrmidons, must look away from its glare (Homer, *Iliad* 18.12–20). At that moment of the Shield's reception, 'what might have been' is fixed into place as 'what is not', reflecting not open possibility but the counterfactuality of Achilles' knowledge of closed alternatives.

Hence Achilles' deepened rage upon seeing his rather narrow human limits reflected in the Shield's divine artifice, that is, in its counterfactual world bounded by the merely physical world-ocean. On this reading, the Shield illustrates how counterfactual worlds could be signified by 'iconic' objects already in ancient poetics: the trope of signifying alternate histories, or divergent theories of history, in works of art is already part of 'classical tradition'. As a result, for a fiction like *Radiance* to repeat that trope is a metapoetic way of signalling its own participation in a long tradition of linking alternate history and classical reception.

A Media Archaeology of Imaginary Ruins: Or, Precessions of Simulacra in *Planets*, plural, *of the Apes*

The line of reading in the preceding section quickly crosses into speculation, and it should be followed thus through later receptions of the Shield, each an alternate history of that paradigmatic moment.[26] Even glancing in that direction, we see that things in ancient epic may be theorized for how they 'theorize' in turn, allowing a 'looking-at' that goes beyond human understanding and temporality: alternatives to traditional explanations of history – that is, not only different events but different causes and indeed divergent metaphysics for causality – and, therefore, alternate-historical theories. Here is ancient precedent for *ekphrasis* of art in context of, and communicating, problems in epistemology: again, 'knowledge fictions'. But how might we proceed to detail the materialities of alternate histories of art?[27]

Near to hand, in other words, is the need to excavate the interconnections between unreal things, tracing via those things' proxy the real links between mutually exclusive theories of history. We may examine different versions of 'the same things' across media, and imaginary objects in particular as transmedia phenomena, for how they reflect variations of theme across divergent metaphysics or across story-modes whose surface similarities belie incommensurable premises. In connection with classical receptions, a step in the direction of that examination has been taken by 'thing theory', the study of discourses about materiality and how material things are entered into discourse, especially with reference to ancient epic poetry.[28] We may go further in that direction by linking ancient epic 'thing theory' to 'media archaeology' as that has been used to study film.[29] This approach can help shed light on the transmedia/ting aspects of fictive things as reflecting alternate-historical metalepsis.

For example, the iconic ruin that ends *Planet of the Apes* is already alternate relative to other versions and mediations of the story. The source, Pierre Boulle's 1963 novel *La planète des singes*, ends with an icon that is neither the 'Statue of Liberty' nor in ruins: 'The Eiffel Tower is still there' ('La Tour Eiffel est toujours là'; Boulle 1963: 189). That hale icon only intensifies the main character's discovery that history has gone rather differently: having set his sights on 'landfall in France', he is startled to learn that *this* Earth, too, is a 'planet of the apes', for out of the first car he sees steps 'a gorilla'.

Again, then, an iconic work of art serves to defamiliarize setting, the more so since the icon has varied across alternate-historical versions of the 'same' story: the novel's Eiffel Tower, the first film's 'Statue of Liberty', the Golden Gate Bridge in the 2011 film *Rise of the Planet of the Apes* (dir. Rupert Wyatt). Crossing, as such icons do, into another filmic 'universe', it as if Boulle's original image, altered for the first movie, has nonetheless been filmed: at the end of the 1997 film *Alien: Resurrection* (dir. Jean-Pierre Jeunet), the protagonists' return to Earth is confirmed when they see, and we are shown, the Eiffel Tower . . . albeit, or perhaps emphatically, in a 'deleted scene': i.e. the view of the Eiffel Tower is an *alternate* ending to *Alien: Resurrection*, redoubling the moment's counterfactual status – it is not historical, nor even simply 'real' in the fiction of the film – in a way that seems to ripple across the fuzzy boundaries between separate realities.[30] In other words, a deleted scene from one film, a scene available for viewing but separate from the story as it stands, shows what might have been the ending of another film that has not only its own story but its own fictional universe, refracting material from an early source in another medium – from novel to film – and (therefore, inexorably) founded on a likewise-different theory of alternate history.

'A Universe of Lenses': The Cinematic Multiverse of *Radiance* and the Reality of *Phantasia*, 'Image in the Mind's Eye'

Such things as iconic objects in alternate-historical films may thus be 'excavated' via media archaeology, revealing their real links across different fictions in various media and signifying divergent theories – visions, literal filmic 'lookings-at' – of history. The particular trope of iconic works of art in connection with planetfall may return us to the solar system of *Radiance* – but in context of what we have seen is that novel's own concluding image for the cosmology that makes possible both space travel and alternate histories, a cinematic multiverse. With an eye thus on the novel's retro-futuristic technologies for filmmaking and/as 'envisioning' other worlds, we may see how examples like the preceding represent what has been called 'forgotten futures' of film: the once and formerly possible, but now counterfactual, future histories of an artform.[31]

Counterfactual in fact, in feeling such past future possibilities – materially embodied but fragmentary, possible only in an alternate future contrary to history – suggests a heightened proximity to the real, an alternate status that registers as close to hand insofar as many such objects, icons all, did exist, in some cases still do. In all cases, they are imaged in relevant fictions as metalepses from worlds that are imagined as alternate but not therefore insignificant.[32] Against a backdrop of alternate cosmology, these ekphrastic objects serve not only as icons but also, perhaps even more, as indices: they point to the alternative, their impossible *physical* presence here suggesting here's nearness to *metaphysically different* there. In terms noted earlier, such counterfactual objects are not historically 'accurate' but only because their 'authenticity' belongs to another history entirely.[33] The implication of their indexicality is that alternate history not only might have been but nearly was – or was not far, just one metaphysically different cosmos over from this one.

This perspective helps confirm how, details aside, in general *ekphrasis* of changed or invented 'thing' is a sign of 'alternate theory of history'. Like fragments of a fictional film named after a line from real fragmentary Sappho, other re-imagined works of art can help alternate history bootstrap up from otherwise bottomless *mise en abyme*, interrupting the *reductio ad absurdum* of incompleteness by signifying a premise – a metaphysics of time and causality – whose reality is of a separate and separately provable order.[34] In other words, and again, insofar as they are only fragments or aspects, alternate-historical depictions of art self-identify as metalepsis and, so, indicate the reality of their current (different) setting since, to get there, they must have crossed impossibly from a different someplace real.

Thus the reality of *Radiance*'s fictive world, its alternate history and different cosmology, is underwritten by the story's metaphysics of metalepsis: the cinematic multiverse, with its veracity guaranteed by autopsy in, precisely, an ancient epic mode. Severin, the filmmaker, sees this for herself, allowed to do so by the metaphysically different being, called a Callowhale, whose capacity to see all the infinite frames of the multiverse is linked in the novel to ancient myths. Thus the Callowhale claims: 'You have never seen like we see. In some places, we look like a camera. Like an eye shared between three women. Like a story about seeing and being seen' (Valente 2015: 428).

Earlier the novel is explicit that the allusion here, in the detail of 'an eye shared between three women', is to the Graeae of classical myth (as with so many others, in Ovid, *Metamorphoses* 4.753–803). As Erasmo, noted above as a lone survivor of the film crew's mysterious disappearance, states: 'They have one eye and one tooth between them. They share it. Pop it out of one sister's socket and into the other'; recalling Severin's voiceover, Erasmo goes on to say that he 'used to dream about it. About the eye' (Valente 2015: 391). He concludes by anticipating the Callowhale's ultimate revelation to Severin and, so, by echoing the novel's other blurrings of dream or fantasy with reality especially in terms of film: 'we're all Graeae. We live in a universe of lenses. We watch and watch. We all share one eye between us, the big black camera iris. We wait for our turn to see what someone else saw on a screen.'

Alternate Histories as Histories of Otherness: Or, 'a Picture That Can Only Ever Come in Parts'

Erasmo has deduced, recalling myth, what the Callowhale declares and reveals to Severin – and what we have been considering as *Radiance*'s underlying idea: historiography, a 'writing of history' which, by definition of its subject, involves movement across media, is a transmedia phenomenon that requires metalepsis and, so, is linked to *mise en abyme*. That idea of movement between separate and inaccessible realities is necessary because the past is gone but not simply so, rather complexly 'lost': in a way it exists still, 'if only' it could be recalled, or things recalling it could be had. We have seen how such things are, therefore, depicted in fictions, alleged past objects – once-were, might-have-been – replaced by present images. A special focus falls on alternate works of art, 'iconic' works which, per that mode of semiosis, may be read as signifying by resembling worlds that are unreachable otherwise. On this reading, alternate works of art are vivid images for the idea that all historiography is meaningfully 'alternate' insofar as metalepsis is implied by representation itself, *mimesis*.[35]

In other words, both mainstream historiography and alternate history depend less on metaphysics of 'accuracy' than on rhetorics of 'authenticity'.[36] This focus on rhetoric shows how vividness of present image is more compelling than veracity of past object. Thus historiography marks itself as current representation of former presence by mobilizing rhetorical devices, including figuring historical inquiry as an act of nearly literal – nearly physical – but still metaphysical recovery of parts and reconstruction of past wholes.[37] The figuration is ancient.

It appears in metapoetic statements, e.g. Herodotus 'wrote down' stories that cannot be verified and by his own account could not have been real; Thucydides proclaims autopsy linked paradoxically to uncertain memory and invented speeches – and harks back to programmatic moments in epic: the Muses tell Hesiod that they can speak the truth and falsehood that seems like truth, and a similar capacity is attributed to other mythic figures like the Sirens and the sea-god Proteus and to legendary storytellers like Odysseus and Helen.[38]

In this chapter, I have tried to show that Catherynne M. Valente is one such storyteller, and her novel *Radiance* a story about how all history is alternate history, all historical 'fact' a matter of 'knowledge fictions'. *Radiance* dramatizes this by combining science-fictional cosmology, alternate film history and classical receptions, doing so – per the allusive sign of the title – in the form of an alternate modern history of ancient poetry: Sappho's poetic description of Aphrodite's 'radiant car' is recalled in Severin's would-be *Radiant Car*. Or rather it would be, if only that lost and fictional film could be seen. In the novel's cinematic multiverse, it may well be, by beings whose metaphysical difference lets them see frames of infinite improbability. Metapoetically, of course, we real-world (?) readers *are* just such beings: as Erasmo intuits, 'we're all Graeae', sharing the Callowhales' capacity to see what might have been . . . if only as *phantasia* or 'image in the mind'. Technically speaking, of course, 'cinema' too only seems to be 'moving' image, a series of still frames perceived as implying motion . . .

There is more to investigate here, including how *Radiance* deepens metapoetry by dramatizing the very need for investigation, framing the diegetic search for alternate-historical fragments of art in terms drawn from real-world *film-noir* detective stories and, by proxy of that genre's literary history, modern visions of discovery and belated recognition in classical tragedy.[39] Recalling, for example, how *noir* dénouements stretch back to mythic Oedipus' unwitting discovery of his own involvement in tragedy, the detective work in *Radiance* ironically solves another – an other, an alternate – mystery: interplanetary travel has increased human prosperity but at a cost to other life, with the carcasses of Callowhales used as fuel.[40]

In *Radiance*, in other words, the search for fragments of film has led to finding a different whole and to seeing wholeness in difference, the meaningfulness of other forms of life. From this perspective, Valente's *Radiance* imagines an alternate history of film in which, ironically, documentary filmmaking is returned to its highest purpose, documenting others' histories and, so, 'writing histories' of otherness. Ironically and critically, for in this way an alternate history of arts can emphasize history-writing, historiography, as critique. Such critical inquiry will, like speculative fiction otherwise, have various targets; in a case like that of exploited Callowhales, a target is modern biopolitics or the tendency of cultures to treat the lives of 'others' as fungible raw material.

In general, however, as embodied in counterfactual arts, alternate history invites meditation on 'history' in just that ancient sense of 'inquiry': as depicted in a scene of ongoing judgement on Achilles' Shield, not a simple, static product but rather a complex, dynamic process that is open to revision over time. Indeed, a focus on alternate arts, emphasizing not only historical differences but aesthetic alternatives, suggests the inevitable incompleteness of any particular set or type of examples from the past. As Valente (2015: 420) has a Callowhale put it, from the cosmic, cinematic-multiversal perspective we readers share, history is therefore like a film now mostly lost: 'We collect the pieces where we can, obsessively assemble and reassemble them, searching for a picture that can only ever come in parts.'

Acknowledgement

I am grateful to the volume's editors for their comments and for their patience as I offered one alternate history of the chapter's delivery date after another. In thinking about alternate history and film, I benefited from discussions with the students in my course on 'Ancient Worlds in Film & Television' at Trinity University, spring 2021; special thanks go to Gloria Gatchel and Rafaela-Seraphina Brenner, both Trinity 2021, whose love of *Radiance* outshines even my own.

Notes

1 *Radiance* begins with a 'Chronology' (Valente 2015: 7–9) listing the first interplanetary launch in 1858. I am grateful to an editor for noting that early (silent) film plays a similarly important role in Robert Charles Wilson's (2009) novel *Julian Comstock: A Story of 22nd-Century America*. On early film in connection with classical receptions, esp. Michelakis and Wyke 2013a and 2013b; cf. Marcus 2007, Gunning 2004.

2 Valente (2009) used the title for an earlier short story, a sort of 'pilot study' for the novel to come, 'The Radiant Car Thy Sparrows Drew'.

3 I am grateful to the editors for noting prominent examples of such metapoetic metalepsis in historical fictions whose stories are claimed to come from lost (fictional/ized) materials: e.g. Umberto Eco's 1980 novel *The Name of the Rose*, whose

main story, a murder mystery centered on a library in 1327 but written down around 1400, is introduced by a frame story about the search for (a translation of) that writing, a search begun in 1968 and written down in 1980. For a similar trope in fantasy, see below, nn. 35–7. In context of film, that literary gesture resembles the device of retroversion or 'flashback'; see Hayward 1996: 122–30, and cf. Stewart 2007.

4 The translation of Sappho is attributed in the novel's front matter to Francis Fawkes. The lines are paired with a second epigraph, 'In the end, everything is a gag', attributed to Charlie Chaplin – and inviting us to read the novel's classical receptions as a kind of joke? Cf. Severin's jocular attitude at the novel's end: '"All right, mister" she says, addressing a being whose consciousness spans the multiverse, "Put me in the picture"' (Valente 2015: 429).

5 Sappho: πάτρος δὲ δόμον λίποισα / χρύσιον ἦλθες / ἄρμ' ὐπασδεύξαισα, κάλοι δέ σ' ἆγον / ὤκεες στροῦθοι περὶ γᾶς μελαίνας / πύκνα δίννεντες πτερ' ἀπ' ὠράνωἴθε-/ρος διὰ μέσσω; edition: Campbell 1967. It is debatable whether 'golden' (χρύσιον) applies to Aphrodite's 'chariot' or rather Zeus' 'house', but the former is possible, allowing for Valente's 'radiant car'.

6 It seems likely that the name 'Anchises' alludes to the story of *katabasis* in Virgil's *Aeneid.* I regret not having the space in this chapter to consider *Radiance*'s or Valente's Underworldliness further: beyond the *Fairyland* series mentioned above, cf. Valente (2021), a retelling of the myth of Orpheus and Eurydice.

7 On 'cinematic epic tradition', esp. Paul (2013: 1–35); cf. Llewellyn-Jones (2018: esp. 15–35).

8 I discuss this possibility more fully in Stevens (2024a).

9 We might compare Milton, *Paradise Lost* 8.175–176, where the archangel Raphael tells Adam to 'dream not of other worlds, what creatures there / Live, in what state, condition, or degree': in a Christian context, implicitly the question of whether life on other worlds is saved; cf., e.g. Lewis' *Chronicles of Narnia* (with Ward 2010), Mary Doria Russell's 1996 novel *The Sparrow.*

10 'Haunted media': Sconce (2000); cf. Marcus (2007: esp. 1-98). On classical receptions as 'haunting', see Uden (2020) and further below.

11 Esp. Rogers and Stevens (2015), Kleu (2019), Bost-Fiévet and Provini (2014), Brown (2008), Liveley (2006). Cf. Valente's (2019) essay 'Just Your Average Tuesday-Morning Minotaur'.

12 On Lucian and/as genre (science) fiction, see Fredericks (1976), and Keen (2015).

13 Transmedia studies: e.g. Deterding and Zagal (2018).

14 Although not an overview, de Kreij (2015) is an illuminating introduction to problems and approaches in Sappho's transmission.

15 In connection with Valente's mention of Zelazny, noted above, the mixture of media may recall Zelazny's 1969 novel *Creatures of Light and Darkness*; I am grateful to Leire Olabarria for reminding me of this similarity.

16 Adapting *Metamorphoses* 1.1–4: *in nova fert animus mutatas dicere formas / corpora; di, coeptis (nam vos mutastis et illa) / adspirate meis primaque ab origine mundi / ad mea perpetuum deducite tempora carmen*. The translation is unattributed (Valente's?).

17 For Ovid's *Metamorphoses* and *Frankenstein*, see Liveley (2018).

18 For figures of Pandora in science fiction, see Stevens (2022). In connection with Ovid, might the rhinoceros be compared with that animal embodying Augustus in Christoph Ransmayr's 1988 novel *The Last World*, a counterfactual history of Ovid's relegation to Roman Tomis featuring visits by an itinerant film projectionist?

19 Ovid's poem, massively influential (e.g. Brown 1999, chapters 15–20 in Hardie 2002), has played a special role in speculative fictions thanks to its trope of fantastical physical change (e.g. Brown 2008; cf. Gildenhard and Zissos 2013) and more recently its theme of constraints on personhood (e.g. Natoli 2017). For Ovid and film, Winkler (2020).

20 Compare *Star Trek*'s alien worlds modelled on historical eras (cf. Kovacs 2015), a modelling reflected in clothing (with Llewellyn-Jones (2018: 197–296) on fashion as image of antiquity).

21 In yet another real-world alternate history, the Statue would have been a lighthouse marking the Suez Canal, recalling the ancient Colossus of Rhodes, and emphasizing the European colonialist and imperialist, and therefore racist, underpinnings of such interpretations of, or rather projections upon, antiquity. See, e.g. Goff (2005), and for a similar analysis of modern science fiction, Rieder (2008).

22 Lowe (2012); cf. Sobchack (1999/2000) for application to artificial ruins left behind by modern historical-epic film.

23 For luxury and foodstuffs in antiquity, see Dalby (2013: 201–3).

24 A related possibility has been studied by Gazis (2018): Hades as a poetic space for alternatives to mainstream traditions of historiography in epic.

25 Esp. Becker (1995). Winkler (2007: 57–63; cf. 2007: 25–9, 31) reads the Shield as 'cinematic', precisely 'a series of static images' which 'present verbal motion pictures'.

26 Perhaps esp. in Virgil, when Aeneas receives his own divine shield and, in ignorance of what it images, responds with 'joyful wonder' (*Aeneid* 8.730: *miratur rerumque ignarus imagine gaudet*).

27 Cf. Dolezel (1998: 1–36 and 199–226).

28 Esp. Canevaro (2018), after Brown (2001).

29 Parikka (2012); cf. Meurer (2020) after Zielinski (2015), and Natale and Balbi (2014).

30 Other icons are nearby; e.g. in context of stories about homecoming, Odysseus – indeed, Boulle's main character is called Ulysse; for Odyssean homecoming in *Alien: Resurrection*, see Rogers (2015, esp. 232–7 on endings).

31 Esp. Gunning (2004); cf. Huhtamo (2011), Mannoni (1994).

32 Jo Walton has emphasized to me that *The Just City* (2015) is not 'alternate' but 'secret history': real but excluded from historical discourse.

33 See further below, n. 36.

34 The standard popularization in English is Hofstadter (1979).

35 Cf. a recurrent metafictional conceit of modern fantasy, foundationally in Tolkien: the 'principal conceit' of his entire Legendarium is self-conscious framing as 'a lost prehistoric tradition' that may be glimpsed in real-world 'myths and legends', which are received as 'echoes, fragments, and transformations' (Fisher 2011: 40); metaphysics aside, the structure again is metalepsis as *mise en abyme*. I have elsewhere suggested that this takes shape in Tolkien's fictions, as later in Valente's, in reference to ancient Underworld stories as those are filtered through Gothic images and imaginings of antiquity (Stevens 2017, 2021, and 2024b).

36 In connection with film, esp. Becker (2013) and Solomon (2007); in the related medium of games, Ghita and Andrikopoulos (2009), Uricchio (2005), and cf. Köstlbauer (2013). I am grateful to Alberto Quiroga for observing that 'authenticity' in this sense and context must recall the role of 'likelihood' or 'probability' in Ancient Greek rhetoric and related philosophy (εἰκώς); cf. Mourelatos (2015), Betegh (2009), Burnyeat (2005).

37 Foundationally, White (1973); cf. Milnor (2008). An important thematization of authenticity in alternate history is in Philip K. Dick's *The Man in the High Castle*; see Evans (2010). Cf. the image of 'salvage' (as in Jesmyn Ward's *Salvage the Bones*, with Stevens 2018) alongside the now more widespread, if watered down, idea of 'deep dive'. 'Salvage' is marked as a decision about the past interacting with the present in James Cameron's 1986 film *Aliens*: finding Ripley alive, a crew leader declares, 'Welp, there goes our salvage, boys', i.e. a potential future is now past, from this point only alternate history.

38 Cf. not necessarily dissimulation but indeterminate signification in cultural practices marking knowledge a matter of superhuman relationship to time, like prophecies, oracles and astrology.

39 E.g. Rushing (2007); I am grateful to Koen Vacano for noting Hoek (2020), Lanouette (2012), and Bordwell (2006).

40 This may recall how mythic Perseus' 'heroic journey' includes stealing the Graeae's single glass eye (Ovid, *Metamorphoses* 4.753–803).

3.2

How Place Creates Time: Imagined Architecture as an Expression of Identity in Ramona Wheeler's *Three Princes*

Leire Olabarria
University of Birmingham

Introduction: Once Upon a Place

Uchronic narratives are, by definition, concerned with the creation of an alternative time as a result of a divergence in the past.[1] In essence, these narratives make use of suspension of disbelief in order to craft an alternative time and allow us to reflect on what could have been. In a literary genre where historical divergence is key to the plot (e.g. Singles 2013: 22–3, 279), the focus is often on those alternate timelines, which are questioned and explored through ideas of inevitability and chance. Narratives of power and the role of 'big men' – or women – in history are arguably some of the most fascinating topics explored through counterfactuals. Some counterfactual narratives, however, seem to be less concerned with an exploration of historical contingence per se, focusing instead on the physical alternate world where the narrative takes place.

Three Princes is an example of this interest in worldbuilding through descriptions of the natural and artificial landscape. In this novel, which presents Egypt as a major imperial power in the nineteenth century CE, we are transported into an imagined world where the streets feel ancient and the temples are eternal, but this reimagining of Egypt is reminiscent of well-known environments that help the reader situate the narrative in a concrete space. Thick descriptions of the urban landscape are here used to craft a convincing characterization of this alternate world, creating a sense of authenticity within a fantastic setting. It is an imagined universe, but one that we seem to know well. The use of traditional architectural forms in this novel, hence, contributes to sustaining on the reader an evocation of a place and, by extension, a culture. In this chapter I discuss how time and place are presented in the novel, arguing that popular perceptions of ancient Egypt as a culture of monumentality allow for a focus on urban spaces in the setting of the narrative. To conclude, I explore how these imagined architectures may unwittingly contribute to the perpetuation of colonial relations of domination.

Three Princes across Three Continents

Ramona Wheeler's *Three Princes* is a perfect example of a counterfactual novel in which the author plays with ideas of power and domination. The main point of divergence in the novel's timeline took place in the first century BCE, when Egypt became the core of the Roman Empire as Julius Caesar married Cleopatra VII.[2] Wheeler does not delve into this alternate historical setting, but the novel implies that, as consequence of this union, Egypt became a political superpower encompassing several kingdoms across Africa, Europe and Asia. The main counterpart to Egypt's power is the land of Tawantinsuyu, an empire that spans South and Central America. Tawantinsuyu is presented as a technologically advanced area, as exemplified by their command of the technique of flying, which they keep a secret. The novel is set in the nineteenth century CE, when Egypt, led by Pharaoh Djoser-George and Queen Sashetah Irene, continues to be one of the most influential stakeholders in international politics, but its supremacy in the area is being questioned. On the one hand, the monarchs of Oesterreich, Victoria and Albert, are rebelling against the Egyptian empire, claiming to be the only defenders of true faith. In their enterprise, they have the unwavering support of their Minister of War, Otto von Bismarck, who is attempting to unite other kingdoms with Oesterreich's militia in a civil war against Egypt.[3] On the other, Tawantinsuyu, under the authority of Viracocha Inca Yupanqui XII, is developing their flying skills even further, and it is rumoured that it is trying to reach the moon. This unprecedented achievement could potentially turn the tables and lead to an imbalance of power between Egypt and Tawantinsuyu that would compromise the political *status quo*. The rulers of Egypt send two men, Lord Scott Oken and Professor-Prince Mikel Mabruke, to secretly investigate the truth behind these rumours. The links between Tawantinsuyu's experiments and Victoria and Albert's rebellion are revealed as our protagonists make their way over the Atlantic by way of Morocco.

Oken and Mabruke are two of the three eponymous princes in the novel, and their adventures in this world of marked steampunk aesthetic (see below) are the focus of the narrative. It is through their eyes that we get a glimpse of Wheeler's reimagination of Victorian times, in which Egypt rules more than half of the world. Oken is a prince of Britannia, the youngest son of the family in the throne of the Spate (province) of Mercia, while Mabruke is a High Nubian prince, so it is interesting that Wheeler has chosen two men hailing from the periphery of Egypt to embody the imperial gaze. They are presented as Egyptian throughout, although a few remarks on Oken's clothing and shaving habits, for example, indicate that there may be some inner conflicts in relation to their ethnic identities, as I explore below. Be that as it may, their own observations and dialogues with other characters along their journey allow Wheeler to introduce striking comparisons between Egypt and Tawantinsuyu that are often framed within a dichotomic framework. For example, whereas in Egypt women are highly respected and treated as equal, in Tawantinsuyu they are subordinate to men; whereas in Egypt slavery is abhorred, in Tawantinsuyu social order and economic activity is based on slave labour. Taking Oken's and Mabruke's point of view, Egypt is presented in contrast to an exoticized Other, yet Egypt may in turn appear as an otherized entity in the eyes of the reader. I develop this idea below in my discussion of Orientalism and imaginative geographies.

The characterization of Egypt as a political power is not only undertaken through the protagonists' observations of cultural traits, which they compare to their own, but also through a painstaking reconstruction of the landscape, which is more than a backdrop to the actions of these characters. In this chapter, I focus on the use of built and natural space as a tool to provide authenticity to this imagined world.

Opera Houses and Bamboo Aircrafts: Monumentality and Technology in *Three Princes*

One of the main features of *Three Princes* is that, despite its being a uchronic novel, the author does not dwell on the historical divergence that gave way to the political *status quo* described in the plot, nor does she present a detailed portrayal of the rulers of the Egyptian empire as a way to reflect on the nature of power.[4] We learn that Gaius Julius Caesar and Cleopatra – referred to as the 'Sacred Couple' (Wheeler 2014: 24) – are remembered as the founders of the so-called

Pharoman empire. The appeal of the 'big man' narrative, in this case a 'big couple', is thus present in the fabric of the novel. However, Wheeler does not provide any further details on this divergence and its consequences. Instead, she describes in depth the world that Oken and Mabruke inhabit. Through their eyes, we discover other cultures and customs, but also the richness and beauty of both built and natural landscapes that they encounter in their journey. This use of ekphrasis, namely 'a demarcated description of a work of visual art, either real or imaginary' (Karastathi 2015: 94), to create an atmosphere of authenticity is the basis of worldbuilding in fantasy and science fiction writing.[5] Character development and plot are also important, but the setting contributes to producing that suspension of disbelief that is needed for a successful description of an alternate world. In those descriptions, Wheeler refers to traditional temples or palaces that are reminiscent of ancient Egyptian buildings. These are combined with unsuspected feats of engineering, such as a highway across the Sahara Desert, in a reinterpretation of Egypt as an international, albeit declining, superpower that maintains some of its traditional architectural forms.

Egypt as a Place of Monumentality

Egypt is often regarded as a place of monumentality, and *Three Princes* capitalizes on this idea. Oken, a prince from Britannia, feels at home at Memphis, which is, he claims, 'the capital of the world' (Wheeler 2014: 26). Wheeler introduces readers to the city as Oken strolls through its busy streets upon his return from a mission on the white plains of Novgorod in Rusland (Wheeler 2014: 22–6). She describes the neighbourhoods and the people who live there, highlighting the deep connection of Memphis to history and the way this is embodied in architecture:

> The Sacred Couple has walked in those courtyards. They had been carried along these very streets in litters made of the finest Lebanese cedar, resting on the shoulders of Roman guards. Altars, artwork, and architecture had remained unchanged here since those days, living tribute to the parents of civilization and of enlightened life.
>
> Wheeler 2014: 24–5

Wheeler not only presents the city as a stage where Julius Caesar and Cleopatra displayed their power, but she also categorizes these urbanistic achievements and monumental landmarks as tokens of civilization. These specific monuments may not have existed, but they evoke a concrete sense of grandeur and historical continuity.

While we get a general glimpse of Memphis as Oken leaves the coach station, it is on the description of specific buildings where Wheeler deploys ekphrasis as a literary device with gusto to transport the reader to an alternate Egypt.[6] Dannenberg (2008: 77) argues that one of the possible strategies of representation of fictional space in counterfactual narratives is the three-dimensionalization of space, which creates a 'concrete and detailed environment in tandem with the depiction of the cognitive process of recognition', and this is precisely what we see at work in *Three Princes*. For example, the Royal Palace is the setting of an audience with the Egyptian queen, in which she charges our protagonist with a secret mission to travel to Tawantinsuyu. In the description of this complex (Wheeler 2014: 43–63), we learn about the monumental scale of the buildings. There are sphinxes 'as big as real lions' (Wheeler 2014: 44) decorating the promenade. The private quarters of the royal family feature a balcony with marble tiles in red and black, and obsidian columns supporting 'scalloped archways above a railing of openwork designs' (Wheeler 2014: 47). This monumentality is accentuated by lavish ornamentation: Oken notes the cedarwood doors (Wheeler 2014: 43), the faience walls (Wheeler 2014: 47), the 'skilfully landscaped' private garden (Wheeler 2014: 56). Overall, Egypt's portrayal in Wheeler's alternate world very much reproduces popular characterizations of Egypt as a culture of monumentality, luxury and excess.

Through these descriptions, Wheeler is appealing to the readers' knowledge on ancient Egypt to set the narrative. Popular portrayals of Egypt – and *Three Princes* is no exception – exploit monumental architecture as a token that stands for Egyptian culture as a whole. The importance of widespread conceptions about Egypt in the construction of this alternate universe should not be underestimated: Singles (2013: 109–11) has emphasized the role of the audience in alternate fiction, highlighting how the perception of a plot as alternate depends on the readers' ability to understand it as such. In other words, something can only be identified as alternate when one is familiar with normative interpretations. While Singles focuses on historical contingency in her argumentation, *Three Princes* illustrates how the characterization of spaces would play a similar role in the evocation of an alternate setting. The spaces presented, such as the Royal Palace mentioned above, do not need to replicate existing architecture in order to be perceived as plausible descriptions of Egyptian settings. In his survey of Egyptianizing features in popular culture, Taterka (2016: 207) has noted that inspiration is often sought not in specific Egyptian monuments, but in a 'general and common image of pharaonic Egypt that we all share'. Evocation, rather than accuracy, is indeed the main focus of many of these cultural products.[7] In her application of 'possible worlds' theory to alternate history writings, Raghunath (2022) reflects on the ontological status of imagined architecture. Taking the Great Hall in Robert Harris' novel *Fatherland* (1992) as a case study, she argues that this building, which actualizes Speer's plan for the urbanism of Berlin, has a different ontological status to the existing architectural plans, but both buildings – the one on the historical plans and the one in the alternate reality described in *Fatherland* – are epistemologically related. This is a thought-provoking framework to assess built spaces in alternate history: they are often meant to evoke a particular setting on the basis of epistemological links.

An interesting observation is that architectural descriptions of the Pharoman empire do not feature pyramids, arguably one of the most widely recognized Egyptian structures, despite their being prominently featured on the book cover. This lack of pyramids contributes to the oddness of this uchronic scenario, eliminating any temptation by the reader to identify them ontologically as the pyramids of Giza. As Singles proposes (see above), our expectations of what Egypt should look like are being challenged so that this setting can be categorized clearly as a counterfactual world. In addition, I suspect that it may also be a narrative device to create a further contrast between Egypt and Tawantinsuyu, as pyramids are presented in Wheeler's descriptions of the latter's built environment. Be that as it may, Egypt's representation in this alternate nineteenth century CE does not seem to be reliant on pyramids, but rather on temples as material embodiments of Egyptian culture both at Memphis and in other cities across the empire. On their way to traverse the Atlantic, Oken and Mabruke arrive at Marrakech, an 'expensive, but friendly' tourist city sprinkled with finely carved alabaster shrines to Egyptian deities (Wheeler 2014: 86). Coincidentally, an opera by Verdi is being premiered at that time, and our protagonists do not miss the opportunity to continue their investigations at this exclusive social event (Wheeler 2014: 105–19).[8] The opera house itself is lavishly decorated, with architecture evoking that of an ancient Egyptian temple: 'the proscenium was Egyptian haeka glass, in the shape of classic Egyptian temple pylons, to show that the stage behind it was sacred ground' (Wheeler 2014: 107). The temple in this description is not only marking the opera house of Marrakech as an Egyptian space, but also as a sacred one.

Thus, temples are presented as the epitome of monumentality and a clear materialization of Egyptian identity. Temples are regarded as sacred spaces, and hence imbued with a sense of changelessness and atemporality that is typical of popular representations of ancient Egypt. Indeed, Wheeler explicitly characterizes temple architecture as an expression of timelessness: 'Memphis, however, was a temple, solemn, stone-cut, clean, and eternal. Melodious deep-throated bells pealing forth the hours and the days wore a pattern of timelessness. The night sky above Egypt was the colour of eternity' (Wheeler 2014: 23). Memphis, the 'capital of the world', is a temple, and this portrayal invites us to see the Egyptian empire as a whole as a place of monumentality, sacredness and monotony. I return to this idea in my discussion of Orientalism and third spaces below.

Egypt as a Place of Technological Advancement

Wheeler reuses shapes and materials expected in Egyptian architecture in order to create a sense of familiarity and continuity, ensuring that her readership finds that connection with ancient Egypt. The setting is, however, actualized and complemented by the introduction of technological developments that place the action in a brave new nineteenth century CE, in line with the steampunk aesthetic of the novel. As defined by Rose (2009: 320), steampunk refers to 'a set of recent speculative fictions (that is, sf, fantasy, horror, and weird stories) that are set in or engage with the nineteenth century in a variety of ways. They are frequently (but not always) alternate history stories where the break from our own history [. . .] is a matter of technology.'[9] The introduction of unsuspected technology contributes to that suspension of disbelief and the construction of a counterfactual world: readers familiarized with normative interpretations would regard these developments not only as anachronistic, but also as particularly surprising because Egypt is seldom presented as a technologically advanced place in popular imagination. Some of those scientific advancements in the case of *Three Princes* include new building and decoration materials, such as 'haeka glass', on which images can be projected (Wheeler 2014: 110), or 'spinglass', lamps based on fibre-optic technology (Wheeler 2014: 61), but perhaps the most striking innovations described are those pertaining to travel.

The Egyptian empire is thoroughly connected by a dense tapestry of elevated highways (Wheeler 2014: 58) that position Memphis at the very heart of that side of the world. It is indicative that, in its association with technology, the Pharoman empire is here presented as essentially more Roman than Egyptian. The statement that 'all roads led to Memphis' (Wheeler 2014: 26) makes an identification with networks of ancient Roman roads all the more explicit. Some of Caesar's highways are a feat of engineering. For example, the Great Sahara

Highway is described as 'soaring over the desert sands on ancient aqueduct structures, a straight line of stonework arches from Memphis to the Atlas Hills' (Wheeler 2014: 65). The hostility of the imposing landscape needs to be tamed and overcome with engineering hacks; for example, windscreens are installed to keep out the desert sands (Wheeler 2014: 66). However, roads eventually deteriorate (Wheeler 2014: 60), so Egypt is torn between either maintaining this imposing but traditional means of transport or embracing future technological innovations.

While Egypt makes use of impressive highways to facilitate communications and transport across the empire, the New World is privy to the secret of flying. Their aircrafts, called Quetzals, are built to resemble living birds; they are made of bamboo and tubes inflated with 'tlalocene', a gas that is lighter than air, that propels the wing-shaped sails (Wheeler 2014: 120–1). Flying technology has been known for centuries, with regular flying routes across major European cities having operated for over a hundred years. The most important aerodrome in this part of the world is located in Casablanca, marking the spot where inhabitants of the New World first landed on the other side of the Atlantic (Wheeler 2014: 118).

Technology is not simply a random addition to enhance the steampunk aesthetic of the novel, but fundamental to the plot itself, as it determines the stakes of the two main political superpowers in Wheeler's universe. Indeed, Egypt is presented as an empire whose power is based on the control of solar energy and light, while Tawantisuyu has a monopoly over air travel with their Quetzals. The queen of Egypt refers to these subtle dynamics as follows:

> We keep our radiance technology as secret as humanly possible – they keep their aeroship technology secret. We sell them spinglass lamps and radiance products. We just don't tell them how we manufacture them. We can build our own aerodromes and mooring towers, but we cannot buy Quetzals from them. We can only lease them. Building and repairing them, and the crew to fly them, are a New World exclusive as well.
>
> Wheeler 2014: 62

Technology, in this way, creates a delicate power balance, which is about to be threatened if Tawantinsuyu succeeds in reaching the moon. Rieder (2008: 29–33) has demonstrated how an 'ideology of progress' lies at the intersection of colonialism and science fiction, not only due to the uneven distribution of technology, but also due to the portrayal of some societies as having – or lacking – an ability to yield scientific innovations. In this way, technology is often used to otherize within science fiction narratives, and *Three Princes* is a good example of this.

Overall, it seems like Egypt's strength does not lie in its current technological prowess, but in their cunning exploitation of natural resources (i.e. solar energy) and the maintenance of their old engineering achievements (i.e. highways). Meanwhile, the rest of the world is moving forward, seeking to overthrow Egyptian supremacy in the name of progress. This contrast between Egypt and the rest of the world is expressed by Oken's reflections as he contemplates the city of Memphis upon this arrival: 'Elsewhere, the world wheeled forward on aqueduct highways and on the spreading sails of Quetzals floating through the skies. In Memphis, time paused, pleased with this eternal moment' (Wheeler 2014: 25). Egypt, embodied in its capital city, is timeless, unchanging, unpreoccupied by the rest of the world. The static nature of Egypt, demonstrated by the continuity of architectural models as well as by the limitations of technological achievements, is illustrative of an Orientalist approach to ancient cultures, which is deployed, perhaps unwittingly, in Wheeler's novel. I discuss the role of Orientalism in the construction of Egypt in *Three Princes* in the following section.

Eternal Egypt: Orientalism and a 'Third Place'

Architecture and engineering are crucial in the construction of this imagined world, which, for the purposes of this novel, needs to be recognizably ancient Egyptian. The actors express and distinguish their identity through architecture in the narrative, and the reader is invited to do likewise. But why would 'modern' Egypt be so readily identified with 'ancient' temples? Why has modern technology had such a limited impact on traditional architectural forms in this alternate nineteenth century CE Egyptian empire? The theoretical framework of Orientalism may help explain the mechanisms at play here.

Orientalism and the Western Gaze

Edward W. Said (1935–2003) was a comparative literature professor of Palestinian descent. He is best known for *Orientalism* ([1974] 2003), a work that would sow the seeds of postcolonial studies for its articulation of how imperialism has influenced subjective perceptions as well as supposedly objective studies of the Orient. Many criticisms of Orientalism can be advanced, but the ideas that Said developed still constitute a thought-provoking interpretative framework to assess and problematize 'Western' representations of 'the East'.

As the name indicates, Orientalism is related to the 'Orient', an analytical category encompassing places that are not connected to each other except through a Western gaze. Said ([1974] 2003: 71–9) explains this lumping together of disparate entities through his idea of imaginative geographies.[10] Imaginative geographies are an important basis for the constructions of spatial as well as social identities; imagined boundaries reaffirm our perceived distinctiveness, separating us from 'the Other'.[11] Despite being theoretically defined through its geographical location, in practice the Orient is constructed through Eurocentric discourses that materialize and reproduce an existing power imbalance. The Orient, Said claims, does not exist as such; what exists is a category that Western scholars created. In this sense, the Orient is not a place but an idea.

According to Said ([1974] 2003: 2–3), Orientalism can be understood in three different yet interrelated ways: an academic discipline; a mindset based on dichotomies; and an idea of domination and subjugation. As an academic discipline, Orientalism shapes Western knowledge of the Orient, which is in turn used to control and justify political domination of the area. As part of these strategies of domination, Orientalist authors would focus on the 'Classical' period of the societies in which they were interested (Said [1974] 2003: 74); in doing so, not only did they seek to contrast their alleged 'present barbarism to [their] former classical greatness' (Said [1974] 2003: 108), but they were also creating that very canon themselves on the basis of their own expectations of what constitutes 'high culture'. Knowledge is power, and, since knowledge is not discovered but constructed, Orientalism self-perpetuates a power dynamic that benefits the West. This evolutionary reading of cultures and search for bygone golden eras should be familiar to anyone involved in the traditional academic study of ancient Egypt. Egyptology is undeniably a product of Orientalism, in the sense that ancient Egypt is a constructed unit of analysis, artificially delineated in geographical as well as chronological terms.[12]

For the purposes of this chapter, I am mostly interested in how Orientalism deploys a binary opposition of East–West in an attempt to assign meaning to those imaginative geographies mentioned above. The East tends to be presented as a (distorted) mirror image of the West on the basis of some tropes of difference (Mitchell [1998] 2009: 409): the East is static where the West is dynamic; the East is religious where the West is secular; the East is passive where the West is active; the East is tyrannical and oppressive where the West is democratic and forward-thinking. These tropes of difference also extend to many other spheres, such as the use of violence, irrational thought and lust.[13] What these dichotomies are doing is effectively otherizing the East by means of a self-affirmation of Western identity as the opposite of 'the Orient'. This otherization – anchored in colonialism and imaginative geographies – is present in a variety of media, ranging from romanticized travellers accounts to artistic representations, scholarly compilations, and, of course, popular culture.[14]

Colonial structures of domination and control are at the heart of much of science fiction. Rieder (2008: 15) goes as far as to claim that colonialism is not a 'hidden truth' of science fiction, but part of the genre's own texture.[15] Indeed, imaginative geographies are also a feature of science fiction, fantasy, and any literary genre that allows for a subversion of reality. The political, emotional and ethical potential of this intellectual exercise should not be underestimated.[16] As Warf (2002: 34) has noted, alternate history could in principle allow for an exploration of altered geographical power dynamics that would show that 'received categories of structuring space are no more "real" or proper than the arbitrary lenses that we use to make sense of our past'. For example, *Three Princes* destabilizes expected power dynamics by presenting Egypt and Tawantinsuyu as unsuspected political actors, hence redrawing Victorian England as a relatively minor subject within this Trans-Atlantic power game.

However, the extent of this subversion needs to be nuanced. New worlds can be created *ex nihilo*, but they will often be based on some existing knowledge in order to appeal to the expectations of the reader. This is because, as Balfe (2004: 76) has noted, these fantasy worlds are 'socially embedded and draw upon pre-existing cultural discourses', which are especially notable in constructions of and encounters with Otherness.[17] In the case of places like Egypt, that pre-existing knowledge will often rely on Orientalist tropes of difference, so any imagined space based on common conceptions of Egypt tends to reproduce the power dynamics described above. I argue that this is the case in Ramona Wheeler's novel, where monumentality can implicitly be a consequence of the static nature of Egypt.

As mentioned in the previous section, Egyptian monumental spaces have been used as a backdrop to express ideas of grandeur and opulence that highlight the perceived exoticism of Egypt. This evocation of place plays a crucial role in *Three Princes*, where descriptions of temples and palaces perpetuate the otherization of Egypt. This allows Wheeler to craft a new world that is indeed based on existing architecture and that plays with the expectations of her readership. In this alternate nineteenth century CE, Egypt is still embodied through the continuity of some architectural models, such as temples, that endorse an essentially Orientalist image of Egypt as a never-changing, static society. However, these architectural expressions are not meant to replicate Egypt, but to recreate an alternative reality – with flying aircrafts and spinglass lamps – inspired by it. In this sense, they are creating a 'third space' that perpetuates those tropes of difference.

Wheeler's Egyptian Empire as a 'Third Space'

One of the main criticisms towards Said's theories is that he emphasizes how the West creates meaning about the East, but he seems to disregard the agency of the latter in that process. Several scholars have claimed that Said's dichotomy should be nuanced, but here I would like to focus on Homi K. Bhabha and his seminal book *The Location of Culture* (1994), because it opens thought-provoking avenues to explore the role of counterfactual worlds in fiction. Bhabha challenges Said's interpretation of Orientalism as something that was mainly formed in the past, finding a line of continuity up to the present. Instead, he is interested in how colonial relations continue to reproduce themselves. In Bhabha's understanding, any impositions or negotiations of cross-cultural contacts occur in what he calls a 'third space of enunciation' (Bhabha 1994: 37). This space is a contradictory 'in-between' place where individuals and communities interact, and cultural identities emerge. A third space cannot be represented, but it 'constitutes the discursive conditions of enunciation that ensure that the meaning and symbols of culture have no primordial unity or fixity; that even the same signs can be appropriated, translated, rehistoricized and read anew' (Bhabha 1994: 55). This means that there is not such a thing as 'pure' cultures, as they will all derive from and create meaning in this fuzzy third space that exists as a consequence of hybridity.

While the idea of third space has often been used to assess power imbalances in colonial relations, I argue that it can productively be employed to elucidate the construction of alternative spaces in counterfactual narratives as well, and that the setting presented to us in *Three Princes* can in fact be understood as a third space. The analysis of imagined worlds as third spaces is not new. Pavlik (2011), for example, rejects conventional dichotomies between 'real' and 'unreal' and sees fantasy worlds in children's literature as a performative 'thirdspaces' arising from social practice.[18] Along the same lines, imaginative geographies in counterfactual fiction are neither real nor unreal, but an in-between space that appeals to the readers' historical (and geographical) understanding. Those settings are often designed to be an evocation of a given culture – or, in Said's terms, a representation of that culture. Since the time described is subverted due to a divergence in the past, physical and cultural settings are our only references as a reader to situate the action. Following Raghunath's reasoning cited above, these worlds are not presented as an ontological alternative, but as an epistemological one. And what role does hybridity play in this context?

The so-called Pharoman empire embraces the idea of hybridity, presenting itself as an amalgam of cultural influences, as reflected in the local architecture of Memphis and its ornamentation. For example, Wheeler highlights the cosmopolitanism of Memphis' population in the following passage:

> He crossed through a residential neighbourhood, street after street of vertical, multistory [*sic*] houses pressed up against each other [. . .]. Hand painted on these housefronts were wildly innocent designs showing the personalities of the owners, family identity tattooed on the skin of their homes. Every kind of art could be found here: ancient hieroglyphics [*sic*] painted alongside Celtic maze designs, Danish realism, and Spanish surrealism. In these neighbourhoods the house art was as well known as the family's name. These were people proud to be in Memphis, even as part of backstreet life.
>
> Wheeler 2014: 24

The capital, and by extension the empire, is seen as a melting pot, where regional trends get subsumed into a reinterpretation of Egypt. In the context of *Three Princes*, Memphis is presented as the ultimate third space: 'Memphis herself was utterly unchanged, changeless, with only the patterns of leaves against the sky and thickened branches of the sycamores lining the avenue to show that time had any hold here' (Wheeler 2014: 25). In this counterfactual narrative, historical progression has been subverted, and Wheeler explores the idea of a hybrid culture based on built environments. This is indeed an alternate time, but it is clear that it is also an alternate place.

Despite explicit references to hybridity in her descriptions of the urban landscape, the identity of the story's protagonists is very much mediated by Egyptian imperialistic efforts. Oken, born in Britannia but brought to Memphis at twelve years of age, is a good example of this tension between regional and imperial identity, as he felt that 'he had been born in the foggy world of Mercia, but Memphis was his home' (Wheeler 2014: 22). Along the same lines, Wheeler notes that 'Oken knew he would always call Memphis home, no matter who he was or where he had been born' (Wheeler 2014: 25). It is interesting to note how some of the aspects discussed in the previous section – namely monumentality and unchangingness – inspire a sense of belonging and identity in this man, who is originally from the fringes of the empire: 'Oken walked down those midnight avenues, feeling the timeless presence of millennia of history. [...] He felt the thrill of association with the grandeur of such ancient lineages and ageless beauty' (Wheeler 2014: 26). The avenues are said to embody the depth of time of the Egyptian empire, shaping the identity of those who walk these streets.

This uchronic scenario is hence presented as a third space that crystalizes the social identity of the protagonists in architectural terms. Third spaces do not base their cultural meanings on Eurocentric historical narratives, because there is no such a thing as a separate, 'pure' culture. In Bhabha's (1994: 54) own words, a third space 'challenges our sense of the historical identity of culture as a homogenizing, unifying force'. This is why his concept of culture is not 'located' in a historical time: 'Cultural diversity is also the representation of a radical rhetoric of the separation of totalized cultures that live unsullied by the intertextuality of their historical locations, safe in the Utopianism of a mythic memory of a unique collective identity' (Bhabha 1994: 50). In this sense, the use of architecture as an expression of identity in counterfactual narratives may serve to redefine the limits and possibilities of cultural interaction in the creation of a historical time that never was. Wheeler's Egypt is a uchronic embodiment of Bhabha's third space: a place where historical narratives – and historical points of divergence – take a back seat, and symbols of culture are re-constructed and acquire new readings.

Conclusions: Ancient Egypt in Modern Egypt

Three Princes is a traditional counterfactual narrative in which we are presented with an altered historical line. However, it does not seem that a questioning of and reflection about the nature of history is the main concern of the author. Instead, the creation of an alternate world on the basis of known architectural landmarks seems to be taking precedence. As Dannenberg (2008: 65) puts it, 'time is so unfathomable and elusive that the human mind often resorts to the more concrete parameters of space to grasp it', so Wheeler is effectively using space to create an alternate time.

Historicity is not the most important aspect of this imagined world. As I point out, *Three Princes* does not elaborate on the point of divergence leading to this moment in time, neither does it dwell on events of this alternate past – of which we only obtain some glimpses through comments *in passim* and artistic representations. It seems that Wheeler is not as interested in what would have happened, but rather in what the world would have looked like had Egypt become a major political stakeholder. This shift from historical narrative to description of space is telling. If, following Singles (2013: 8), we understand alternate history as an active genre where the reader is required to 'complete' the narrative and identify parts of it as subversive, it is easy to see that those worlds that never were are indeed a reflection of our own.

Overall, the world created by Wheeler may seem contradictory. On the one hand, it presents a new historical line with Egypt in a position of dominance. On the other, it fails to challenge Orientalist tropes of difference by presenting Egypt as a declining superpower whose authority is being questioned on different fronts. This goes in line with Balfe's (2004: 77–9) observations about fantasy as a genre: even though in theory the sky is the limit when it comes to constructing fantasy worlds, in practice we often encounter Western heroes battling against an Eastern evil Other. Wheeler attempts to subvert this balance, but her characterization of Egypt is embedded within a contemporary discourse that continues to present Egypt as an eternally static Other.

Notes

1 For a concise introduction to alternate history as a genre, including a classification according to the nature of the historical divergence (or 'nexus') presented, see Hellekson (2001: 3–9). See also Singles (2013: 14–26) on the limitations of these taxonomies.

2 In this sense, *Three Princes* would be a 'true alternate history' according to Hellekson's categorization (2001: 7–8), because the narrative takes place years (in this case centuries) after a crucial 'nexus event' would have changed the course of history.

3 For a discussion of how and why historical entities (including historical characters) remain constant in counterfactual narratives despite changes to the timeline, see Gallagher (2018: 11–15).

4 Singles (2013: 281) refers to these kinds of alternate history that do not focus on contingency and necessity tentatively as 'meta-alternate history'.

5 For a topofocal reading of fantasy settings, see e.g. Ekman (2013), who argues that place is as important as character or plot.

6 Karastathi (2015: 95) has proposed that one of the main uses of ekphrasis is the spatialization of narrative fiction. In this case, the description of architecture has a similar purpose.

7 On a similar use of architecture to create an alternative Egypt, see Cromwell's (2022: 5–15) analysis of the Egyptian 'palace' on the gamescape of *Persona 5*, where

the combination of ruins and known architecture create a recognizable space that, however, does not conform to reality.

8 The opera itself deals with the rescue of the Anasazi from starvation 600 years before the present (in the novel) and the role played by an Inca-Egyptian coalition to save them, thus providing a rare window into the history of this alternate universe by means of art and performance. On the use of imagined art within uchronic narratives, see Stevens in this volume.

9 While I have highlighted the steampunk *aesthetic* of this novel, I hesitate to categorize it as stereotypical steampunk. First, and following Rose's definition, the main departure from our timeline is not technological; instead, technological difference seems to be a consequence of a historical divergence in the past (in this case, the union of Julius Caesar and Cleopatra). Second, steampunk takes pride on presenting historical details – or 'easter eggs' – with minute accuracy, inviting readers to engage in the practice of microhistory (Rose 2009: 324–5). As argued in this chapter, Wheeler does not seem interested in historical accuracy, and the inclusion of a couple of historical characters (e.g. Otto von Bismarck) may not warrant the classification of this novel as traditional steampunk.

10 Said built on Bachelard ([1958] 2014) in his development of 'imaginative geographies' as a category of analysis.

11 On this point, see Gregory (1994).

12 I have explored the links of Orientalism and conceptions of ancient Egypt – with a focus on their impact on popular representations of Egypt – elsewhere (see Olabarria 2019: 190–3; 2020: 5–7).

13 On the use of industrial advances to define an opposition of East and West, see the concept of 'techno-Orientalism' (e.g. Roh, Huang, and Niu 2015), which is transmedially recurrent in science fiction.

14 See, for example, Gregory's (1995) fascinating study of the imaginative geographies produced by Florence Nightingale and Gustave Flaubert in their respective travels in Egypt in the mid-nineteenth century.

15 On the role that colonialism, and especially the 'colonial gaze', played in the emergence of science fiction as a genre, see Rieder (2008: 6–12).

16 See Gilbert and Lambert (2010) on how to approach counterfactual geographies from an emotional and ethical point of view.

17 On the centrality of 'the Other' in both science fiction and postcolonial literature, see Hoagland and Sarwal (2010: 7–15) and Kerslake (2010: 8–24).

18 Here Pavlik (2011: 239–40) follows Edward W. Soja (1996), who reinterprets Bhabha's concept from the perspective of cultural geography.

3.3

Antiquity Interrupted: Partial Receptions as Counterfactuals

Jesse Weiner
Hamilton College

Introduction

As the case studies in this volume testify, counterfactuals provide points of departure for narratives of alternate history, and, in my own study, of literary history. In this chapter, I explore the potential of counterfactual reworkings of specific works of literature, rather than properly historical narratives. In so doing, I aim to highlight the power of 'terminal' and 'partial' receptions (as I call them) to redirect and reflect back upon the narratives of their source texts. After some theoretical scaffolding where I clarify my use of 'terminal' and 'partial' receptions, as well as 'interruptions', I present three case studies. The first is Hélisenne de Crenne's sixteenth-century translation into French of the first four books of Virgil's *Aeneid*. The second is Kurt Vonnegut's *Cat's Cradle*, which I argue (and have previously argued) presents a sustained reception of Homer's *Odyssey*, but one in which the Odysseus-figure never escapes Calypso's island. The third case study is Ferdinando Baldi's western film, *Il Pistolero dell'Ave Maria*, which adapts Aeschylus' *Oresteia*, as well as the *Electra*s of Sophocles and Euripides, to nineteenth-century Mexico, but excises the *Eumenides* from its narrative. I suggest that these alternative narratives – which essentially alter their source texts by 'interrupting' them before their canonical ending and proposing a new development of the story – are transformative in their presentation of alternate literature with dynamics similar to their counterparts in speculative history. In all three case studies, I argue that what I call the 'interruptions' of ancient narratives function as counterfactuals, inviting us to revisit and reflect upon classical literature by denying the resolution of their source texts.

Partial Receptions and Literary Counterfactuals

The mechanics of historical counterfactuals often follow a pattern.[1] First, it is imagined that an historical event did not happen, or something that never happened did happen. For example, Niall Ferguson's (1999: 2) opening to *Virtual History* asks, 'What if there had been no English Civil War? What if there had been no American War of Independence? . . . What if the Russians had won the Cold War? What if Kennedy had lived?'[2] In Classics we might ask, 'What if the Greeks had lost at Marathon, or Caesar at Pharsalus?' 'What if the Pisonian conspiracy (a failed plot to assassinate Nero in 65 CE, for which Seneca and the twenty-five-year-old Lucan lost their lives) had succeeded (with implications both for the principate and for literary output)?' Second, the narrative proceeds to speculate what would have or might have happened in the aftermath of this historical counterfactual, a mutation in the *series causarum* ('series of causes'). Frederick Pohl's short story 'The Deadly Mission of Phineas Snodgrass' (1962) provides a representative and classically engaged exemplum of a historical counterfactual: with the best of intentions, the allusively named Phineas travels back in time to Augustan Rome, where he introduces modern medicine (the counterfactual), which thus initiates an uchronia (alternative timeline). In the aftermath, the planet suffers from exponentially increased overpopulation and ecological collapse. As resolution – spoiler alert – someone else later travels back in time and assassinates Snodgrass on the Palatine, and so prevents this dystopian alternative future/history from coming into fruition. As Pohl's story concludes, 'To the great (if only potential) joy of some quintillions of never-to-be-born persons, Darkness blessedly fell'.[3] As this example demonstrates, counterfactuals provide an opportunity to reimagine the past and reflect on the present, raising questions about determinism, contingency and causality.

But what if (to adapt the speculative template of counterfactuals) the concept of counterfactuals were applied not only to history but also, perhaps metatextually, to fictional and mythological literature? And what if these counterfactuals were not triggered by the points of departure but rather by the termini of their stories? Taking up these questions and building on some of my previous work (especially Weiner 2015 and 2018), this chapter explores the dynamics of partial receptions. By partial receptions, I refer to works that display sustained engagement (as opposed to passing allusions) to a particular source text, but which only adapt, translate, or allude to a portion of the source text, rather than the whole. How are the classics transformed when that focus on only one portion of the text ('partial' reception) allows us to explore new alternative endings of the ancient narratives? What if an *Iliad* ends with Patroclus' death? What if the speech of Aristophanes concludes a rewriting of Plato's *Symposium*, without Socrates ever given his turn to speak?

At the outset, I wish to distinguish the reception of a text from the reception of myth. I treat a finished work of artistic production (at least most works) as a more or less fixed material object (the *Iliad* as it comes down to us; a sculpture of Bernini) in its moment of reception. Of course, art is always subject to reinterpretation, manuscripts have textual variants and lacunae, a sculpture might break or lose its paint; such is the nature of materiality. However, no reasonable reader of any edition of the *Iliad* (at least that I know of) that contained all twenty-four books would question that Patroclus dies by Hector's hand, and I suspect that the fact of Antigone's burial of Polynices in Sophocles' *Antigone* has never been a point of contention. These are basic plot points within a specific narrative. In this sense, literary counterfactuals bear much in common with historical ones. Of course, the target texts, films, etc. are themselves 'literary'. But I here distinguish between alternative history (to return to the Pohl example, what if Augustus had been gifted with modern medical technology?) and alternative literature (what if Odysseus, received from the *Odyssey*, never leaves Calypso's island?). In both cases the target (receiving) texts are literary, but in the Pohl example, the point of reference is historical, while in the second example (which points towards my Kurt Vonnegut case study below) the source is literary.

Greek and Roman myth was always malleable, mutable and multiple in its versions and forms, and Richard Buxton (1994: 219) emphasizes 'the seemingly endless variations of Greek mythology'. Hesiod and Ovid present different creation myths. Some ancient authors and sculptors present Prometheus as *plasticator* – the moulder of humans – while others suggest that human beings came into being in some other way. And so on. We might think of Iphigenia, Agamemnon's daughter, whom he sacrificed at the outset of Trojan war, according to the mythological tradition (Agamemnon had offended the goddess Artemis, who grounded the Argive ships until the human sacrifice was completed). It is one thing to consider Iphigenia's death in Euripides' *Iphigenia in Aulis* (she is sacrificed) counterfactual to her survival in his earlier *Iphigenia among the Taurians* (which one might argue is counterfactual to her death in Aeschylus' *Agamemnon* and other texts), but it is a somewhat different thing in my view to argue that either play is properly counterfactual to the *myth* in its canonical versions. I confine what follows to counterfactuals in inter*textual* relationships and receptions.

I present three brief case studies in classical reception, which we might consider terminal literary counterfactuals, in that the target text truncates the narrative of its source text in ways that prove dynamic: an *Aeneid* that ends with the fourth book, and so concludes with Dido's suicide and erases Aeneas' later accomplishments (Hélisenne de Crenne's sixteenth-century translation of Virgil; Weiner 2018; 2024); an *Odyssey* in which the Odysseus-figure never escapes Calypso's island (Kurt Vonnegut's 1963 novel *Cat's Cradle*; Weiner 2015); an *Oresteia* that cuts off abruptly with the murders of its Clytemnestra- and Aegisthus-figures and so lacks the *Eumenides*' explorations of justice, democracy, and the civilizing transformations of the rule of law (Ferdinando Baldi's 1969 film, *Il Pistolero dell'Ave Maria*). Each post-classical work offers a sustained and transformative intertextual relationship with an ancient antecedent, and yet they are varied not only in their genres but also in their modes of reception. Hélisenne's *Eneydes* is a translation, albeit one in which the translator asserts her authority over the text.[4] *Cat's Cradle* is more subtle in its intertextuality, but it nevertheless offers a sustained pattern of allusion to its Homeric source. *Il Pistolero dell'Ave Maria* is, in Hardwick's (2003: 9) framework, an 'adaptation': 'a version of the source developed for a different purpose or insufficiently close to count as a translation'. All of these works might fall into Hardwick's (2003: 10) category of 'refiguration', by 'selecting and reworking material from a previous or contrasting tradition'. In all of these works, I view their partial receptions as counterfactual, in that they imagine an alternate ending for their source narratives.

By exploring these three works, I argue that terminal, literary counterfactuals perform critical interventions on their source texts, interventions that have the radical power to transform ancient themes, messages and genres. Each partial reception, I suggest, asks counterfactual 'what if' questions of ancient literature with profound implications. These interventions, in my view, function as historical counterfactuals, albeit on a literary plane. Whereas historical counterfactuals invite us to think through the contingent 'what ifs' of the historical record, literary counterfactuals invite us to revisit the themes, ethics and structures behind art and storytelling. As Tony Keen (2006) writes, 'alternate history . . . makes us ask new questions about the ancient world', questions that often prompt reflections on our own society and our relationship with antiquity. The literary counterfactuals for which I argue prompt similar questions, albeit through interventions upon the storytelling, rather than the historical record, of the past.

What if the *Aeneid* Ended with Dido's Death?

In the mid-sixteenth century, Marguerite Briet translated the first four books of the *Aeneid* into French prose under her pseudonym, Hélisenne de Crenne.[5] In her own day, Hélisenne (most scholars refer to Hélisenne by her forename, rather than 'de Crenne') was a successful novelist and epistolary writer, publishing with the prominent Denys Janot. Today, however, Hélisenne's *Aeneid* (*Les Quatre premiers livres des Eneydes du treselegant poete Virgile, traduictz de Latin en prose Françoyse*; 1541) is little known and less read (only three manuscripts are known to survive), yet it marks a vitally important moment in feminism, translation and the classics.[6] As Diane S. Wood argues in her study of Hélisenne, the author was 'a woman on the cutting edge of her era who both exploited and innovated literary tradition', and, through her writing, Hélisenne positioned herself as a learned and noncompliant *virago* – a female warrior – and 'attempted to achieve parity for her gender' in a radically patriarchal age.[7]

Sharon Marshall (2011: 9) argues that Hélisenne performed 'a very specific type of reception; one in which the translator occupies a particularly authoritative position as a stand-in for the author and is able to exert their influence over the interpretation of the text'. Hélisenne's pen name adapts Elissa, the Phoenician name of Dido, and Hélisenne thus signals deep interest and personal investment in the Carthaginian queen.[8] This relationship is sustained throughout her work since, in her novel *Les Angoisses douloureuses qui procèdent d'amours* ('*The Torments of Love*'; 1538), Hélisenne calls her female protagonist by the same name.[9]

. . . *avec les vents s'envola sa jeune vie* ('her young life flew away with the winds'; 4.34). Thus ends Hélisenne's *Eneydes* with her rendering of Virgil's *in ventos vita recessit* ('her life withdrew into the winds'; *Aeneid* 4.705). By severing her narrative at the end of the fourth book, Hélisenne's *Aeneid* concludes with Dido's abandonment and suicide, and Hélisenne erases Aeneas' later triumphs and Rome's imperial destiny from the text. The final image is of Dido, while Aeneas becomes 'a feckless and manipulative lover', in the words of Marshall (2011: 13), and 'Hélisenne challenges Virgil's presentation of the hero'. Wood notes:

> . . . her [Hélisenne] statement in the 'Epistre dédicatoire' that the *Aeneid* recounted 'les gests de illustrissimes Troyens, Et principalement de'Enée' (EN fol. 1v.), [the actions of the most illustrious Trojans, and principally of Aeneas]. Departing from Virgil's emphasis on Aeneas' quest to found Rome, she makes Dido the central figure of her account. Reversing the traditional subject-object relation, Aeneas is reduced to being the object of Dido's obsession.
>
> Wood 2000: 148[10]

Hélisenne's *Eneydes* partial translation represents a transformative counterfactual. By translating only the first four books of the *Aeneid*, Hélisenne produced not an incomplete translation but rather a radical intervention, or even interruption, upon Virgil's epic. While she does not use the term specifically of reception, I find Rena Fraden's (2012) 'interruption' valuable for thinking about the dynamics of partial receptions; this notion refers to meaningful engagements between author, audience and source text in the construction of new and varied interpretations of works of art. The '*premiers*' of Hélisenne's title is important, in that it signals this erasure. Hélisenne calls attention to the full narrative of Virgil's *Aeneid*, while effectively performing a *damnatio* on Aeneas' life after Dido. Through this counterfactual, the *Aeneid* becomes not a celebration of Roman nationalism but instead a proto-feminist tale of tragic romance and male perfidy (*homme perfide*), which problematizes the victimization of women (cf. Broomhall 2002: 207). Hélisenne's full phrase (voiced through Dido) to describe Aeneas at the outset of *Aeneid* 4.15, *homme perfide desloyal et impiteux* ('perfidious, disloyal, and impetuous man') amplifies Virgil's more concise *perfide* at *Aeneid* 4.305. Likewise, in the above quotation, Hélisenne's *jeune vie* ('young life') goes beyond Virgil's simpler *vita* ('life') to emphasize the tragic pathos of the heroine's life interrupted in its prime (Marshall 2011: 192 n. 123; Worth-Stylianou 2002: 156). Hélisenne conditions her readers to sympathize with Dido and 'the much prolonged suffering of the unfortunate woman' (*la trop longue peine e l'infoelice dame*; summary, *Aeneid* 4.34) amplifying and extending the final thirteen lines of *Aeneid* (4.693–705). In Virgil, women are frequently an obstacle to or a distraction from the fulfilment of male ambition; leaving aside divine figures, in addition to Dido, we might think of Creusa in *Aeneid* 2, the burning of the ships in *Aeneid* 5, and the role of Amata in the epic's second half. Hélisenne adapts the same poem to defend women and to contribute to the *querelle des femmes* ('the woman question'), a broad cultural debate beginning in the Renaissance about the nature of women and their place in society.[11] Jerry C. Nash (2000: 376) suggests that Hélisenne 'plead[s] for ... what we call today literary equality feminism'. Rather than one of several of Virgil's exempla of the unfortunate human cost of empire, Dido becomes a central figure of the *Eneydes*, and, through her structural intervention upon the *Aeneid*, Hélisenne amplifies Dido's abandonment, heartbreak and suicide to the climax of the entire translation.

Susan Broomhall (2021) finds Hélisenne's translation of 'Virgil ... radical, creatively embellishing the original from a female perspective with a highly sympathetic presentation of Dido's plight and women's loyalty in love'. The very form of Hélisenne's translation underscores this shift in focus and tone, working in tandem with the work's terminal counterfactual; by electing to write in prose with a chapter format rather than in epic verse, Hélisenne transmutes martial epic – a traditionally masculine genre with deep roots in imperialism – into a work more closely resembling a tragic romantic novel.[12]

What if Odysseus Never Escaped Ogygia?: Kurt Vonnegut's *Cat's Cradle*

Kurt Vonnegut's novel, *Cat's Cradle* ([1963] 1988), is a post-Second World War apocalyptic tale, which satirizes the Cold War arms race while expressing very serious technoscientific fears of weapons of mass destruction and ecocatastrophe. As I have previously argued, Vonnegut subtly structures the novel's plot through Homer's *Odyssey* and Odysseus' 'heroic' journey (Weiner 2015). I argue that Vonnegut's allusive programme should not be seen as an illustration of Tony Keen's (2006) concept of 'ghosting', in which 'no direct influence of classical materials can be detected'; rather, it channels at least three intertextual dynamics from Lorna Hardwick's (2003: 9) reception lexicon: the novel demonstrates 1) 'correspondences', 'aspects of a new work that which directly relate to the characteristic of the source'; 2) 'dialogue', 'mutual relevance of source and receiving texts and contexts'; and 3) 'hybrid intervention', referring to 'a fusion of material from classical and other cultures reworking the source to create a political, social or aesthetic critique of the receiving society'. It is due to the existence of these sustained intertextual dynamics that I argue that *Cat's Cradle* is a good example of interrupted reception.

The novel's protagonist, John (allusively, 'Call me Jonah'; Vonnegut [1963] 1988: 11) identifies as a fraternity member at Cornell University ('I am a Cornell DU' [Delta Upsilson]; Vonnegut [1963] 1988: 14). John travels to Ilium (again in New York) in the pursuit of knowledge as he researches a book. Afterwards, as he continues his research, John winds up terminally trapped on an island with a beautiful young woman, an island culturally dominated by a calypso singer and his spiritual influence.[13] Thus, I argue, John is an Odysseus-figure as a Greek from Ithaca, who travels to Troy and winds up confined on Calypso's island.[14] Promethean themes of technology and pursuit of scientific knowledge for curiosity's sake dominate the novel, which somewhat mirror Odysseus' own motives during the *Odyssey*'s *apologoi* (books 9–12). The forms of intertextuality are more understated than those of Hélisenne's translation and Baldi's adaptation, but Vonnegut's allusions do structure the novel in a sustained way, and they serve as a terminal counterfactual, in that they offer an *Odyssey* with no homecoming and no familial reconciliation. Motivated by the pursuit of knowledge after leaving Ithaca and Troy, John finds himself on an Ogygia of sorts (Ogygia being the island where Calypso lived). However, in contrast to Homer's Odysseus, John never makes it home. There is no raft, no divine intervention, and the novel ends with death, suicide in despair, and the implication that John himself will terminate his own life in defiance of a god who may or may not exist: 'I would take from the ground some of the blue-white poison that makes statues of men; and I would make a statue of myself, lying on my back, grinning horribly, and thumbing my nose at You Know Who' (Vonnegut [1963] 1988: 191).

Cat's Cradle's allusive system offers a literary counterfactual. Whereas Hélisenne's *Eneydes* is more neatly structural in terminating its source text with Virgil's fourth book, Vonnegut's *Cat's Cradle* effects something similar with its sustained reception of the *Odyssey*. If we read John as a failed Odysseus-figure who never gets off the island, this *Odyssey* becomes not a celebration of human ingenuity and technological innovation but instead a critique of twentieth-century technoscientific development. The atom bomb and the nuclear arms race loom in the background, introduced on the very first page: 'I began to collect material for a book to be called *The Day the World Ended* ... The book was to be an account of what important Americans had done on the day when the first atomic bomb was dropped on Hiroshima, Japan' (Vonnegut [1963] 1988: 11).

Odysseus never builds his raft, nor does he find a technological solution to listen to the Sirens' song of universal knowledge. In Homer, shipbuilding and navigation are emblematic of technology and hallmarks of civilization, and watercraft are the means of the hero's salvation.[15] In Vonnegut by contrast, a small boat unleashes a weapon of mass destruction ('ice-nine'), which triggers apocalyptic catastrophe (Vonnegut [1963] 1988: 174). The boat is suggestive of Odysseus' raft, but, whereas in Homer a small watercraft is Odysseus' instrument of escape from Ogygia, in Vonnegut it is the catalyst for permanent, lethal entrapment on an island. John, *Cat's Cradle*'s narrator, describes the event in Biblical terms ('Call me Jonah'). Like Odysseus, John is a survivor; he makes it through the initial catastrophe and lives long enough to write about its aftermath ('Here it is, the end of the world; and here I am, almost the very last man'; Vonnegut [1963] 1988: 190). Yet technology has created a world in which John no longer wants to live, and shortly before his implied suicide, John once again invokes the technoscientific horrors of the Second World War, making his narrative a ring composition of sorts. John quotes the Bokonon, the calypso singer and religious figure: 'Let us start our Republic with a chain of drug stores, a chain of grocery stores, a chain of gas chambers, and a national game. After that, we can write our Constitution' (Vonnegut [1963] 1988: 190). With this partial reception, Vonnegut reconfigures the *Odyssey*'s celebration of human ingenuity into a pessimistic tale of human folly and a caution against the pursuit of certain types of knowledge.[16]

Vonnegut thus presents a sustained but partial reception of the *Odyssey* and its mythological backstory, one in which its Odysseus-figure remains terminally trapped on Calypso's island. Like my other case studies, Vonnegut stages an interruption on his Homeric source text. Through the counterfactual erasure of Odysseus' escape, homecoming and triumph, technological ingenuity is turned from a Homeric marker of civilization and human development into a post-war harbinger of hubris and apocalyptic destruction.

What if the *Oresteia* Had No Third Act?: Ferdinando Baldi's *Il Pistolero dell'Ave Maria*

The Italian director Ferdinando Baldi's *Il Pistolero dell'Ave Maria* (1969, released for Anglophone audiences as *The Forgotten Pistolero* [hereafter *Il Pistolero*]) adapts Aeschylus' *Oresteia* to the silver screen. Baldi had previously taught as a professor of Classics (Wong 2018: 56), and the film also incorporates elements from the *Electras* of Sophocles and Euripides (Luschnig 2015: 229).[17] A 'spaghetti western' set in nineteenth-century Mexico in the wake of the Second Mexican Empire (Kabatchnik 2014: 17),[18] the film presents a story of familial violence and revenge, whose plot is easily recognizable to those familiar with myths surrounding the House of Atreus.

Aeschylus' *Oresteia* was first staged in Athens at the festival of Dionysus in 458 BCE. *The Oresteia* was an immediate classic and is the only full trilogy of Attic tragedy to have survived into modernity. The *Oresteia*'s first play, *Agamemnon*, depicts the titular king's return home from the Trojan War to Mycenae, only to be ambushed and murdered by his wife Clytemnestra and her lover Aegisthus, who is also Agamemnon's cousin. Both Clytemnestra and Aegisthus claim vengeance for previous interfamilial violence as motives for their bloody coup. In *The Libation Bearers*, the second play of the *Oresteia*, Agamemnon's son Orestes returns to Mycenae from exile/custodianship abroad. Goaded both by his sister Electra and the god Apollo, Orestes kills Clytemnestra and Aegisthus. Thus, *The Libation Bearers* features another cycle of interfamilial violence and blood feud, since, in order to avenge his father, Orestes must murder his mother. The trilogy's final play, *Furies/Eumenides* (depending on the edition/translation), begins with Orestes haunted and hunted by the Erinyes (commonly known as the Furies), chthonic goddesses of vengeance, for his matricide. Orestes seeks refuge in Athens from Athena, who presides over Greece's first trial. The specifics of the rhetorical arguments and forensic evidence are complicated and lie beyond the scope of this paper, but the play provides an etiological myth for Athenian democracy and its judicial system, as well as a transition from blood feud and vigilantism to a model of justice based on third-party arbitration.

At *Il Pistolero*'s opening, Rafael Garcia (Pylades-figure, played by Peter Martell) escapes bandits in his pursuit and finds his childhood friend, Sebastian Carrasco (Orestes-figure, played by Leonard Mann). In an early scene that recalls the *Oresteia*'s iconic recognition scene in *The Libation Bearers* and its subsequent rewritings by Sophocles and Euripides (both plays called *Electra*), Sebastian takes the wounded Raphael into his home, where a cloth emblazoned with a family emblem clues Raphael into Sebastian's identity. Somewhat implausibly, Sebastian has amnesia and has no recollection of his father's murder or his rescue by his domestic nurse. As Martin Winkler notes, 'That his nurse saves Sebastian from certain death after his father's assassination parallels the versions mentioned by Pindar', Sophocles and Euripides (Winkler 2022: 97, with n. 13). This first recognition episode partially takes place by a familial grave, and Baldi amplifies focalization on the Pylades-figure (Rabinowitz 2020: 310 notes the film's focus 'on the relationships between men').

Sebastian reunites with his sister Isabella (Electra-figure, played by Pilar Velázquez) at their father's tomb, which mimics the scene's setting in Greek tragedy. Baldi follows Euripides by having Isabella punitively married to Juanito, a kindly peasant (played by Luciano Rossi). The film suggests that Isabella had earlier fallen in love with Rafael. As punishment for and prevention of any possible procreation from the union, Anna Carrasco's (Clytemnestra-figure, played by Luciana Paluzzi) henchman (Francisco, played by Piero Lulli), castrated Rafael. Rafael's revenge is thus joined to Sebastian's.

Despite its clear incorporation of elements from Sophocles and Euripides, as well as its own innovations upon the myth's dramatic traditions, I treat *Il Pistolero* as an *Oresteia*, rather than a standalone *Electra*. The film's exposition of General Juan Carrasco's (Agamemnon-figure, played by José Suárez) *nostos* ('homecoming'), betrayal and murder is too expansive to be relegated as mere backstory.[19] The scene occupies a significant portion of the film's running time, and its story spans Carrasco's return, Anna and Tomás' (Aegisthus-figure, played by Alberto de Mendoza) plotting, and the murder itself. When Anna first stabs Juan, she wears a white dress with a geometric pattern that conjures Greek art, and the act occurs over a couch upholstered with deep red fabric that recalls the red tapestries Clytemnestra ominously lays out for her husband's fatal re-entry into the domestic life in the *Agamemnon* (910–930, 944–957). *Il Pistolero*'s *Agamemnon*-scene may be backstory related through flashback, but Baldi does not focalize the episode through an internal narrator's memories. Instead, the scene works as a *mise en abyme* with an omniscient lens, showing events no living character in the film could have seen in their totality.

Thus, the *Agamemnon* plays a rich and self-contained role, framed within *Il Pistolero*'s broader *Electra* narrative as a film within the film. The same cannot be said of the *Eumenides*. *Il Pistolero*'s climactic final scene, depicting Sebastian and Rafael's vengeance against Anna and Tomás, concludes with the main home of the Carrasco hacienda burning down against a dark night sky. C. W. Marshall (2017: 58) reads the imagery as a recollection of Aeschylus' motif of light and dark. After the killings, there is no more story to tell; after the fire, there is no patrimony for Sebastian to reclaim. The narrative ends abruptly, and the *Eumenides* receive nothing of the treatment given to the *Agamemnon* in *Il Pistolero*. Thus, the terminal counterfactual is that *Il Pistolero* structures itself through sustained engagement with the *Oresteia*, but that engagement truncates with the conclusion of *The Libation Bearers*, namely, the work is interrupted in the second part of the trilogy's end, leading to a counterfactual where the Erinyes do not seem to have a crucial role.

The film *may* give brief nods to the Erinyes. Anna's henchmen pursue Rafael relentlessly, and there are subtle suggestions that Rafael suffers from insomnia. But the henchmen are hardly agents of justice, quite the opposite. In *Il Pistolero* it is not the Orestes-figure but the Pylades-figure who is hunted, and Rafael is haunted by past traumas suffered as a victim long before the events of the *Electra* narrative, not for his own violent acts (he commits many, ostensibly without remorse). In any case, in contrast to the film's transmedial retelling of the *Agamemnon*, the *Eumenides* occupies no part of *Il Pistolero*'s narrative, and Baldi's story leaves no room for the Erinyes to adjudicate or avenge interfamilial killing. In a final plot twist, just before her death in the burning house, Anna confesses that she is not Rafael and Isabella's biological mother (she is apparently infertile), thereby removing the miasma of blood-guilt (perhaps its own counterfactual). In a sense, we might read this plot twist to mirror the strange logic of Aeschylus' *Eumenides* without restaging the play, since Orestes' defence rests on the forensic argument that mothers are not biologically related to their children (*Eumenides* 606, 657–666). After the final image of the house on fire, *Il Pistolero*'s end credits show Isabella, Sebastian and Rafael riding on horseback into the desert.

In short, *Il Pistolero* presents an adaptation of the *Oresteia*, one which truncates with the deaths of Aegisthus and Clytemnestra. The results are transformative. In Aeschylus, the *Eumenides*' trial expiates and, perhaps, offers closure for Orestes. The *Oresteia*'s third act presents a much larger, civilizing shift in ethics and the performance of justice, replacing vigilantism and blood-vengeance with a system of arbitration and trial by third-party members of the community. The Erinyes are tamed and transformed into the Eumenides. In a sense, Aeschylus' *Eumenides* works as metaphor for the settling of the 'Wild West'. By ending the narrative where he does, Baldi removes all such 'progress' from his *Oresteia*. Vengeance has been executed, but there is no shift towards the rule of law or a less violent means of or approach towards justice. This *Oresteia* leans into the *Agamemnon* and *Electra*'s themes of familial betrayal, violence and revenge, and, in part through its laconic protagonists, its focalization on Sebastian's amnesia (he doesn't remember what he is supposed to avenge) and Rafael's own motives for vengeance, refuses to move beyond that. The film's denouement reflects this lack of progress or character development. The film ends where it started: the *pistoleros* (and Isabella) riding on horseback across a barren landscape. *Il Pistolero*'s closing shot is ambiguous and, in my view, ambivalent. It remains unclear where the trio are going, whether they even know where they are going, or whether their revenge has healed past emotional wounds (Isabella faints during the revenge scene and Rafael carries her from the burning house). Rafael and Isabella are reunited, but their partnership can never be sexually reproductive, and the nature of any future relationship is left unknown. Their inability to produce a next generation mirrors Anna's and is suggestive of this *Eumenides*-less *Oresteia* to progress beyond gunslinger justice. Despite the dramatic visual of the hacienda on fire, there is no suggestion that the cyclical system of vigilante justice has been broken. Such is the counterfactual effect of interrupting the *Oresteia* narrative by excising the *Eumenides*.

Through its terminal reception of the *Oresteia*, *Il Pistolero* thus turns an origin myth for democracy and civilizational progress into a simpler revenge story that remains ambivalent in its lack of closure. Generically, the spaghetti western and the first two plays of the *Oresteia* are excellent fits for one another. As Bert

Fridlund 2014: 8–9 collates and distils critical approaches to defining the spaghetti western genre:

> The characters in a spaghetti Western are inhabitants of a cruel, anarchist universe, where might is right. The institutions of society are inefficient and/or corrupt. The hero is an alienated expert at weapons and a ragged outsider. He is cool and controlled and cares for his own interests in an environment that does not allow for moral scruples. To achieve his goals he has to temporarily waive his own personality and integrity. He is an expert in killing and achieves his goals through superior technical skills and tactics ... the characters are driven by greed or vengeance ... the characters are defined by their actions without emotional depth ...

Working with Fridlund's definition of the genre, even as it turns Aeschylean tragedy into a spaghetti western – what Winkler calls an 'opera of violence' – *Il Pistolero*'s reception of the first two plays reflects back onto the *Oresteia* and its moral ambiguities.[20] The *Agamemnon*'s chorus of elders may cry out against the pollution of justice, but they are powerless to stop it (πρᾶσσε, πιαίνου, μιαίνων τὴν δίκην, ἐπεὶ πάρα ['Speak, fatten yourself while you can, polluting justice]; *Agamemnon* 1669). Orestes, of course, returns to Argos as an outsider. He theatrically abandons his personality and, at least to an extent, his integrity when he declares that in his 'eye for an eye', or rather 'trick (*dolos*) for a trick', approach to justice, he must kill through stealth and trickery (*Libation Bearers* 556–558). Orestes adopts the persona of a stranger (ξένος μέν εἰμι Δαυλιεὺς ἐκ Φωκέων ('I am a stranger, Daulian of the Phocians'; *Libation Bearers* 674), announcing his death in a feigned Phocian accent (ἄμφω δὲ φωνὴν ἥσομεν Παρνησσίδα, / γλώσσης ἀυτὴν Φωκίδος μιμουμένω ['We'll each assume a Parnassian voice, mimicking a Phocian toungue']; *Libation Bearers* 564–565). In *Il Pistolero* Sebastian, too, adopts an alter ego and accent when returning to his Oaxaca hacienda (the dubbed English pronunciation of Oaxaca is cringeworthy throughout the film). Aeschylus' Orestes perhaps anticipates the ethos of the spaghetti western, since monetary loss as well as vengeance motivates his violence (*Libation Bearers* 273–275).

Thus, I suggest that the terminal literary counterfactual – an *Oresteia* truncates without *The Furies* – bends tone and genre well beyond the obvious shift in media from stage to screen, allowing for explorations of alternative themes. The partial *Oresteia* turns a civilizing origin myth of judicial arbitration into a revenge drama, in which there appears no alternative to vigilante justice and no apparent end to cycles of interfamilial violence.

Conclusion

Terminal intertextual counterfactuals can be just as transformative and imaginative as speculative histories. With these three post-classical receptions, it is difficult to say how effective or not these counterfactual interventions and interruptions were at engaging their audiences with the source texts. In the case of Hélisenne, her *Eneydes* appears to have been a commercial flop, though scholars of her work praise its transformation of the *Aeneid* into a genre-bending, proto-feminist work. *Cat's Cradle* was a great success but, perhaps because of the subtlety of its allusive system, I am (to my knowledge) the first to have traced its deep engagement with the *Odyssey*. Despite its international release, *Il Pistolero* was not a huge box office success. In its afterlife, it has become something of a cult classic, and viewers and scholars are keenly aware of its restaging of Greek tragedy. I note not only its inclusion in compendia on the spaghetti western genre but also Martin Winkler's (2022) recent chapter on the film. But, regardless of audience reception, all three works adapt and interrupt ancient literary narratives. Through sustained but partial reception of their source texts, Hélisenne de Crenne's *Eneydes*, Kurt Vonnegut's *Cat's Cradle* and Ferdinando Baldi's *Il Pistolero dell'Ave Maria* radically transform ancient narratives. These transformations are not only generic (into prose, into a science fiction novel, into a 'spaghetti western' film) but also substantive. By translating only the first four books of the *Aeneid*, Hélisenne turns a martial and nationalist epic into a proto-feminist novel with a focus on romantic desire and love gone wrong. Vonnegut's *Cat's Cradle* imagines an *Odyssey* in which Odysseus never makes it home, and in which the pursuit of knowledge and technological development are not hallmarks of civilization but rather harbingers of its downfall and of ecological apocalypse. Ferdinando Baldi's *Il Pistolero* creates an *Oresteia* without a *Eumenides*, which reduces the trilogy to a revenge drama with a seemingly unending cycle of violence and without any pretence of optimism for a peaceful or bloodless mechanism of justice. In so doing, these counterfactual alternative narratives highlight distinctive elements of their (interrupted) source texts, poignant in their absence: the *Aeneid*'s privileging of political duty over private desire, the *Odyssey*'s celebration of technoscientific human ingenuity and the pursuit of knowledge, and the *Oresteia*'s treatment of blood feud as a negative model that has no place in a just and civil society. Such is the imaginative power of terminal counterfactuals and partial receptions.

Notes

1 On counterfactuals, see Hellekson (2001), Singles (2013), Gallagher (2018).
2 While Ferguson (1999: 3) suggests that science fiction and, if only by implication, other popular fiction genres are unworthy of scholarly attention, I share no such reservations (quite the opposite), and scholarship on counterfactuals and uchronias notes their prevalence in science fiction. See, for example, Hills (2009) and Roberts (2009).
3 Frederick Pohl's story has been reprinted many times. It originally appeared in *Galaxy Magazine* (June 1962: 5–8; Pohl was managing editor).
4 Hardwick (2003: 10) defines translation as 'literally from one language to another. Literal, close, free are words used to pin down the relationship to the source as are phrases like "in the spirit rather than the letter"... Free translations sometimes merge into adaptations or versions'.
5 At the outset I want to acknowledge that I first learned of Hélisenne's *Aeneid* from Sharon Marshall years ago when we each gave papers at the Classical Association / Classical Association of Scotland's 2009 meeting in Glasgow on a 'Reception of Virgil' panel, and my thoughts on Hélisenne lean heavily on Marshall's (2011) dissertation. I adapt this case study from Weiner (2018; 2024).
6 Focusing on the publishing business surrounding Hélisenne, Chang (2009: 60) suggests that the *Eneydes* may well have been a commercial failure. Worth-Stylianou (2002: 148) notes that there is no trace of Hélisenne's translation having been reprinted. Cf. Broomhall (2002: 203).
7 Wood (2000: 138): '... the *Eynedes* [is] an example of an "oeuvre virile" [manly work] created by a virago'. See also Wood (1991). Broomhall (2021) notes that, in part by suggesting Cicero as her model, Wood claims a place in a male-dominated tradition. Broomhall (2021, citing Broomhall 2002: 1) also notes that 'Women represented less than 1% of all identifiable published authors in 16th-century France'. Also Broomhall (2002: 81) argues that in her *Angoysses*, Hélisenne 'emphasized her "boldness"'.
8 Chang (2009: 165) notes the significance of Hélisenne's pseudonym and suggests that Dido was her primary interest in Virgil's epic. Nash (2000: 380–1) traces this association back to Hélisenne's *Epistres* and suggests that the 'identity posits Hélisenne/Dido as *la femme forte*'. Also Wood (1992).
9 Chang (2009: 139) notes that the novel capitalizes on Hélisenne 'as a writer, narrator, and protagonist'.
10 Wood (1992) also speculates that Hélisenne's readership might not have been interested in Aeneas' mission to found Rome.
11 On the *querelle des femmes*, see, for example, Kelly (1982).
12 Worth-Stylianou (2002: 156) writes, '... the translation turns the *Aeneid* into a romance, with Dido as the tragic heroine'. See also Wood (2000: 135): 'Her

[Hélisenne] choice of the first four books of the epic is consistent with her own penchant for popular novels, since these books contain the legendary tale of Dido's tragic love for Aeneas'.

13 Weiner (2015). *Cat's Cradle*'s allusive opening sentence invites a multi-layered reading of the novel by imitating the first line of Herman Melville's *Moby Dick* while simultaneously signalling the biblical book of Jonah.

14 Weiner (2015: 118): Vonnegut 'has been shown to engage with the *Odyssey* in several of his later works, including *Happy Birthday, Wanda June* (1971), *Breakfast of Champions* (1973), and *Bluebeard* (1987)', with note 5, citing Godshalk (1973), Hume (1982), Klinkowitz (1982), Andrews (2001). Marvin (2002) suggests that the *Odyssey* figures into Vonnegut's work as early as *Player Piano* (1952).

15 On Odysseus and technology in the *Odyssey*, see, for example, Dougherty (2001); Horkheimer and Adorno (2002); Weiner (2015).

16 In my fuller reading of *Cat's Cradle* through the *Odyssey* in Weiner (2015), I suggest that Vonnegut's post-Second World War reception of Homer and reflections on technoscientific pursuit dovetail with Horkheimer and Adorno (2002).

17 All three of my case studies are transmedial, which is, of course, common of many receptions. Here, Baldi adapts Attic tragedy into film, whereas Hélisenne and Vonnegut adapt epic poetry into novelistic prose. Partial receptions and literary counterfactuals often work in tandem with shifts in media and genres.

18 While this list is hardly exhaustive and, for the sake of this chapter's anticipated readership, confined to Anglophone scholarship, on 'spaghetti westerns' and the term's definition, see, for example, see Brizio-Skov (2019) and Fridlund (2014). There is, of course, a considerable body of scholarship in Italian (and other languages).

19 Marshall (2017: 58) notes the film's retelling of *Agamemnon* in flashback.

20 Winkler (2022: 98), drawing on the title of Staig and Williams (1975).

References

Ancient sources

Aeschylus (2008), *Oresteia. Agamemnon. Libation-Bearers. Eumenides*, ed. and trans. A. H. Sommerstein, London-Cambridge, MA: Cambridge University Press.

Ammianus Marcellinus (1940), *History. Volume II*, trans. J. C. Rolfe, London-Cambridge, MA: Cambridge University Press.

Ammianus Marcellinus (1999), *Rerum Gestarum Libri Qui Supersunt, vol 1, libri XIV–XXV*, ed. W. Seyfarth, L. Jacob-Karau and I. Ulmann, Munich: Teubner.

Aristotle (1929), *Physics. Books 1–4*, trans. P. H. Wicksteed and F. M. Cornford, London-Cambridge, MA: Harvard University Press.

Aristotle (1965–70), *History of Animals. Books I–III and IV–VI*, trans. A. L. Peck, London-Cambridge, MA: Harvard University Press.

Aristotle (1991), *History of Animals. Books VII–X*, ed. and trans. D. M. Balme, London-Cambridge, MA: Harvard University Press.

Aristotle (1995), *Poetics*, ed. and trans. S. Halliwell, London-Cambridge, MA: Harvard University Press.

Arrian (1976), *Anabasis of Alexander. Books 1–4*, trans. P. A. Brunt, London-Cambridge, MA: Harvard University Press.

Augustine (2010), *De opere monachorum*, Turnhout: Brepols.

Augustine (2016), *Confessions. Books 1–8*, ed. and trans. C. J. B. Hammond, London-Cambridge, MA: Harvard University Press.

Aurelius (1911), *De viris illustribus*, ed. F. Pichlmayr, Leipzig: Teubner.

Cicero (1949), *On invention. Best kind of orator. Topics*, trans. H. M. Hubbell, London-Cambridge, MA: Harvard University Press.

De rebus bellicis (2017), ed. and trans. P. Fleury, Paris: Les Belles Lettres.

Diodorus Siculus (1954), *The Library of History. Books 16.66–17*, trans. C. B. Welles, London-Cambridge, MA: Harvard University Press.

Diogenes Laertius (1925), *Lives of Eminent Philosophers. Books 1–5*, London-Cambridge, MA: Harvard University Press.

Euripides (1998), *Suppliant Women. Electra. Heracles*, ed. and trans. D. Kovacs, London-Cambridge, MA: Harvard University Press.

Euripides (1999), *Trojan Women. Iphigenia among the Taurians. Ion*, ed. and trans. D. Kovacs, London-Cambridge, MA: Harvard University Press.

Euripides (2002), *Bacchae. Iphigenia at Aulis. Rhesus*, ed. and trans. D. Kovacs, London-Cambridge, MA: Harvard University Press.

Eusebius of Caesarea (1926), *Ecclesiastical History*, trans. K. Lake and J. E. L. Oulton, London-Cambridge, MA: Harvard University Press.

Eusebius of Caesarea (1999), *Life of Constantine*, trans. Av. Cameron and S. G. Hall, Oxford: Clarendon Press.

Florus (1819), *Epitome rerum Romanorum*, ed. F. N. Titze, Prague: Kraufs.

Fragmenta historicorum graecorum (1878–85), ed. K. O. Müller, Paris: Ambrosio Firmin-Didot.

Herodotus (1908), *Historiae, 2 vol*, ed. K. Hude, Oxford: Scriptorum Classicorum Bibliotheca Oxoniensis.

Homer (1919), *Odyssey*, trans. A. T. Murray, London-Cambridge, MA: Harvard University Press.

Homer (1998–2000), *Iliad*, ed. M. L. West, Stuttgart: Teubner.

Julian (1913a), *Volumes I (Panegyric in Honour of Constantius; The Heroic Deeds of Constantius; Panegyric in Honour of Eusebia; Hymn to the King Helios; Hymn to the Mother of the Gods)*, trans. W. C. Wright, London-Cambridge, MA: Harvard University Press.

Julian (1913b), *Volumes II (To the Uneducated Cynics; To the Cynic Heracleios; Consolation upon the Departure of Sallust; Letter to Themistius the Philosopher; Letter to the Senate and People of Athens; Fragment of a letter to a Priest; The Caesars; Misopogon)*, trans. W. C. Wright, London-Cambridge, MA: Harvard University Press.

Julian (1923), *Volume III: Letters. Epigrams. Against the Galilaeans. Fragments*, trans. W. C. Wright, London-Cambridge, MA: Harvard University Press.

Lactantius (1984), *De mortibus persecutorum*, ed. J. L. Creed, Oxford: Clarendon Press.

Libanius (1969), *Selected Orations. Vol I*, ed. and trans. A. F. Norman, London-Cambridge, MA: Harvard University Press.

Livy (1926), *History of Rome. Books 8–10*, trans. B. O. Foster, London-Cambridge, MA: Harvard University Press.

Livy (2021), *History of Rome. Books 28–30*, ed. and trans. J. C. Yardley, London-Cambridge, MA: Harvard University Press.

Lucian (1913), *Complete Works. Volume I*, trans. A. M. Harmon, London-Cambridge, MA: Harvard University Press.

Menander Rhetor (1981), *On Epideictic Speeches*, ed. and trans. D. A. Russell and N. G. Wilson, Oxford: Clarendon Press.

Ovid (1916), *Metamorphoses, 2 vols*, trans. F. J. Miller, London-Cambridge, MA: Harvard University Press.

Plato (2022), *Lysis. Symposium. Phaedrus*, ed. and. trans. C. Emlyn-Jones and W. Preddy, London-Cambridge, MA: Harvard University Press.

Pliny (1940), *Natural History. Books 8–11*, trans. H. Rackham, London-Cambridge, MA: Harvard University Press.

Pliny (1945), *Natural History. Books 12–16*, trans. H. Rackham, London-Cambridge, MA: Harvard University Press.

Plutarch (1914), *Lives. Themistocles and Camaillus. Aristides and Cato Major. Cimon and Lucullus*, trans. B. Perrin, London-Cambridge, MA: Harvard University Press.
Plutarch (1919), *Lives. Demosthenes and Cicero. Alexander and Caesar*, trans. B. Perrin, London-Cambridge, MA: Harvard University Press.
Polybius ([1979] 2003), *The Rise of the Roman Empire*, trans. I. Scott-Kilvert, annot. F. W. Walbank, London: Penguin Books.
Progymnasmata (2003), *Greek Textbooks of Prose Composition and Rhetoric (Aelius Theon; Attributed to Hermogenes; Aphtonius; Nicolaos the Sophist)*, trans. G. A. Kennedy, Atlanta: Society of Biblical Literature.
Pytheas of Massalia (2022), trans. L. Scott, London: Routledge.
Quintus Curtius (1946), *History of Alexander, 2 vols*, trans. J. C. Rolfe, London-Cambridge, MA: Harvard University Press.
Rhetorica ad Herennium (1954), trans. H. Caplan, London-Cambridge, MA: Harvard University Press.
Sappho (1967), *Greek Lyric Poetry: A Selection of Early Greek Lyric, Elegiac and Iambic Poetry*, trans. D. A. Campbell, Bristol: Bristol Classical Press.
Sophocles (1994a), *Antigone. The Women of Trachis. Philoctetes. Oedipus at Colonus*, ed. and trans. H. Lloyd-Jones, London-Cambridge, MA: Harvard University Press.
Sophocles (1994b), *Ajax. Electra. Oedipus Tyrannus*, ed. and trans. H. Lloyd-Jones, London-Cambridge, MA: Harvard University Press.
Sozomen (2004), *Historia Ecclesiastica: Kirchengeschichte, 4 vols*, ed. and trans. G. H. Hansen, Turnhout: Brepols.
Strabo (1844), *Geographica, vol 1*, ed. G. Kramer, Berlin: F. Nicolai.
Suetonius ([1913] 1998), *Lives of the Caesars, vol 1*, trans. J. C. Rolfe, London-Cambridge, MA: Harvard University Press.
Themistius (2021), *Themistius and Valens. Orations 6–13*, trans. S. Swain, Liverpool: Liverpool University Press.
Theodoret (1864), *Historia Ecclesiastica*, ed. J. Ludwig, Paris: Migne.
Thucydides (2009), *History of the Peloponnesian War*, trans. M. Hammond, annot. P. J. Rhodes, Oxford: Oxford University Press.
Virgil (1901), *Aeneid*, ed. A. Hirzel, Oxford: Clarendon Press.
Vitruvius (2019), *On Architecture*, trans. M. H. Morgan, Hastings: Delphi Classics.
Zonaras (1868–71), *Epitome Historiarum*, ed. L. Dindorf, Stuttgart: Teubner.

Works of fiction

Amis, K. (1976), *The Alteration*, London: Jonathan Cape.
Anderson, P. (1955), 'Delenda Est', *The Magazine of Fantasy and Science Fiction*, 9 (6): 3–35 (revised in 1960, *Guardians of Time*), 133–76, London: Gollancz.
Anderson, P. ([1957] 1982), *Cold Victory*, London: Pinnacle Press.

Asimov, I. (1949), 'The Red Queen's Race', *Astounding Science Fiction*, 42 (5): 65–85.
Atkinson, K. (2013), *Life After Life*, London: Penguin.
Atwood, M. (2005), *Penelopiad*, New York: Canongate.
Austen, J. (1813), *Pride and Prejudice*, London: T. Egerton.
Barker, P. (2018), *The Silence of the Girls*, London: Hamish Hamilton.
Barker, P. (2021), *The Women of Troy*, London: Penguin Books.
Benét, V. (1935), *The Curfew Tolls*. Available online: www.shortstoryproject.com/stories/the-curfew-tolls/ (accessed 8 February 2022).
Bennett, A. (2004), *The History Boys*, London: Faber and Faber.
Bester, A. (1958), 'The Men Who Murdered Mohammed', *The Magazine of Fantasy and Science Fiction*, 15 (89): 118–28.
Binet, L. (2019), *Civilisations*, trans. S. Taylor, London: MacMillan.
Bishop, M. (1987), 'For Thus Do I Remember Carthage', in B. Preiss (ed.), *The Universe*, 209–25, New York: Bantam Spectra.
Boulle, P. (1963), *La planète des singes*, Paris: Julliard.
Bradbury, R. (1952), 'A Sound of Thunder', *Collier's*, June 28: 20–32.
Chaudhry, T. S. (2014), *The Queen of Sparta*, Winchester: John Hunt Publishing.
Christopher, J. (1981), *Fireball*, London: Gollancz.
Clarke, S. (2004), *Jonathan Strange & Mr Norrell*, London: Bloomsbury.
Cohen-Scali, S. (2016), *Max*, London: Walker Books.
de Camp, L. S. (1937), 'The Isolinguals', *Astounding Science Fiction*, 20 (1): 108–19.
de Camp, L. S. (1939), 'Lest Darkness Fall', *Unknown*, 3 (4): 9–86.
de Camp, L. S. (1940), 'The Wheels of If', *Unknown*, 4 (2): 9–68.
de Camp, L. S. (1951), 'The Care and Feeding of Mad Scientists', *Astounding Science Fiction*, 47 (5): 128–39.
de Camp, L. S. ([1958a] 2002), 'Aristotle and the Gun', in Aristotle and the Gun and Other Stories, Waterville: Five Stars, 12–56.
de Camp, L. S. ([1958b] 2013), *An Elephant for Aristotle*, Rockville: Phoenix Pick..
de Camp, L.S. (1960), *The Bronze God of Rhodes*, New York: Doubleday.
de Camp, L. S. ([1963] 1993), *The Ancient Engineers*, London: Barnes & Noble Books.
de Camp, L. S. (1965), *The Arrows of Hercules*, New York: Doubleday.
de Camp, L. S. (1969), *The Golden Wind*, New York: Doubleday.
de Camp, L. S. (1992), 'The Round-Eyed Barbarians', *Amazing Stories*, 66 (9): 9–15
de Camp, L. S. (1993), *Rivers of Time*, Wake Forest: Baen Books.
Dick, P. K. (1962), *The Man in the High Castle*, New York: Putnam.
Eco, U. (1980), *The Name of the Rose*, Milan: Bompiani.
Farneti, M. (2009), *Imperium Solis*, Milan: Editrice Nord.
Farneti, M. (2012), *Gladius Imperii*, Milan: Editrice Nord.
Fry, S. (1996), *Making History*, London: Hutchinson.
Garfinkle, R. (1996), *Celestial Matters*, New York: Tor Books.
Garrison, E. (2011), *The Milesian Mistress: The Autobiography of Aspasia of Miletus*, Independently Published.

Golding, W. (1956), 'Envoy Extraordinary', in *Sometime, Never*, 117–78, London: Eyre & Spottiswoode.

Graves, R. (1934), *I, Claudius*, London: Arthur Barker.

Hale, E. E. (1881), 'Hands Off', *Harper's New Monthly Magazine*.

Hanson, V. D. (2000), 'No Glory that was Greece: The Persians Win at Salamis, 480 B.C.', in R. Cowley (ed.), *As What If? The World's Foremost Military Historians Imagine What Might Have Been*, 15–35, New York: Berkley Trade.

Harris, R. (1992), *Fatherland*, London: Hutchinson.

Haynes, N. (2017), *Children of Jocasta*, London: Pan Macmillan.

Heinlein, R. A. (1940), 'The Roads Must Roll', *Astounding Science Fiction*, 25 (4): 9–37.

Hélisenne de Crenne (1538), *Les Angoisses douloureuses qui procèdent d'amours*, Paris.

Hélisenne de Crenne (1539), *Les Epistres familières et invectives*, Paris.

Hélisenne de Crenne (1541), *Les Quatre premiers livres des Eneydes du treselegant poete Virgile. Traduictz de Latin en prose Françoyse*, Paris.

Ibsen, H. ([1873] 1986), *Emperor and Galilean*, trans. M. Meyer, London: Heinemann.

Kipling, R. (1926), 'The Eye of Allah', *Strand Magazine*, September: 215–26.

Leiber, F. (1958), 'Try and Change the Past', *Astounding Science Fiction*, 61 (1): 93–8.

Leinster, M. (1934), 'Sidewise in Time', *Astounding Science Fiction*, 13 (4): 10–46.

Levinson, P. (2006), *The Plot to Save Socrates*, New York: Tor Books.

Lewis, C. S. (1950–6), *The Chronicles of Narnia*, London: Geoffrey Bles (books 1–5) and The Bodley Head (books 6–7).

Manfredi, V. (2002), *Spartan*, trans. C. Feddersen-Manfredi, London: Pan Macmillan.

Mayhew, J. (2015), *The Big Lie*, London: Hot Key Books.

Melville, H. (1851), *Moby Dick*, London: Richard Bentley.

Merezhkovsky, D. ([1895] 1901), *The Death of Gods*, trans. H. Trench, Westminster: Archibald Constable & Co.

Miller, F. and L. Varley (1998), *300*, Milwaukie, OR: Dark Horse Books.

Miller, M. (2018), *Circe*, New York: Little, Brown & Co.

Milton, J. (1667), *Paradise Lost*, London: Samuel Simmons.

Moore, W. (1953), *Bring the Jubilee*, New York: Ballantine Books.

Poe, E. A. (1842), 'The Pit and the Pendulum', *The Gift: a Christmas and New Year's Present*, 133–51, Philadelphia: Carey and Hart.

Pohl, F. (1962), 'The Deadly Mission of Phineas Snodgrass', *Galaxy Magazine*, 20 (5): 5–8.

Pressfield, S. (1998), *Gates of Fire*, New York: Doubleday.

Ransmayr, C. ([1988] 1990), *The Last World*, trans. J. E. Woods, London: Chatto & Windus.

Renault, M. (1969), *Fire from Heaven*, New York: Pantheon Books.

Renault, M. (1972), *The Persian Boy*, London: Longman.

Renault, M. (1981), *Funeral Games*, New York: Pantheon Books.

Renouvier, C. (1876), *Uchronie. Utopie dans l'histoire*, Paris: Bureau de la critique philosophique.

Robinson, K. S. (2002), *The Years of Rice and Salt*, New York: Bantam Books.

Roth, P. (2004), *The Plot Against America*, Boston: Houghton Mifflin.

Russell, M. D. (1996), *The Sparrow*, New York: Villard.

Saint, J. (2021), *Ariadne*, London: Headline Publishing Group.

Schachner, N. (1933), 'Ancestral Voices', *Astounding Stories*, 12 (4): 70–82.

Schrader, H. P. (2006), *Are They Singing in Sparta?*, Lincoln: iUniverse.

Schrader, H. P. (2007), *Spartan Slave, Spartan Queen*, Lincoln: iUniverse.

Schrader, H. P. (2010a), *The Olympic Charioteer*, Lincoln: iUniverse.

Schrader, H. P. (2010b), *A Boy of the Agoge*, Tucson: Wheatmark.

Schrader, H. P. (2011), *A Peerless Peer*, Tucson: Wheatmark.

Schrader, H. P. (2012), *A Heroic King*, Tucson: Wheatmark.

Scott, M. (1984), *The Game Beyond*, New York: Baen Books.

Scott, M. (1986), *A Choice of Destinies*, New York: Baen Books.

Scott, M. (1987), *The Kindly Ones*, New York: Baen Books.

Sell, W. (1938), 'Other Tracks', *Astounding Stories*, 22 (2): 56–68.

Silverberg, R. (2004), *Phases of the Moon*, Burton, MI: Subterranean Press.

Silverberg, R. (2013), *Roma Eterna*, London: Gateway.

Słonimski, A. (1924), *Torpeda czasu*, Używana: Towarzystwo Wydawnicze "IGNIS".

Smale, A. (2015), *Clash of Eagles*, London: Del Rey.

Solomon, R. (2019), *The Deep*, New York: Gallery Publishing.

Stålenhag, S. (2014), *Tales from the Loop*, Los Angeles: Desing Studio Press.

Stevenson, R. L. (1886), 'Kidnapped', *Young Folks*, 28 (810).

Swanwick, M. (2007), 'Urdumheim', *Magazine of Fantasy and Science Fiction*, 113 (4–5): 207–37.

Thornton, S. (2015), *The Conqueror's Wife*, London: Penguin Random House.

Tidhar, L. (2011), *Osama*, Hornsea: PS Publishing.

Tilton, L. (1994), *Betrayal*, New York: Pocket Books.

Tilton, L. (1995), *Babylon 5: Accusations*, London: Pan Macmillan.

Tilton, L. (2004), 'The Gladiator's War: A Dialog', *Asimov's Science Fiction*, 28 (4): 20–43.

Tilton, L. (2005), 'Pericles the Tyrant', *Asimov's Science Fiction*, 29 (10–11): 88–103.

Tolstoy, L. ([1869] 2016), *War and Peace*, trans. L. Maude and A. Maude, Oxford: Oxford University Press.

Turtledove, H. (1989), 'Counting Potsherds', *Amazing Stories*, 63 (6): 12–36.

Valente, C. M. (2007), *The Glass Town Game*, New York: Margaret K. McElderry Books.

Valente, C. M. (2009), 'The Radiant Car Thy Sparrows Drew', *Clarkersworld Magazine*, 35.

Valente, C. M. (2011–16), *Fairyland*, New York: Tor Books.

Valente, C. M. (2015), *Radiance*, New York: Tor Books.

Valente, C. M. (2019), 'Just Your Average Tuesday-Morning Minotaur', in B. M. Rogers and B. E. Stevens (eds), *Once and Future Antiquities in Science Fiction and Fantasy*, 199–203, London: Bloomsbury.

Valente, C. M. (2021), *L'Esprit de L'Escalier*. Available online: https://www.tor.com/2021/08/25/lesprit-de-lescalier-catherynne-m-valente/ (accessed 20 October 2022).

Vidal, G. (1964), *Julian*, Boston: Little, Brown & Co.
Vidal, G. ([1981] 2002), *Creation*, New York: Doubleday.
von Däniken, E. ([1968], 1969), *Chariots of the Gods? Unsolved Mysteries of the Past*, trans. M. Heron, London: Souvenir.
Vonnegut, K. (1952), *Player Piano*, New York: Charles Scribner's Sons.
Vonnegut, K. ([1963] 1988), *Cat's Cradle*, New York: Dell Press.
Vonnegut, K. (1973), *Breakfast of Champions*, New York: Dell Press.
Vonnegut, K. (1987), *Bluebeard*, New York: Dell Press.
Walton, J. (2006), *Farthing*, New York: Tor Books.
Walton, J. (2015), *The Just City*, London: Corsair.
Wells, H. G. (1895), *The Time Machine*, London: Heinemann.
Wheeler, R. (2014), *Three Princes*, New York: Tor Books.
Wilson, R. C. (2009), *Julian Comstock: A Story of the 22nd-Century America*, New York: Tor Books.
Wu Ming (2007), *Manituana*, London-New York: Verso Books.
Zelazny, R. (1965), '. . .And call me Conrad', *Magazine of Fantasy and Science Fiction*, 29 (4): 5–57.
Zelazny, R. (1969), *Creatures of Light and Darkness*, New York: Doubleday.

Secondary sources

Adcock, F. E. (1946), 'Delenda est Carthago', *The Cambridge Historical Journal*, 8 (3): 117–28.
Andrews, D. (2001), 'Vonnegut and Aesthetic Humanism', in K. A. Boon (ed.), *At Millennium's End: New Essays on the Work of Kurt Vonnegut*, 17–47, Albany: SUNY Press.
Attebury, B. (2003), 'The magazine era: 1926–1960', in E. James and F. Mendlesohn (eds), *The Cambridge Companion to Science Fiction*, 32–47, Cambridge: Cambridge University Press.
Azoulay, A. A. (2019), *Potential History: Unlearning Imperialism*, London: Verso.
Bachelard, G. ([1958] 2014), *The Poetics of Space*, trans. M. Jolas, New York: Penguin.
Bakogianni, A. (2015a), 'Introduction: War as Spectacle: A Multi-sensory Event Worth Watching?', in A. Bakogianni and V. M. Hope (eds), *War as Spectacle: Ancient and Modern Perspectives on the Display of Armed Conflict*, 1–21, London: Bloomsbury Academic.
Bakogianni, A. (2015b), 'The Anti-War Spectacle: Denouncing War in Michael Cacoyannis' Euripidean Trilogy', in A. Bakogianni and V. M. Hope (eds), *War as Spectacle: Ancient and Modern Perspectives on the Display of Armed Conflict*, 291–311, London: Bloomsbury Academic.
Bal, M. (2017), *Narratology: Introduction to the Theory of Narratology*, 4th edn, Toronto-Buffalo-London: University of Toronto Press.

Balfe, M. (2004), 'Incredible Geographies? Orientalism and Genre Fantasy', *Social and Cultural Geography*, 5: 75–90.

Baxter, S. (2019), 'Foreword', in G. Morgan and C. Palmer-Patel (eds), *Sideways in Time: Critical Essays on Alternate History Science Fiction*, 1–9, Liverpool: Liverpool University Press.

Baynham, E. and T. Ryan (2018), '"The Unmanly Ruler": Bagoas, Alexander's Eunuch Lover, Mary Reanault's *The Persian Boy*, and Alexander Reception', in K. R. Moore (ed.), *Brill's Companion to the Reception of Alexander the Great*, 615–39, Leiden-Boston: Brill.

Becker, A. (1995), *The Shield of Achilles and the Poetics of Ekphrasis*, Lanham, MD: Rowman and Littlefield.

Becker, M. (2013), 'On visual cogency: the emergence of an antiquity of moving images', in P. Michelakis and M. Wyke (eds), *The Ancient World in Silent Cinema*, 37–52, Cambridge: Cambridge Univesity Press.

Berrens, S. (2004), *Sonnenkult und Kaisertum von den Severern bis zu Constantin I. (193-337 N. Chr.)*, Stuttgart: Franz Steiner.

Berry, R. (2021), *Doing English Grammar: Theory, Description, and Practice*, Cambridge: Cambridge University Press.

Betegh, G. (2009), 'What Makes a Myth *eikôs*? Remarks inspired by Myles Burnyeat's Eikôs Mythos', in R. Mohr and B. Sattler (eds), *One Book, The Whole Universe: Plato's Timaeus Today*, 213–24, Las Vegas: Parmenides Publishing.

Bhabha, H. K. (1994), *The Location of Culture*, London: Routledge.

Bigwood, J. M. (1993), 'Aristotle and the Elephant again', *American Journal of Philology*, 114 (4): 537–55.

Black, J. (2015), *Other Pasts, Different Presents, Alternative Futures*, Bloomington & Indianapolis: Indiana University Press.

Bond, S. E. (2019), 'The False Narratives of the Fall of Rome Mapped onto America', *Hyperallergic*, 3 July. Available online: https://hyperallergic.com/505776/the-false-narratives-of-the-fall-of-rome-mapped-onto-america/ (accessed 27 July 2023).

Bordwell, D. (2006), *The Way Hollywood Tells It: Story and Style in Modern Movies*, Berkeley: University of California Press.

Bost-Fiévet, M. and S. Provini, eds (2014), *L'Antiquité dans l'imaginaire contemporaine: Fantasy, science-fiction, fantastique*, Paris: Classiques Garnier.

Bould, M., A. M. Butler, A. Roberts and Sh. Vint, eds (2009), *The Routledge Companion to Science Fiction*, London: Routledge.

Bowersock, G. (1978), *Julian the Apostate*, Cambridge, MA: Harvard University Press.

Bowman, F. O. (2021), 'What the Founders Would Have Done with Trump', *Washington Monthly*, 18 January (accessed 20 July 2022).

Braun, R. and J. Richer, eds (1978), *L'Empereur Julien: De l'histoire à la légende*, 2 vols, Paris: Les Belles Lettres.

Brioni, S. (2015), 'Fantahistorical vs Fantafascist Epic: "Contemporary" Alternative Italian Colonial Histories', *Science Fiction Studies*, 42 (2): 305–21.

Brizio-Skov, F. (2019), 'Spaghetti Westerns and Their Audience', in P. Bondanella (ed.), *The Italian Cinema Book*, 181–7, London: Bloomsbury Academic.

Brockell, G. (2020), 'Wait, so who is Nero, and why are people comparing him to Trump?', *The Washington Post*, 9 March (accessed 20 July 2022).

Broderick, D. (2019), *The Time Machine: Extreme Science Meets Science Fiction*, New York: Springer.

Broomhall, S. (2002), *Women and the Book Trade in Sixteenth-Century France*, Burlington, VT: Ashgate.

Broomhall, S. (2021), 'Hidden women of history: Hélisenne de Crenne, the first French novelist to tell her own story', *The Conversation*, 28 March. Available online: https://theconversation.com/hidden-women-of-history-helisenne-de-crenne-the-first-french-novelist-to-tell-her-own-story-108249 (accesed 24 February 2022).

Brown, B. (2001), 'Thing Theory', *Critical Inquiry*, 28 (1): 1–22.

Brown, P. (1971), *The World of Late Antiquity: AD 150–750*, London: Thames and Hudson.

Brown, S. A. (1999), *The Metamorphosis of Ovid: Chaucer to Ted Hughes*, London: Bloomsbury.

Brown, S. A. (2008), '"Plato's Stepchildren": SF and the Classics', in L. Hardwick and C. Stray (eds), *A Companion to Classical Reception*, 415–27, Malden, MA: Wiley-Blackwell.

Bullari, D. (2020), 'The Visionary Leadership of Alexander the Great', *The Foreign Journal*, 30 November. Available online: https://theforeignjournal.medium.com/the-visionary-leadership-of-alexander-the-great-e17cf327c867 (accessed 22 February 2023).

Bunzl, M. (2004), 'Counterfactual History: A User's Guide', *American Historical Review*, 109 (3): 845–58.

Burnyeat, M. F. (2005), 'Eikôs Mythos', *Rizai*, 2 (2): 143–65.

Buxton, R. (1994), *Imaginary Greece: The Contexts of Mythology*, Cambridge: Cambridge University Press.

Caillois, R. ([1958] 1992), *Les jeux et les hommes*, Paris: Gallimard Education.

Canevaro, L. G. (2018), *Women of Substance in Homeric Epic: Objects, Gender, Agency*, Oxford: Oxford University Press.

Carpenter, H., ed. (1981), *The Letters of J.R.R. Tolkien*, London: George Allen & Unwin.

Carr, E. H. (2001), *What Is History?*, 2nd edn, Basingstoke: Palgrave.

Carrère, E. (1986), *Le Détroit de Behring*, Paris: P.O.L.

Carroll, J. (2002), *Constantine's Sword: The Church and the Jews: A History*, Boston: Houghton Mifflin.

Cartledge, P. A. (2002), *Sparta and Lakonia. A regional history 1300 to 362 BC*, 2nd edn, Abingdon: Routledge.

Chang, L. L. (2009), *Into Print: The Production of Female Authorship in Early Modern France*, Newark, DE: University of Delaware Press.

Comberiati, D. (2019), 'Dystopic Worlds and the Fear of Multiculturalism', in S. Brioni and D. Comberiati (eds), *Italian Science Fiction. The Other in Literature and Film*, 163–82, London: Palgrave Macmillan.

Cooke, B. (2022), 'Lessons for Leaders: Destiny, Devotion, and Self-Deception', in A. Augoustakis and M. S. Cyrino (eds), *Screening Love and War in Troy: Fall of A City*, 211–21, London: Bloomsbury.

Cowley, R. (2000), *What If? The World's Foremost Military Historians Imagine What Might Have Been*, 2nd edn, London: Pan Macmillan.

Cowley, R. (2002), *More What If? Eminent Historians Imagine What Might Have Been*, 2nd edn, London: Pan Macmillan.

Cribiore, R. (2013), *Libanius the Sophist: Rhetoric, Reality, and Religion in the Fourth Century*, Ithaca: Cornell University Press.

Crick, N. (2014), *Rhetoric and Power: The Drama of Classical Greece*, Columbia: University of South Carolina Press.

Cromwell, J. (2022), 'From Pyramids to Obscure Gods: The Creation of an Egyptian World in *Persona 5*', *Thersites*, 14: 1–40.

Dalberg-Acton, J. E. E. ([1887] 1907), *Historical Essays & Studies*, J. N. Figgis and R. V. Laurence (eds), London: MacMillan and Co.

Dalby, A. (2013), *Food in the Ancient World from A to Z*, London-New York: Routledge.

Dannenberg, H. P. (2008), *Coincidence and Counterfactuality: Plotting time And Space in Narrative Fiction*, London-Lincoln, NE: University of Nebraska Press.

Davis, W. D. (1907), *A Victor of Salamis: A Tale of The Days of Xerxes, Leonidas and Themistocles*, New York: Macmillan.

de Camp, L. S. ([1996] 2011), *Time and Chance: An Autobiography*, London: Gateway / Orion.

De Donno, F. (2014), 'Wu Ming's Reformation: Mythopoesis, Utopia, and Global Politics', in F. De Donno and S. Gilson (eds), *Beyond Catholicism: Heresy, Mysticism, and Apocalypse in Italian Culture*, 239–71, New York: Palgrave Macmillan.

de Groot, J. (2010), *The Historical Novel*, London-New York: Routledge.

de Kreij, M. (2015), 'Transmission and Textual Variants: Divergent Fragments of Sappho's Songs Examined', in A. Lardinois, S. Levie, H. Hoeken and C. Lüthy (eds), *Texts, Transmissions, Receptions*, 17–34, Leiden-Boston: Brill.

De Pascale, G. (2009), *Wu Ming: non soltanto una band di scrittori*, Geneve: Il melangolo.

Deterding, S. and J. P. Zagal, eds (2018), *Role-Playing Game Studies: A Transmedia Approach*, London: Routledge.

Deuermoth, Q. and P. Singaravélou (2016), *Pour une histoire des possibles*, Paris: Seuil.

Dolezel, L. (1998), *Heterocosmica: Fiction and Possible Worlds*, Baltimore: The Johns Hopkins University Press.

Dougherty, C. (2001), *The Raft of Odysseus: The Ethnographic Imagination of Homer's* Odyssey, Oxford: Oxford University Press.

Duncan, A. (2003), 'Alternate History', in E. James and F. Mendelsohn (eds), *The Cambridge Companion to Science Fiction*, 209–18, Cambridge: Cambridge University Press.

Eco, U. (1995), 'Ur-Fascism', *The New York Review of Books*, 22 June: 1–9 (accessed 28 July 2022).
Eddington, A. (1929), *The Nature of the Physical World*, Cambridge: Cambridge University Press.
Edwards, E. and B. M. Stableford (2017), 'Time Paradoxes', *Science Fiction Encyclopedia*. Available online: https://sf-encyclopedia.com/entry/time_paradoxes (accesed 8 February 2022).
Effingham, N. (2021), 'The Metaphysical Possibility of Time Travel Fictions', *Erkenntnis*, 88 (3): 1309–29.
Ekman, S. (2013), *Here Be Dragons: Exploring Fantasy Maps and Settings*, Middletown, CT: Wesleyan University Press.
Elitzur, A. C. and E. Cohen (2022), 'Some Notes on Counterfactuals in Quantum Mechanics', *Entropy*, 22 (3): 266.
Evans, R. J. (2014), *Altered Pasts: Counterfactuals in History*, London: Little, Brown & Co.
Evans, T. H. (2010), 'Authenticity, Ethnography, and Colonialism in Philip K. Dick's *The Man in the High Castle*', *Journal of the Fantastic in the Arts*, 21 (3): 366–83, 499.
Feeley, G. (2004), 'The way it wasn't', *Washington Examiner. The Weekly Standard*, 6 September (accessed 28 July 2022).
Ferguson, N., ed. (1997), *Virtual History: Alternatives and Counterfactuals*, London: Picador.
Ferguson, N. (1997), 'Afterword: A Virtual History, 1646–1996', in N. Ferguson (ed.), *Virtual History: Alternatives and Counterfactuals*, 416–40, London: Picador.
Ferguson, N. (1999), *Virtual History*, New York: Basic Books.
Fernández-Camacho, P. (2022), 'Carthaginians Beyond the Ocean: Comparison, Justification, and Inversion in the Hypothesis of the Carthaginian Discovery of America', *Classical Receptions Journal*, 14 (2): 141–58.
Fisher, J. (2011), 'Tolkien and Source Criticism: Remarking and Rethinking', in J. Fisher (ed.), *Tolkien and the Study of His Sources*, 29–44, Jefferson, NC: McFarland & Co.
Flatt, M. (2018), 'Is the future female? Fixing sci-fi's women problem', *The Guardian*, 29 August. Available online: https://www.theguardian.com/books/2018/aug/29/is-the-future-female-fixing-sci-fis-women-problem (accessed 24 November 2022).
Fletcher, K. F. B. and O. Umurhan, eds (2019), *Classical Antiquity in Heavy Metal Music*, London: Bloomsbury Academic.
Fotheringham, L. (2020), 'Doing justice to the past through the representation of violence: *Three* and ancient Sparta', in I. Hague, I. Horton and N. Mickwitz (eds), *Contexts of Violence in Comics*, 17–33, New York: Routledge.
Fraden, R. (2012), *Imagining Medea: Rhodessa Jones and Theater for Incarcerated Women*, Chapel Hill, NC: University of North Carolina Press.
Fredericks, S. C. (1976), 'Lucian's *True History* as SF', *Science Fiction Studies*, 3 (1.8): 49–60.
Fridlund, B. (2014), *The Spaghetti Western: A Thematic Analysis*, London-Jefferson, NC: McFarland & Company.

Frow, J. (2005), *Genre*, London: Routledge.

Gagarin, M. (2014), '*Eikos* arguments in Athenian forensic oratory', in V. Wohl (ed.), *Probabilities, Hypotheticals and Counterfactuals in Ancient Greek Thought*, 15–29, Cambridge: Cambridge University Press.

Gallagher, C. (2018), *Telling It Like It Wasn't: The Counterfactual Imagination in History and Fiction*, Chicago-London: University of Chicago Press.

Gazis, G. A. (2018), *Homer and the Poetics of Hades*, Oxford: Oxford University Press.

Geoffroy, L. (1836), *Napoléon et la Conquête du Monde, 1812–1832*, Paris: H-L Delloye.

Gertler, P. J., S. Martínez, P. Premand, L. B. Rawlings and C. M. J. Vermeersch (2016), *Impact Evaluation in Practice*, 2nd edn, Washington, DC: The World Bank Group.

Ghita, C. and G. Andrikopoulos (2009), 'Total War and Total Realism: A Battle for Antiquity in Computer Game History', in D. Lowe and K. Shahabudin (eds), *Classics for All: Reworking Antiquity in Mass Culture*, 109–26, Newcastle upon Tyne: Cambridge Scholar Publishing.

Gibson, C. A. (2004), 'Learning Greek History in the Ancient Classroom: The Evidence of the Treatises on Progymnasmata', *Classical Philology*, 99 (2): 103–29.

Gilbert, D. and D. Lambert (2010), 'Counterfactual geographies: worlds that might have been', *Journal of Historical Geography*, 36: 245–52.

Gildenhard, I. and A. Zissos, eds (2013), *Transformative Change in Western Thought: A History of Metamorphosis from Homer to Hollywood*, London: Legenda.

Godshalk, W. L. (1973), 'Vonnegut and Shakespeare: Rosewater at Elsinore', *Critique*, 15: 37–48.

Goff, B., ed. (2005), *Classics & Colonialism*, London: Bloomsbury Academic.

Gomel, E. (2010), *Postmodern Science Fiction and Temporal Imagination*, New York: Continuum.

Gould, S. (1989), *Wonderful Life: The Burgess Shale and the Nature of History*, New York: W. W. Norton & Co.

Greenwood, D. N. (2021), *Julian and Christianity: Revisiting the Constantinian Revolution*, Ithaca: Cornell University Press.

Gregory, D. (1994), *Geographical Imaginations*, Oxford-Cambridge, MA: Blackwell.

Gregory, D. (1995), 'Between the Book and the Lamp: Imaginative Geographies of Egypt, 1849–50', *Transactions of the Institute of British Geographers*, 20: 29–57.

Gunning, T. (2004), '"Animated Pictures": Tales of the Cinema's Forgotten Future, after 100 Years of Film', in V. R. Schwartz and J. M. Przyblyski (eds), *The Nineteenth-Century Visual Culture Reader*, 100–13, London-New York: Routledge.

Hardie, P., ed. (2002), *The Cambridge Companion to Ovid*, Cambridge: Cambridge University Press.

Hardwick, L. (2003), *Reception Studies*, Oxford: Oxford University Press.

Hardwick, L. and C. Stray, eds (2008), *A Companion to Classical Receptions*, Malden, MA-Oxford: Wiley-Blackwell.

Hardy, B. C. (1968), 'The Emperor Julian and His School Law', *Church History*, 37 (2): 131–43.

Harrison, N. (2016), 'Sci-fi media coverage dominated by men, survey shows', *The Guardian*, 12 May. Available online: https://www.theguardian.com/books/booksblog/2016/may/12/sci-fi-media-coverage-dominated-by-men-survey-shows (accessed 24 November 2022).

Hayward, S. (1996), *Key Concepts in Cinema Studies*, London-New York: Routledge.

Helbig, J. (1988), *Der parahistorische Roman: Ein literaturhistorischer und gattungstypologischer Beitrag zur Allotopieforschung*, Frankfurt: Klostermann.

Hellekson, K. (2001), *The Alternate History: Refiguring Historical Time*, Kent, OH: The Kent State University Press.

Henriet, B. (2011), *L'histoire revisitée: l'Uchronie dans toutes ses forms*, 2nd edn, Paris: Belles Lettres.

Hills, M. (2009), 'Time, Possible Worlds, and Counterfactuals', in A. Butler and M. Bould (eds), *The Routledge Companion to Science Fiction*, 455–63, London: Routledge.

Hoagland, E. and R. Sarwal (2010), 'Introduction: Imperialism, the Third World, and Postcolonial Science Fiction', in E. Hoagland and R. Sarwal (eds), *Science Fiction, Imperialism and the Third World: Essays on Postcolonial Literature and Film*, 5–19, Jefferson, NC: McFarland & Company.

Hoek, L. (2020), '"Tools for Shaping Stories? Visual Plot Models in a Sample of Anglo-American Advice Handbooks', in A. Masschelein and D. De Geest (eds), *Writing Manuals for the Masses: The Rise of the Literary Advice Industry from Quill to Keyboard*, 171–98, London-New York: Palgrave Macmillan.

Höfler, M. (2005), 'Causal inference based on counterfactuals', *BMC Medical Research Methodology*, 5: article 28.

Hofstadter, D. (1979), *Gödel, Escher, Bach: An Eternal Golden Braid*, New York: Basic Books.

Horkheimer, M. and T. W. Adorno (2002), *Dialectic of Enlightenment*, trans. E. Jephcott, Stanford, CA: Stanford University Press.

Hugill, P. J. (2010), 'The shaping of the American Empire', *Journal of Historical Geography*, 36: 261–5.

Huhtamo, E. (2011), 'Natural Magic: A Short Cultural History of Moving Images', in W. Guynn (ed.), *The Routledge Companion to Film History*, 3–15, London: Routledge.

Hume, K. (1982), 'Vonnegut's Self-Projections: Symbolic Characters and Symbolic Fiction', *Journal of Narrative Technique*, 12: 177–90.

Huntington, J. (1975), 'Science Fiction and the Future', *College English*, 37 (4): 345–52.

Hutcheon, L. (2013), *A Theory of Adaptation*, 2nd edn, London: Routledge.

Kabatchnik, A. (2014), *Blood on the Stage, 480 B.C. to 1600 A.D.: Milestone Plays of Murder, Mystery, and Mayhem: An Annotated Repertoire*, Lanham, MD: Rowman and Littlefield.

Kahlos, M. (2013), *Forbearance and Compulsion: The Rhetoric of Religious Tolerance and Intolerance in Late Antiquity*, London: Bloomsbury.

Karastathi, S. (2015), 'Ekphrasis and the Novel/Narrative Fiction', in G. Rippl (ed.), *Handbook of Internemdiality: Literature – Image – Sound – Music*, 92–112, Berlin-Boston: Walter de Gruyter.

Keen, A. (2015), 'Mr. Lucian in Suburbia: Links between the *True History* and *The First Men in the Moon*', in B. M. Rogers and B. E. Stevens (eds), *Classical Traditions in Science Fiction*, 105–20, Oxford: Oxford University Press.

Kelly, J. (1982), 'Early Feminist Theory and the "Querelle des Femmes", 1400–1789', *Signs*, 8 (1): 4–28.

Kerslake, P. (2010), *Science Fiction and Empire*, Liverpool: Liverpool University Press.

Kettle, M. (2023), 'What would Britain look like today if we'd chosen to follow the roads not taken?', *Guardian*, 31 May 2023. https://www.theguardian.com/commentisfree/2023/may/31/britain-germany-alternative-history-brexit-falklands-second-world-war (accessed 1 June 2023).

Kirsch, J. (2005), *God Against the Gods: The History of the War Between Monotheism and Polytheism*, London: Penguin.

Kleu, M., ed. (2019), *Antikenrezeption in der Science Fiction*, Essen: Oldib Verlag.

Klinkowitz, J. (1982), *Kurt Vonnegut*, London: Methuen.

Köstlbauer, J. (2013), 'The Strange Attraction of Simulation: Realism, Authenticity, Virtuality', in M. W. Kapell and A. B. R. Elliott (eds), *Playing with the Past: Digital Games and the Simulation of History*, 169–84, London: Bloomsbury.

Kovacs, G. and C. W. Marshall, eds (2011), *Classics and Comics*, Oxford: Oxford University Press.

Kovacs, G. (2015), 'Moral and Mortal in *Star Trek: The Original Series*', in B. M. Rogers and B. E. Stevens (eds), *Classical Tradition in Science Fiction*, 199–216, Oxford: Oxford University Press.

Lamoreaux, N. R. (2011), 'Taking Counterfactual History Seriously', *California History*, (89) 1: 39–50, 70–1.

Lanouette, J. ([1999] 2012), 'A History of Three-Act Structure', *Screentakes*, 24 December. Available from: https://www.screentakes.com/an-evolutionary-study-of-the-three-act-structure-model-in-drama/#1 (accessed 6 July 2021).

Lebow, R. N. (2007), 'Counterfactual Thought Experiments: A Necessary Teaching Tool', *The History Teacher*, 40 (2): 153–76.

Lefkowitz, M. (2014), 'Sophocles: Literary Biography', in H. M. Roisman (ed.), *The Encyclopedia of Greek Tragedy*, vol 3: S-Z., 1291–5, Oxford-Malden, MA: Wiley-Blackwell.

Levy, J. S. (2015), 'Counterfactuals, Causal Inference, and Historical Analysis', *Security Studies*, 24: 378–402.

Little, C. E. (1934), 'The Authenticity and Form of Cato's Saying "Carthago Delenda Est"', *Classical Journal*, 29: 429–35.

Liveley, G. (2006), 'Science Fiction and Cyber Myths: or, Do Cyborgs Dream of Dolly the Sheep?', in V. Zajko and M. Leonard (eds), *Dancing with Medusa: Classical Myth and Feminist Thought*, 275–94, Oxford: Oxford University Press.

Liveley, G. (2018), 'Patchwork Paratexts and Monstrous Metapoetics: "After tea, M reads Ovid"', in J. Weiner, B. E. Stevens and B. M. Rogers (eds), *Frankenstein and Its Classics: The Modern Prometheus from Antiquity to Science Fiction*, 25–41, London: Bloomsbury.

Llewellyn-Jones, L. (2018), *Designs on the Past: How Hollywood Created the Ancient World*, Edinburgh: Edinburgh University Press.

Lowe, D. (2012), 'Always Already Ancient: Ruins in the Virtual World', in T. S. Thorsen (ed.), *Greek and Roman Games in the Computer Age*, 53–90, Trondheim: Akademika Publishing.

Luckhurst, R. (2006), *Science Fiction*, Cambridge: Polity.

Luisi, P. L. (2003), 'Contingency and determinism', *Philosophical Transactions: Mathematical, Physical, and Engineering Sciences*, 361: 1141–7.

Luschnig, C. E. (2015), 'Electra', in R. Lauriola and K. Demetriou (eds), *Brill's Companion to the Reception of Euripides*, 201–37, Leiden-Boston: Brill.

Maar, A. (2014), 'Possible Uses of Counterfactual Thought Experiments in History', *Principia*, 18 (1): 87–113.

Makridis, O. (2011), 'The Austere Demagogue: Thucydides on the Uses and Abuses of Periclean Rhetoric', *Atlantic Journal of Communication*, 19: 268–84.

Malvestio, M. (2018), 'Cronache del *fantafascismo*: l'ucronia in Italia e il revisionismo storico', *The Italianist*, 38 (1): 89–107.

Mandel, D. R., D. J. Hilton and P. Castellani, eds (2005), *The Psychology of Counterfactual Thinking*, London-New York: Routledge.

Mannoni, L. (1994), *Le grand art de la lumière et de l'ombre: archéologie du cinéma*, Paris: Nathan.

Marcus, L. (2007), *The Tenth Muse: Writing about Cinema in the Modernist Period*, Oxford: Oxford University Press.

Marra, E. (2014), 'Il caso della letteratura ucronica italiana: Ucronia e propaganda nella narrativa italiana', *Between*, 4 (7): 1–21.

Marshall, C. W. (2017), *Aeschylus: Libation Bearers*, London: Bloomsbury.

Marshall, S. (2011), 'The *Aeneid* and the Illusory Authoress: Truth, fiction, and feminism in Hélisenne de Crenne's *Eneydes*', PhD diss., University of Exeter, Exeter.

Martindale, C., and R. F. Thomas, eds (2006), *Classics and the Uses of Reception*, Oxford- Malden, MA: Blackwell.

Marvin, T. F. (2002), *Kurt Vonnegut: A Critical Companion*, Westport, CT: Greenwood Press.

Marx, K. (1848), *The Manifesto of the Communist Party*. Available online: https://www.marxists.org/archive/marx/works/1848/communist-manifesto/ch01.htm (accessed 8 February 2022).

Marx, K. and F. Engels ([1845] 2010), 'The Holy Family, or Critique of Critical Criticism', in Karl Marx and Frederick Engels, *Collected Works*, vol 4, 5–211, London: Lawrence & Wishart.

McDonagh, E. (2001), 'A Post-Christian Ireland? An Introduction', *The Irish Review*, 27: 1–6.

McFarlane, A. (2019), 'Time and Affect After 9/11: Lavie Tidhar's Osama: A Novel', in G. Morgan and C. Palmer-Patel (eds), *Sideways in Time: Critical Essays on Alternate History Fiction*, 92–106, Liverpool: Liverpool University Press.

Mendelsohn, F. (2008), *Rhetorics of Fantasy*, Middletown, CT: Wesleyan University Press.

Menke, R. (1998), 'Narrative Reversals and the Thermodynamics of History in Martin Amis's *Time's Arrow*', *Modern Fiction Studies*, 44 (4): 959–80.

Meurer, U. (2020), '"The Shards of Zadar": A (Meta-)Archaeology of Cinema', in P. Michelakis (ed.), *Classics and Media Theory*, 187–210, Oxford: Oxford University Press.

Meyer, E. (1901), *Geschichte des Altertums. Dritter Band: Das Perserreich und die Griechen. Erste Hälfte: Bis zu den Friedensschlüssen von 448 und 446 v. Chr.*, Stuttgart: Cotta.

Michelakis, P. and M. Wyke, eds (2013a), *The Ancient World in Silent Cinema*, Cambridge: Cambridge Univesity Press.

Michelakis, P. and M. Wyke (2013b), 'Introduction: silent cinema, antiquity, and the exhaustless urn of time', in P. Michelakis and M. Wyke (eds), *The Ancient World in Silent Cinema*, 1–24, Cambridge: Cambridge Univesity Press.

Millender, E. (2018), 'Spartan Women', in A. Powell (ed.), *A Companion to Sparta*, 2 vols, 500–24, Hoboken, NJ: Wiley Blackwell.

Miller, A. H. (2012), '"A Case of Metaphysics": Counterfactuals, Realism, *Great Expectations*', *English Literary History*, 79 (3): 773–96.

Milnor, K. (2008), 'Making the Material Matter: Objects and Accuracy in Classics and Film', *Classical and Modern Literature*, 28 (1): 5–20.

Mitchell, T. ([1998] 2009), 'Orientalism and the exhibitionary order', in D. Preziosi (ed.), *The Art of Art History: A Critical Anthology*, new edn, 409–23, Oxford-New York: Oxford University Press.

Morgan, G. and C. Palmer-Patel, eds (2019a), *Sideways in Time: Critical Essays on Alternate History Fiction*, Liverpool: Liverpool University Press.

Morgan, G. and C. Palmer-Patel (2019b), 'Introduction', in G. Morgan and C. Palmer-Patel (eds), *Sideways in Time: Critical Essays on Alternate History Science Fiction*, 11–28, Liverpool: Liverpool University Press.

Morley, N. (2010), *The Roman Empire: Roots of Imperialism*, London: Pluto Press.

Morley, N. (2017), 'What can Karl Marx tell us about comparing Donald Trump to Roman Emperors?', *Eidolon* 6 March. Available online: https://eidolon.pub/what-can-karl-marx-tell-us-about-comparing-donald-trump-to-roman-emperors-b124ff281023 (accessed 19 July 2022).

Morley, N. (2019), 'Counterfactualism and Anticipation,' in R. Poli (ed.), *Handbook of Anticipation*, 595–613, London: Springer.

Morowitz, H. J. (1993), *Beginnings of Cellular Life: Metabolism Recapitulates Biogenesis*, New Haven, CT: Yale University Press.

Moshenka, G. (2017), 'Archaeologists in popular culture', in G. Moshenka (ed.), *Key Concepts in Public Archaeology*, 151–65, London: University College of London Press.

Mourelatos, A. P. D. (2014), 'The Conception of *eoikos/eikos* as Epistemic Standard in Xenophanes, Parmenides, and Plato's *Timaeus*', *Ancient Philosophy*, 34: 169–91.
Mumford, L. (1934), *Technics and Civilization*, London: Routledge.
Murdoch, A. (2008), *The Last Pagan: Julian the Apostate and the Death of the Ancient World*, Rochester, VT: Inner Traditions/Bear.
Murphy, C. (2007), *Are We Rome? The Fall of an Empire and the Fate of America*, Boston-New York: Mariner.
Nash, J. C. (2000), 'Constructing Hélisenne de Crenne: Reception and Identity', in C. M. Jones and K. Busby (eds), '*Por Le Soie Amisté*': *Essays in Honor of Norris J. Lacy*, 371–83, Leiden-Boston: Brill.
Natale, S. and G. Balbi (2014), 'Media and the Imaginary in History: The Role of the Fantastic in Different Stages of Media Change', *Media History*, 20 (2): 203–18.
Natoli, B. A. (2017), *Silenced Voices: The Poetics of Speech in Ovid*, Madison, WI: University of Wisconsin Press.
Nisbet, G. (2008), *Ancient Greece in Film and Popular Culture*, 2nd edn, Exeter: Bristol Phoenix Press.
ODEG = Aarts, B., S. Chalker and E. Weiner (2014), *The Oxford Dictionary of English Grammar*, 2nd edn, Oxford: Oxford University Press.
Olabarria, L. (2019), '"When the world was milk and honey and the magic was strong and true": Edward Said, ancient Egypt, and heavy metal', in K. Fletcher and O. Umurhan (eds), 173–99, *Classical Antiquity in Heavy Metal Music*, London: Bloomsbury Academic.
Olabarria, L. (2020), *Kinship and Family in Ancient Egypt: Archaeology and Anthropology in Dialogue*, Cambridge: Cambridge University Press.
Pak, C. (2019), '"It Is One Story": Writing a Global Alternate History in Kim Stanley Robinson's The Years of Rice and Salt', in G. Morgan and C. Palmer-Patel (eds), *Sideways in Time: Critical Essays on Alternate History Science Fiction*, 46–61, Liverpool: Liverpool University Press.
Parikka, J. (2012), *What is Media Archaeology?*, Cambridge-Malden, MA: Polity Press.
Paul, J. (2013), *Film and the Classical Epic Tradition*, Oxford: Oxford University Press.
Pavlik, A. (2011), 'Being There: The Spatiality of "Other World" Fantasy Fiction', *International Research in Children's Literature*, 4: 238–51.
Pinkerton, J. (1979), 'Backward Time Travel: Alternate Universes, and Edward Everett Hale', *Extrapolations*, 20 (2): 168–75.
Postclassicisms Collective (2020), *Postclassicisms*, Chicago: The Chicago University Press.
Potter, D. (2009), *Rome in the Ancient World – From Romulus to Justinian*, London: Thames & Hudson.
Prendergast, C. (2019), *Counterfactuals: Paths of the Might Have Been*, London: Bloomsbury.
Rabinowitz, N. S. (2020), 'Iphigenia among the Taurians', in A. Markantonatos (ed.), *Brill's Companion to Euripides*, 2 vols, 299–319, Leiden-Boston: Brill.

Raghunath, R. (2020), *Possible Worlds Theory and Counterfactual Historical Fiction*, London: Springer.

Raghunath, R. (2022), 'Possible worlds theory, accessibility relations, and counterfactual historical fiction', *Journal of Literary Semantics*, 51: 1–18.

Rieder, J. (2008), *Colonialism and the Emergence of Science Fiction*, Middletown, CT: Wesleyan University Press.

Roberts, A. (2009), 'The Copernican Revolution', in A. Butler and M. Bould (eds), *The Routledge Companion to Science Fiction*, 3–12, London: Routledge.

Roberts, A. (2016), *The History of Science Fiction*, 2nd edn, London: Palgrave Macmillan.

Roberts, A. (2019), 'Napoleon as Dynamite: Geoffroy's Napoléon Apocryphe and Science Fiction as Alternate History', in G. Morgan and C. Palmer-Patel (eds), *Sideways in Time: Critical Essays on Alternate History Science Fiction*, 31–45, Liverpool: Liverpool University Press.

Roberts, S. L. (2011), 'Using Counterfactual History to Enhance Students' Historical Understanding', *The Social Studies*, 102 (3): 117–23.

Rodiek, C. (1997), *Erfundene Vergangenheit. Kontrafaktische Geschichtsdarstellung (Uchronie) in der Literatur*, Heidelberg: Klostermann.

Rogers, B. M. (2015), 'Hybrids and Homecomings in the *Odyssey* and *Alien Resurrection*', in B. M. Rogers and B. E. Stevens (eds), *Classical Tradition in Science Fiction*, 217–42, Oxford: Oxford University Press.

Rogers, B. M. and B. E. Stevens (2015), 'Introduction', in B. M. Rogers and B. E. Stevens (eds), *Classical Traditions in Science Fiction*, 1–25, Oxford: Oxford University Press.

Rogers, B. M. and B. E. Stevens, eds (2019), *Once and Future Antiquities in Science Fiction and Fantasy*, London-New York: Bloomsbury.

Roh, D. S., B. Huang and G. A. Niu, eds (2015), *Techno-Orientalism: Imagining Asia in Speculative Fiction, History, and Media*, London-New Brunswick, NJ: Rutgers University Press.

Roland, A. (2010), 'Was the Nuclear Arms Race Deterministic?', *Technology and Culture*, 51 (2): 444–61.

Rollinger, C. (2020), *Classical Antiquity in Videogames: Playing with the Ancient World*, London-New York: Bloomsbury.

Rose, M. (2009), 'Extraordinary Pasts: Steampunk as a Mode of Historical Representation', *Journal of the Fantastic in the Arts*, 20: 319–33.

Rosenfeld, G. D. (2005), *The World Hitler Never Made: Alternate History and the Memory of Nazism*, Cambridge: Cambridge University Press.

Rosenfeld, G. D. (2022), 'What's in a name? Past possibilities and the challenges of historicizing counterfactual history', *History & Theory*, 61 (3): 514–23.

Rushing, R. A. (2007), *Resisting Arrest: Detective Fiction and Popular Culture*, New York: Other Press.

Ryan, M.-L. (1980), 'Fiction, non-factuals, and the Principle of Minimal Departure', *Poetics*, 9: 403–22.

Ryan, M.-L. (1991a), *Possible worlds, Artificial Intelligence, and Narrative Theory*, Bloomington: Indiana University Press.

Ryan, M.-L. (1991b), 'Possible worlds and accessibility relations: A semantic typology of Fiction', *Poetics Today*, 12: 553–76.

Ryan, M.-L. (2006), 'From Parallel Universes to Possible Worlds: Ontological Pluralism in Physics, Narratology, and Narrative', *Poetics Today*, 27 (4): 633–74.

Said, E. W. ([1974] 2003), *Orientalism*, Penguin Books: London.

Sarton, G. ([1952] 1993), *Ancient Science through the Golden Age of Greece*, New York: Dover.

Saylor, S. (1981), 'Classical Gore'. Available online: http://www.stevensaylor.com/Creation.html (accessed 6 December 2022).

Scalzi, J. (2015), 'The Big Idea: Catherynne M. Valente'. Available online: https://whatever.scalzi.com/2015/10/20/the-big-idea-catherynne-m-valente-4/ (accessed 20 October 2022).

Schiavone, A. (2021), *What Is Progress*, New York: Europa Editions.

Schmid, G. (2009), 'Counterfactuals and Futures Histories: Retrospective Imagining as an Auxiliary for the Scenarios of Expectance', *Historical Social Research*, 34 (2): 74–87.

Schneider-Mayerson, M. (2009), 'What Almost Was The Politics of Contemporary Alternate History Novel', *American Studies*, 50 (3–4): 63–83.

Schwartz, G. M. and J. J. Nichols, eds (2006), *After Collapse: The Regeneration of Complex Societies*, Tucson: The University of Arizona Press.

Schweitzer, D. (2010), *The Fantastic Horizon: Essays and Reviews*, San Bernardino: Wildside Press.

Sconce, J. (2000), *Haunted Media: Electronic Presence from Telegraphy to Television*, Durham, NC: Duke University Press.

Seed, D. (1999), *American Science Fiction and the Cold War*, Chicago: Fitzroy Dearborn.

Senholt, J. C. (2013), 'Radical Politics and Political Esoterism. The Adaptation of Esoteric Discourse within the Radical Right', in E. Asprem and K. Granholm (eds), *Contemporary Esoterism*, 244–64, Sheffield: Equinox.

Shippey, T. (1973), 'Science Fiction and History', *Foundation*, 4: 4–19.

Shuldiner, D. P. (1999), *Of Moses and Marx: Folk Ideology and Folk History in the Jewish Labor Movement*, Westport: Bergin & Garvey.

Sicher, E and N. Skradol (2006), 'A World Neither Brave nor New: Reading Dystopian Fiction', *Partial Answers: Journal of Literature and the History of Ideas*, 4 (1): 151–79.

Singles, K. (2013), *Alternate History: Playing With Contingency and Necessity*, Berlin-Boston: Walter de Gruyter.

Slatkin, L. M. (2019), 'Counterfactuals and the Plot of *The Iliad*', in B. M. King and L. Doherty (eds), *Thinking the Greeks: A Volume in Honor of James M. Redfield*, 13–23, London: Routledge.

Sobchack, V. (1999/2000), 'What is Film History? or the Riddle of the Sphinxes', *Melbourne Art Journal*, 4: 25–36.

Soja, E. W. (1996), *Thirdspace: Journeys to Los Angeles and Other Real-and-Imagined Places*, Oxford-Cambridge, MA: Blackwell.

Solomon, J. (2007), 'Viewing *Troy*: Authenticity, Criticism, Interpretation', in M. M. Winkler (ed.), *Troy: From Homer's Iliad to Hollywood Epic*, 85–98, Oxford-Malden, MA: Blackwell.

Sorensen, D. R. and B. E. Kinser, eds (2013), *Thomas Carlyle: On Heroes, Hero Worship, and the Heroic in History*, Yale: Yale University Press.

Spedo, G. (2009), 'The Plot Against the Past: An Exploration of Alternate History in British and American Fiction', PhD diss., University of Padua, Padua.

Spencer, H. (1996), *Collected Writings*, in M. W. Taylor (ed.), London-New York: Routledge.

Stableford, B. (2006), *Science Facts and Science Fiction: An Encyclopaedia*, London: Routledge.

Staig, L. and T. Williams (1975), *Italian Western: The Opera of Violence*, London: Lorrimer-Odeon.

Starr, W. (2022), 'Counterfactuals', in E. N. Zalta and U. Nodelman (eds), *The Stanford Encyclopedia of Philosophy*. Available online: https://plato.stanford.edu/archives/win2022/entries/counterfactuals (accessed 21 November 2022).

Stevens, B. E. (2017), 'Ancient Underworlds in J. R. R. Tolkien's *The Hobbit*', in B. M. Rogers and B. E. Stevens (eds), *Classical Traditions in Modern Fantasy*, 121–44, Oxford: Oxford University Press.

Stevens, B. E. (2018), 'Medea in Jesmyn Ward's *Salvage the Bones*', *International Journal of the Classical Tradition*, 25: 158–77.

Stevens, B. E. (2021), 'Middle-earth as Underworld: from *Katabasis* to *Eucatastrophe*', in H. Williams (ed.), *Tolkien and the Classical World*, 105–30, Jena and Zurich: Walking Tree.

Stevens, B. E. (2022), '"The beautiful trap inside us": Pandoran Science Fiction and Posthuman Personhood', in L. Maurice and T. Bibring (eds), *Gender, Creation Myths and their Reception in Western Civilization: Prometheus, Pandora, Adam and Eve*, 169–81, London: Bloomsbury.

Stevens, B. E. (2024a), 'Film Translations of Greek and Roman Epic', in R. Armstrong and A. Lianeri (eds), *A Companion to Translation Studies and Ancient Epic*, Malden, MA: Blackwell.

Stevens, B. E. (2024b), '"All … that walk the world in these after-days": Classical Receptions as Gothic 'Haunting' in J.R.R. Tolkien', in D. Maillard (ed.), *Tolkien et l'Antiquité: Passé et Antiquités en Terre du Milieu*, 69–90, Paris: Classiques Garnier.

Stewart, G. (2007), *Framed Time: Toward a Postfilmic Cinema*, Chicago, IL: University of Chicago Press.

Suvin, D. (1983), 'Victorian Science Fiction: The Rise of Alternative History Sub-Genre', *Science Fiction Studies*, 10: 148–69.

Taterka, F. (2016), 'Egyptianizing Motifs in the Products of Popular Culture Addressed to Younger Recipients', in K. Dominas, E. Wesołowska and B. Trocha (eds), *Antiquity in Popular Literature and Culture*, 205–21, Newcastle upon Tyne: Cambridge Scholars Publishing.

Tattersdill, W. (2023), 'Towards a Counterfactual Criticism: Alternate History and the Study of English Literature', *Textual Practice*.

Teitler, H. C. (2017), *The Last Pagan Emperor: Julian the Apostate and the War Against Christianity*, Oxford: Oxford University Press.

Tetlock, P. E. and A. Belkin, eds (1996), *Counterfactual Thought Experiments in World Politics: Logical, Methodological, and Psychological Perspectives*, Princeton: Princeton University Press.

Tetlock, P. E., R. N. Lebow and G. Parker, eds (2006), *Unmaking the West: 'What-If?' Scenarios That Rewrite World History*, Ann Arbor, MI: University of Michigan Press.

Thiess, D. J. (2014), *Relativism, Alternate History, and the Forgetful Reader: Reading Science Fiction and Historiography*, Lanham, MD: Lexington Books.

Thorpe, C. (2006), *Oppenheimer: The Tragic Intellect*, Chicago: Chicago University Press.

Tobin, P. D. (1978), *Time and the Novel: The Genealogical Imperative*, Princeton: Princeton University Press.

Tordoff, R. (2014), 'Counterfactual History and Thucydides', in V. Wohl (ed.), *Probabilities, Hypotheticals and Counterfactuals in Ancient Greek Thought*, 101–21, Cambridge: Cambridge University Press.

Trevor-Roper, H. (2000), *Hitler's Table Talk: 1941–1944*, New York: Enigma Books.

Trudelle Schwarz, M. (2013), *Fighting Colonialism with Hegemonic Culture: Native American Appropriation of Indian Stereotypes*, New York: State University of New York Press.

Uden, J. (2020), *Spectres of Antiquity: Classical Literature and the Gothic, 1740–1830*, Oxford: Oxford University Press.

Umachandran, M. (2019), 'More than a Common Tongue: Dividing Race and Classics Across the Atlantic', *Eidolon* 11 June. Available online: https://eidolon.pub/more-than-a-common-tongue-cfd7edeb6368 (accessed 9 June 2023).

Uricchio, W. (2005), 'Simulation, History, and Computer Games', in J. Raessens and J. Goldstein (eds), *The Handbook of Computer Game Studies*, 327–38, Cambridge, MA: The Massachusetts Institute of Technology Press.

Vaidman, L. (1999), 'The Meaning of Elements of Reality and Quantum Counterfactuals: Reply to Kastner', *Foundations of Physics*, 29 (6): 865–76.

VanderWeele, T. J. (2020), 'Counterfactuals in Social Epidemiology – Thinking Outside of "the Box"', *American Journal of Epidemiology*, 189 (3): 175–8.

Ward, M. (2010), *Planet Narnia: The Seven Heavens in C.S. Lewis' Imagination*, Oxford: Oxford University Press.

Warf, B. (2002), 'The way it wasn't: alternative histories, contingent geographies', in R. Kitching and J. Kneale (eds), *Lost in Space: Geographies of Science Fiction*, 17–38, London-New York: Continuum.

Warren, J. W. (2018), 'Avoiding Nation Building in Afghanistan: An Absent Insight from Alexander', in K. R. Moore (ed.), *Brill's Companion to the Reception of Alexander the Great*, 739–53, Leiden-Boston: Brill.

Watts, E. (2015), *The Final Pagan Generation*, Oakland, CA: University of California Press.

Watts, E. J (2021), *The Eternal Decline and Fall of Rome: The History of a Dangerous Idea*, Oxford: Oxford University Press.

Weiner, J. (2015), 'Mapping Hubris: Kurt Vonnegut's *Cat's Cradle* and Odysseus' *Apologoi*', *International Journal of the Classical Tradition*, 22 (1): 116–37.

Weiner, J. (2018), 'Rewriting the Classics: A translator alters more than a text's language, turning the process into a political statement', *History Today*, 68 (7): 12–14.

Weiner, J. (2024), ''The Master's Tools?: Towards a Politics of Reception Studies', in A. Bakogianni and L. Unceta Gómez (eds), *Classical Recteption: State of the Discipline and New Directions*, 23–39, Berlin: Walter De Gruyter.

Weiss, P. (2003), 'The vision of Constantine', *Journal of Roman Archeology*, 16: 237–59.

Weiss, H. (2013), *Literature, History, Choice: The Principle of Alternative History in Literature* (S. Y. Agnon, *The City with All That is Therein*), Newcastle upon Tyne: Cambridge Scholars Publishing.

Wendell, J. (2020), 'Qualifying counterfactuals: Students' use of counterfactuals for evaluating historical explanations', *History Education Research Journal*, 17 (1): 50–66.

White, H. (1973), *Metahistory: The Historical Imagination in 19th-Century Europe*, Baltimore, MD: The Johns Hopkins University Press.

Whitehead, A. N. (1925), *Science and the Modern World*, Cambridge: Cambridge University Press.

Whitmarsh, T. (2013), *Beyond the Second Sophistic: Adventures in Greek Postclassicism*, Berkeley, CA: University of California Press.

Winkler, M. M. (2007), 'The *Iliad* and the Cinema', in M. M. Winkler (ed.), *Troy: From Homer's Iliad to Hollywood Epic*, 43–67, Oxford-Malden, MA: Blackwell.

Winkler, M. M. (2020), *Ovid on Screen: A Montage of Attractions*, Cambridge: Cambridge University Press.

Winkler, M. M. (2022), 'Clytemnestra and Electra under Western Skies', in S. Matheson (ed.), *Women in the Western*, 91–105, Edinburgh: University of Edinburgh Press.

Winthrop-Young, G. (2009), 'Fallacies and Thresholds: Notes on the Early Evolution of Alternate History', *Historische Sozialforschung*, 34 (2): 99–117.

Wittenberg, D. (2013), *Time Travel: The Popular Theory of Narrative*, New York: Fordham University Press.

Wohl, V. (2014), 'Introduction: *eikos* in Ancient Greek Thought', in V. Wohl (ed.), *Probabilities, Hypotheticals and Counterfactuals in Ancient Greek Thought*, 1–14, Cambridge: Cambridge University Press.

Wong, A. S. (2018), *Spaghetti Westerns: A Viewer's Guide*, Lanham, MD: Rowman & Littlefield.

Wood, D. S. (1991), 'The Evolution of Hélisenne de Crenne's Persona', *Symposium: A Quarterly Journal in Modern Literatures*, 45 (2): 140–51.

Wood, D. S. (1992), 'Dido as Paradigm of the Tragic Heroine in the Works of Hélisenne de Crenne', *Explorations in Renaissance Culture*, 18: 125–36.

Wood, D. S. (2000), *Hélisenne de Crenne: At the Crossroads of Renaissance Humanism*, London: Associated University Presses.

Worth-Stylianou, V. (2002), 'Translations from Latin into French in the Renaissance', in G. Sandy (ed.), *The Classical Heritage in France*, 137–64, Leiden-Boston: Brill.

Zaccaria, P. (2016), 'Rediscovering Theopompos: neglected evidence of the Meropis', *Aevum*, 90 (1): 51–70.

Zielinski, S. (2015), 'Why and How Anarchaeology and Variantology of Arts and Media Can Enrich Thinking about Film and Cinema: Nine Miniatures', in A. Beltrame, G. Fidotta and A. Mariani (eds), *At the Borders of (Film) History: Temporality, Archaeology, Theories*, 21–32, Udine: Forum.

Webgraphy

Alternate Historian (2013–), *Today in Alternate History*. Available online: http://www.todayinah.co.uk/ (accessed 30 November 2022).

Alternative History Wiki. Available online: https://althistory.fandom.com/wiki/Main_Page (accessed 30 November 2022).

Amazon Customer Reviews:

K. Gilligan (2007): https://www.amazon.com/gp/customer-reviews/R1X4VXYV4V1Y90/ref=cm_cr_dp_d_rvw_ttl?ie=UTF8&ASIN=0671655639, posted 19 June 2007 (accessed 22 November 2022).

A. Barre (2015): https://www.amazon.ca/gp/customer-reviews/RSWU20H3ECFZG/ref=cm_cr_dp_d_rvw_ttl?ie=UTF8&ASIN=B00QUBUFG2, posted 17 January 2015 (accessed 9 July 2022).

Mrs. K. (2015): https://www.amazon.co.uk/gp/customer-reviews/R2VMIY4N4X96Q5/ref=cm_cr_dp_d_rvw_ttl?ie=UTF8&ASIN=B00QUBUFQ2, posted 30 December 2015 (accessed 9 July 2022).

Oh My Bookness (2016): https://www.amazon.com/gp/customer-reviews/RR88KLI38AAN3/ref=cm_cr_dp_d_rvw_ttl?ie=UTF8&ASIN=B00QUBUFG2, posted 21 December 2016 (accessed 9 July 2022).

The Encyclopedia of Science Fiction (SFE). Available online:

Edwards, M. and B. M. Stableford (2017), 'Time Paradoxes', https://sf-encyclopedia.com/entry/time_paradoxes (accessed 8 February 2022).

Clute, J. (2022), 'Melissa Scott', https://sf-encyclopedia.com/entry/scott_melissa (accessed 20 November 2022).

Langford, D. (2013), 'Sidewise Award', https://sf-encyclopedia.com/entry/sidewise_award (accessed 20 November 2022).

ISFDB (Internet Speculative Fiction Database). Available online: https://www.isfdb.org/cgi-bin/ea.cgi?Melissa_Scott (accessed 20 November 2022).

John Hunt Publishing. Available online: https://johnhuntpublishing.com (accessed 9 July 2022).

Jones, T. (2005), *The Tony Jones Alternate History Page*. Available online: https://www.clockworksky.net/alternate_history_top.html (accessed 30 November 2022).

Keen, Tony (2006), Blog. Available online: http://tonykeen.blogspot.com/2006/04/t-stands-for-tiberius-models-and.html

Schmunk, R. B. (1991–2022), *Uchronia. The Alternate History List*, available online: http://www.uchronia.net (accessed 30 November 2022).
Introduction: http://www.uchronia.net/intro.html (accessed 17 November 2022).
Divergence chronology: http://www.uchronia.net/bib.cgi/diverge.html (accessed 17 November 2022).

Today in Alternate History. Available online: http://www.todayinah.co.uk/ (accessed 30 November 2022).

Index

The letter *f* after an entry indicates a page with a figure.

Milton Keynes UK
Ingram Content Group UK Ltd.
UKHW020017091124
450615UK00003B/68

9 781350 281622